CHESTERTON AND THE
EDWARDIAN CULTURAL CRISIS

Hull University Press

LAMPADA FERENS

CHESTERTON AND THE EDWARDIAN CULTURAL CRISIS

JOHN COATES

Lecturer in Literature and Drama
Department of Adult Education
University of Hull

HULL UNIVERSITY PRESS
1984

Phototypeset in 11 on 12pt Baskerville by
Computape (Pickering) Ltd, Pickering, North Yorkshire.

For Carole and Charlotte

CONTENTS

ACKNOWLEDGEMENTS

The author would like to thank Miss D.E. Collins for permission to use the quotations from Chesterton which appear in this book. He is also grateful to the editors of several periodicals who have allowed him to use material from his own previously published articles. Acknowledgement is made to the editor of the *Chesterton Review* for permission to use 'Symbol and Structure in *The Flying Inn*' (vol. IV, no. 2 (1978) 246–60), 'Chesterton and the Meaning of Adventure' (vol. V, no. 2 (1979) 278–99), 'The Restoration of the Past and the War of Values' (vol. VI, no. 2 (1980) 280–304), and 'The Reaction against Impressionism' (vol. IX, no. 4 (1983) 314–33). The author would also like to thank the editor of *English Literature in Transition* for permission to use 'The Return to Hugo: a discussion of the intellectual context of Chesterton's view of the grotesque' (vol. 25, no. 2 (1982) 86–103), the editor of *Mosaic* for permission to use 'Philosophical and Literary Hostility to Myth: Chesterton and his contemporaries' (vol. XV, no. 4 (1982) 91–105), and the editor of *Prose Studies* for permission to use 'The Fleet Street Context and the Development of Chesterton's Prose Style' (vol. 6, no. 1 (1983) 57–74). He wishes to acknowledge the painstaking work of his colleague Dr Joyce Bellamy in copy-editing his manuscript.

Chronology of Chesterton's Life and Chief Works

1874   Gilbert Keith Chesterton born 29 May in Kensington; eldest son of Edward and Marie Louise Chesterton (née Grosjean).

1887   Began to attend St Paul's School.

1892   Entered Slade School of Art.

1892–4   Emotional and intellectual crisis.

1895–9   Introduction to journalism. Worked for two publishing firms and began to publish poems and articles.

1896   Meeting with Frances Blogg.

1899   Began to write for the *Speaker*.

1900   *Greybeards at Play* and *The Wild Knight*. Came to public notice through opposition to the Boer War. Met Hilaire Belloc.

1901   Began to write for the *Daily News*.
        Marriage to Frances Blogg.
        The Defendant

1902   *Twelve Types*

1903   *Robert Browning*

1904   *The Napoleon of Notting Hill*
        G.F. Watts

1905   *The Club of Queer Trades*
        Heretics
        Began to write for the *Illustrated London News*

1906   *Charles Dickens*

1906–14   Steady disillusionment with Liberal Party.

1908   *The Man who was Thursday*
        Orthodoxy
        All Things Considered

1909   *George Bernard Shaw*
        Tremendous Trifles

1910   *The Ball and the Cross*
        What's Wrong with the World
        Alarms and Discursions

1911   *Appreciations and Criticisms of the Works of Charles Dickens*
        The Innocence of Father Brown
        The Ballad of the White Horse

1912   *Manalive*
        Simplicity and Tolstoy
        A Miscellany of Men

1912–13   The Marconi Case.
        Trial of Cecil Chesterton.

1913   G.K. Chesterton leaves the *Daily News*.
        The Victorian Age in Literature

1914   *The Wisdom of Father Brown*
        The Flying Inn

1914–15   Very serious nervous and physical illness.

1917   *A Short History of England*

1918	Death of Cecil Chesterton.
1919	Trip to Palestine.
	Irish Impressions
1920	*The Superstition of Divorce*
	The New Jerusalem
1922	Received into the Catholic Church.
	Eugenics and Other Evils
	What I saw in America
	The Man who knew too much
1923	*St. Francis of Assisi*
	Fancies Versus Fads
1925	*The Everlasting Man*
	William Cobbett
	Tales of the Long Bow
	G.K.'s Weekly started.
1926	*The Outline of Sanity*
	The Incredulity of Father Brown
1927	*The Return of Don Quixote*
	Collected Poems
	The Secret of Father Brown
	Robert Louis Stevenson
1928	*Generally Speaking*
1929	*The Thing*
	The Poet and the Lunatics
1930	*Four Faultless Felons*
	Come to think of It
1931	*All is Grist*
1932	*Chaucer*
	Began radio talks on BBC.
1933	*All I survey*
	St. Thomas Aquinas
1934	*Avowals and Denials*
1935	*The Scandal of Father Brown*
	The Well and the Shallows
1936	*As I was saying*
	G.K. Chesterton died 14 June at Beaconsfield.

Some Posthumous Works

1936	*Autobiography*
1937	*The Paradoxes of Mr Pond*
1950	*The Common Man*
1953	*A Handful of Authors*
1955	*The Glass Walking Stick*
1958	*Lunacy and Letters*
1958	*Essays and Poems
1964	*The Spice of Life*
1971	*Chesterton on Shakespeare*

*This is a selection of previously published writing.

I INTRODUCTION

I

It has, perhaps, been inevitable that, in searching for what in Chesterton's work was of permanent value, critics had tended towards anthologising or at least towards selection. They have been inclined to take passages or even complete works, as much as possible out of the context of the local and temporary controversies, conditions and journalistic pressures which helped to produce them and to read them as classic statements of a point of view or, at most, as expressions of Chesterton's own fascinating and many-sided personality. Such a method of Chesterton criticism, adopted by Hugh Kenner, W.H. Auden and Marshall McLuhan among others, has proved useful and is inherently plausible, given the vast bulk and unevenness of his work, and the admittedly ephemeral circumstances and characters which often provoked it. One object of this book, however, is, in looking at him as a controversial cultural influence, to help to restore the balance. Whatever may be said of some of the individuals against whom he contended, it cannot be said that the currents of opinion they embodied were themselves trivial. My intention in seeking to restore some of the partially lost cultural context is to throw light on Chesterton's concerns, persona and style, but, even more, by showing him as a voice of sanity sadly needed in the battle against the mythopoeic currents of thought of the new twentieth century, evolutionary, racialist and historicist, which have helped to mould our present life and thought; as the restorer, too, of a true view of lost 'popular' elements of sensibility,

1

especially in the areas of myth, the grotesque and adventure, which the intellectuals of his time neglected.

I am concerned with the cultural, rather than the specifically religious or political aspects of his work. These latter areas have been amply studied and there are excellent books on them. While it is undoubtedly true that Chesterton's writings will be best appreciated by those who are, broadly, in sympathy with his religious and political views, this is not an essential ticket of admission to his work. His attempts to halt an ideological flood, habits of thinking through myth and false analogy, a yielding to inevitability and fatalism whether through evolutionary fantasy or through historicism or through pseudo-science and his concern to link the intellectuals of his time with the world of popular thought and feeling from which they were cut off, a concern untainted with a disparagement of reason or the higher products of 'minority culture' are matters of interest not necessarily yoked to any particular religious position. They will concern anyone disturbed by the history of ideas in the twentieth century. The forces against which Chesterton struggled have shaped our time and are still very much alive.

Chapter II is an attempt to set the scene, to examine Chesterton's perception of the ideological nature of the twentieth century and the defective inherited attitudes with which his contemporaries were about to meet the storm. Chapter III deals with the journalistic arena in which most of his battles were fought, and seeks to establish the reasons for his choice of profession, its significance and something of the way in which and the background against which his work in it was conducted. The fourth and fifth chapters pursue the attack on the ideology of inevitability in two areas; first, the evolutionary fantasy in its most lethal form, the Superman cult, through an examination of the major novel dealing with Nietzscheanism, *The Flying Inn*, and secondly, the problem of human freedom of action and historical inevitability, focused on Chesterton's long standing concern with the image of Don Quixote, and the theme of restoring the past.

In the next three chapters, I deal with Chesterton as the healer of a cultural split, with his attempt to recover for literature and for intellectual discourse generally, areas of feeling, needs, and kinds of

2

response, in three specific areas, adventure, myth or fable, and the grotesque which contemporary educated opinion despised, ignored or perversely misinterpreted. In Chesterton's view it was partly this narrowness of base in the culture of his time which weakened its defence against the dangers which threatened.

Finally, the next two chapters sketch some of those, not primarily religious, aspects of Chesterton's scheme of sanity; first, his, somewhat misunderstood, view of the visual arts, in what was to be their most revolutionary century, which was far from being merely reactionary, but which rather contained the elements of a distinct, and in many ways original, view of perception; secondly, Chesterton's plan of the non-ideological mind, his 'survival kit' for the twentieth century in the form of suggestions for the ways in which intellectual balance might be recovered and maintained. The book ends with a hint of ways in which Chesterton's intellectual influence may have operated. Before considering these aspects of Chesterton's work, however, it is possible that some readers who are not familiar with the shape of his career may find a brief account of it helpful.

II

Chesterton is a writer known and yet not known. He is a widely recognised figure whose aphorisms are often quoted, several of whose books are still reprinted and whose Father Brown stories, at least, are much read. There is perhaps a widespread sense that he is in some way significant and he certainly has not been eclipsed in the minds of both the academic and the general reader as his friend and intellectual ally Belloc probably has. Yet he is almost unrepresented in university syllabuses of English Literature. Nor, in spite of a small but intellectually very substantial body of critical work on him, including a recently-founded periodical and the gold-mine of material provided by over a hundred of his books, two hundred easily accessible essays as well as hundreds of uncollected ones, is there any evidence that he attracts the extensive attention of scholarly researchers. The number of articles for the last twenty years listed in the standard bibliographies is surprisingly small, when one considers the often obscure and marginal topics which are pursued. The reasons for the neglect of Chesterton probably include the sheer amount of what the critic feels he must master to discuss him and the notion that as a polemicist or 'man of ideas' he has dated and was, in any case, too little of a serious artist to merit close attention. A more effective obstacle than these, however, is the reader's impression that he does know Chesterton, the notion of a tiresomely rollicking and roistering 'character', with more than a whiff of anti-Semitism about him, a romantic reactionary, or at best a writer interesting only to Catholics of the older generation. Since this appallingly inaccurate stock image so obscures the facts about Chesterton, there is an added reason, before exploring some aspects of his achievement, to recall briefly the main points of his life and career.

The main sources for Chesterton's biography are his *Autobiography* (1936), Maisie Ward's *Gilbert Keith Chesterton* (1944) with its supplement *Return to Chesterton* (1952), Dudley Barker's *G.K. Chesterton: a biography* (1973), and, *The Outline of Sanity: a life of G.K. Chesterton* (1983) by A. Stone Dale. Laurence J. Clipper's *G.K. Chesterton* (1974) is arguably the best general survey of his work. Of these, the *Autobiography* is especially valuable for the account of his childhood and of his adolescent crisis. Maisie Ward's life is the cornerstone of any understanding of his career, very well-documented and full of facts. It is, however, while certainly not hagiography, written with the warm sympathy of a personal friend and co-religionist. Dudley Barker's book contains some interesting new material on the adolescent crisis but it suffers from an absence of sympathy with Chesterton's religious milieu and a strong dislike of Hilaire Belloc.

Gilbert Keith Chesterton was born in 1874. He was the son of Edward Chesterton 'the head of a hereditary business of house agents and surveyors, which had already been established for some three generations in Kensington'[1] but who, possessed of a private income and an imaginary heart condition, passed over most of his work to his brother and devoted himself to his family, to woodcarving, painting and playing with toy theatres. G.K. Chesterton's home was a secure and kindly world presided over by a father who 'serene, humorous and full of hobbies' knew all his English literature backwards. His mother, born Marie Louise Grosjean, of a family

4

originally Swiss in origin, was an energetic warm-hearted woman of sparkling wit and more unconventional views than her husband. She did not allow herself to be troubled by domestic concerns: 'Her clothes thrown on anyhow. . . . The house too was dusty and untidy.'[2] The Chesterton's were Liberal in politics, mildly Unitarian, if anything, in religion, affectionate and most indulgent parents who shared none of the supposedly typical Victorian rigour. They were, however, acutely conscious of the difference between themselves and the lower classes. Chesterton shocked his family as a child when screaming to be given a hat, 'If you don't give it me, I'll say 'at.'[3]

This happy childhood seems to have given Chesterton a lasting sense of wonder and delight in the mere existence of things: 'It was not merely a world full of wonders; it was a miraculous world.'[4] His father's toy-theatre provided a first vision of fantasy, a vivid romantic world, with its highly-coloured sharp-edged figures 'a sort of symbol of all I happen to like in imagery and ideas.'[5] He attributed to this early 'glimpse of some incredible paradise' his feeling for everything that emphasises a fine shade of distinction between one thing and another.

He was educated as a day-boy at St Paul's School and until around fifteen was a backward, day-dreaming, introverted lad. Uninterested in his schoolwork, he read avidly among the English classics, committing to memory pages of his favourite authors, especially Shakespeare, Scott and Dickens. In his later schooldays he struck up a close friendship with E. C. Bentley, later an author of light verse and of the classic detective story *Trent's Last Case*. They gathered round them a circle of boys of literary tastes who formed their own debating club in which Chesterton sharpened the skill in argument he displayed so markedly in later life. His schoolfriends eventually ran their own magazine, the *Debater*, most issues of which contained prose and verse by Chesterton. This material, much of it precocious and of high quality, was wholly unexpected from a boy his teachers had regarded as a near idiot.

Chesterton did not follow most of his friends to university but went instead to the Slade School of Art. His time there, the unhappiest and most troubled in his life, was of great significance in the development of his thought. A number of experiences, both intellectual and emotional convinced him of the reality of evil. The least serious of these involved a dabbling with Spiritualism but, he remarked:

> I have sometimes thought that this practice, of the true psychology of which we really know so little, may possibly have contributed towards the disturbed or even diseased state of brooding or idling through which I passed at that time.[6]

The period, it is fairly clear, corresponded with Chesterton's belated sexual maturation and his first encounters in the conversation of the idler students of the Slade, with the 'very negative and even nihilistic philosophy' of the time. To a boy from a loving, but perhaps over-protected background whose liberal optimistic decencies had almost passed over the existence of evil, the result was, in Maisie Ward's word 'crucifying'.[7]

Chesterton mentions a 'Congestion of imagination' in which he had 'an overpowering impulse to record and draw horrible ideas and images; plunging deeper and deeper as in a blind spiritual suicide.'[8] Dudley Barker, who has examined what by chance remains of these early notebooks, most of which Chesterton destroyed, suggests that several of the drawings record fantasies of sadistic sexual violence. Outwardly there was nothing to see of this but for Chesterton it was a dreadful revelation of his own and perhaps of all mens' inner nature: 'There is something truly menacing in the thought of how quickly I could imagine the maddest, when I had never committed the mildest crime.'[9] Although these impulses gradually passed away, they left an understanding of spiritual darkness all the more striking in a man whose gentleness, warmth and sheer goodness, attested by so many witnesses, seem to have bordered on the saintly and whose jovial insistence on the joy of life and the value of laughter offended grave men like the Anglican C. F. G. Masterman and the atheist Robert Blatchford.

Perhaps more significant than these adolescent sexual disorders was the effect of the sceptical and solipsistic intellectual trends of the period in philosophy and in art, picked up in conversation or casual hints or because they were in the air at the Slade. Artistic impressionism and subjectivist ideas lent themselves to the 'metaphysical suggestion that things only exist as we perceive them, or things do not exist at all.'[10] For Chesterton these notions contributed to a mood of unreality and 'sterile isolation', to a loss of the distinction between sleeping and waking, to the 'metaphysical doubt' of the world's reality.

This crisis, intellectual and emotional and accompanied by great unhappiness seems to have lasted for three years. In Chesterton's words he 'dislodged the incubus' by thinking it out for himself with little help from philosophy and none from religion. Since he had dug low enough in his own mind to discover the devil, he was unimpressed by sceptical arguments about the relativity of evil or meaninglessness of sin. He countered suggestions of the unreality of existence by an insistence on its wonder:

> Anything was magnificent compared with nothing. Even if the very daylight was a dream, it was a day-dream; it was not a nightmare.[11]

He was confirmed in this looking at things with a 'mystical minimum of gratitude' by his reading of Stevenson and Browning. The latter was to be the subject of the book which, more than any other, launched his reputation. When his career as a writer began five years after the crisis at the Slade, he was 'full of a new and fiery resolution to write against the Decadents and Pessimists who ruled the culture of the age.'[12] Chesterton worked for two successive publishers, moving over gradually from the second, Fisher Unwin, into journalism. In the autumn of 1899 he started his first full-time journalistic employment with the *Speaker*, a weekly which had been taken over by a group of young, advanced Liberals, members of that small and courageous minority opposed to the Boer War. Chesterton's determined attacks on the war in a number of articles in the *Speaker* began to make his name widely known.

It was at this time that he formed the two most significant relationships of his life, striking up a close friendship with Hilaire Belloc in 1900, and marrying Frances Blogg after an engagement of three years in 1901. Belloc was by all accounts a strong intellectual influence on Chesterton, if only in selected areas, notably history, politics and sociology. Chesterton's style, philosophy, theology and approach to literature, already defined in embryonic form as his early notebooks show, remained unaffected by his friend. Belloc is in some ways a difficult figure to treat justly. His once considerable reputation has almost evaporated and critical neglect is flavoured, as it is not in Chesterton's case, with a dismissive hostility. Even many of those interested in Chesterton see the association with Belloc as a liability and its effect as wholly negative.

Chesterton's own account, found mainly in 'The Portrait of a Friend' chapter in *Autobiography*, makes it clear that he admired Belloc's range of information, his distinctly 'French' logic and wit, his practical knowledge of military and political technique. He was a man who knew how as well as why he would fight and his French connections represented a window on to another culture and a wider European world. Belloc's travel books, especially *The Path to Rome*, his biographies of *Danton* and *Marie Antoinette*, the short study of *The French Revolution* and the historical sketches in *The Eye Witness*, among much else, still have the power to move and stir the reader. Their beautifully cadenced, artfully simple, if somewhat mannered prose remains effective in an age less indulgent than the Edwardian to self-conscious rhetorical effect. They all possess, to a high degree, the power to make Belloc's vision of the past a living reality, convincing by the force of his imagination and the cogency of the arguments which support it. His major political polemic, *The Servile State*, displays, even more clearly, powers of close reasoning and an almost Swiftian energy and spareness. Altogether a much more formidable figure than critical received opinion currently allows, Belloc certainly widened the range of his friend's knowledge both of European culture and history. Together, they were to form a mutually complementary and highly effective intellectual partnership.

However, along with real advantages, Belloc's influence did indeed have its drawbacks. His logic and intellectual rigour could lend itself to a narrow fanaticism, his trenchancy in argument become a harsh, bitter, inexorable bullying. His love of Europe and the weight he put on its significance blinded him to the value of other cultures. Belloc had, besides, in spite of much warmth and a debonair gaiety, the capacity for intense personal hatred foreign to Chesterton. (It is witnessed, for example, by his unedifying and blatantly unfair feud with Masterman from which Chesterton

8

deliberately distanced himself). Belloc's radicalism and social concern, so passionate and sincere, were flawed by that obsession with Jewish conspiracies characteristic of the Third Republic and which reached its nadir in the Dreyfus case. It is arguable that these unattractive features of Belloc's mind had some influence on Chesterton, especially in the overheated period between the Marconi case and his physical and nervous breakdown in 1914. Nevertheless, it is difficult to sum up all the effects of a close friendship and intellectual alliance of more than thirty years. Belloc cannot be left out of the account or swept under the carpet as an embarrassment. Perhaps his biggest contribution to Chesterton's career lay in the increased intellectual confidence he gave him. In challenging settled historical and cultural attitudes, such as the Whig view of history or the various widely canvassed theories of Socialism and in urging alternative views, Chesterton could call on a powerful and scholarly mind, which, if it was much less original than his own, was well furnished with facts and endowed with more accuracy in detail than he could manage.

Chesterton's wife, a devout Anglo-Catholic, was influential in his movement, completed by *Orthodoxy* (1908), if not before, towards a fully developed Christian position. She was a strong-minded woman, a rebel against the conventional Bohemianism of her home in Bedford Park, then something of an artists' colony, and the 'Saffron Park' of *The Man who was Thursday*. Devoted to her husband, she did not share his expansive, high-spirited nature or convivial habits. His friends blamed her for persuading him to leave his Fleet Street life and settle in Beaconsfield in 1911. Her inability to have children, in spite of an operation to enable her to do so, her years of pain through arthritis and her proneness to nervous depression caused them both much sorrow. It was, nevertheless, a loving marriage. She gave Chesterton emotional support and did much to curb his carelessness with money, and occasional excessive drinking.

Chesterton's spate of books began with a volume of nonsense verse *Greybeards at Play* and one of serious poetry *The Wild Knight* (both 1900). These are of some interest as throwing light on themes in his later work, but not much marked at the time. *The Defendant*

(1901), made up of essays already published in the *Speaker*, created more of a stir. Chesterton's distinctive style, blending the humorous and serious, was not approved by all the reviewers, but it marked the appearance of a new voice in the contemporary war of ideas. Chesterton began to reach a wider public after he moved from the *Speaker* to employment with the mass-circulation paper the *Daily News* (1901). *Twelve Types* (1902), again drawn from articles published in periodicals, aroused an increasing attention but it was with his first full length critical study *Robert Browning* (1903) that Chesterton's reputation was, in a true sense, launched. *Robert Browning* marked a change of direction in appreciation and understanding of the poet, throwing new light on his 'obscurity' and the nature of his grotesque art and of the grotesque in general. The book showed characteristics found in the later critical works, extreme originality, and a fresh and fruitful view of the subject, combined with casual inaccuracies. (Chesterton even invented a line of 'Mr Sludge the Medium'). He trusted to his excellent memory in quotations, feeling that to verify references was pedantic and blurred the image of the poem or novel already existing in his mind. It was a habit irritating to scholars.

In 1904 came the first of his novels: *The Napoleon of Notting Hill*, exploring his social ideals and conception of adventure. The monograph on *G.F. Watts* of the same year is an interesting examination of a now unfashionable painter, a statement of Chesterton's own artistic views but, most of all, along with the work on Browning and Dickens, testifies to his understanding of one of his abiding interests, the mind of the Victorian age.

The Club of Queer Trades, another fantastic novel was published in 1905 together with *Heretics*, a good humoured but exceedingly effective dissection of the 'philosophies' advanced by some of his contemporaries. The chapters on Shaw and Kipling are especially perceptive. The following year saw the emergence of a more significant work, *Charles Dickens*. Chesterton's views on Dickens, advanced in the study of 1906, and a series of prefaces to the novels published as *Appreciations and Criticisms of the Works of Charles Dickens* in 1911, were as exciting and innovative as his work on Browning. He succeeded in changing the direction of Dickens studies, in deepening an understanding of the mythic nature of Dicken's art and in contributing to a revival of his critical reputation.

These early books and his *Daily News* articles were substantial reasons for the growth of Chesterton's reputation. Like Shaw and other Edwardian writers he developed a public image of persona during these years. It is worth noting, however, that Chesterton's 'props', his long cloaks and slouch hat, regarded as reprehensible now by sober scholars, were not a pose but adopted at the insistence of his wife, who sensibly felt that if he could not look tidy, he might as well look picturesque.

Two of Chesterton's most important works, his greatest novel *The Man who was Thursday* and the first of his two major apologetics, *Orthodoxy*, appeared in 1908. *The Man who was Thursday* is, among much else, a richly suggestive allegory, at times reminiscent of Kafka, at times suggesting, as one of Chesterton's friends remarked, that the publisher had commissioned him to write a version of *The Pilgrim's Progress* in the style of *The Pickwick Papers*.[13] *Orthodoxy* is an intellectual autobiography, a history of the development of Chesterton's mind up to his thirty-fourth year and the picture of a soul's search for truth in the modern world. It is also particularly interesting for its exploration of religious and psychological truths incarnate in myths, folk-tales or fairy stories, for its working out of a Christian philosophy as a perilous balance of many conflicting claims and appetites and for a persuasive argument that the ills of the modern world stem from its passion for facts and the inductive method. *Orthodoxy* and *The Man who was Thursday* mark a new profundity and subtlety in Chesterton's thought.

In 1909 Chesterton published a study of his friend and controversial opponent in *George Bernard Shaw*, an amusing, good-tempered but searching critique of Shavianism and, still, perhaps, among the best books on the subject. *Tremendous Trifles*, a collection of essays republished from periodicals, appeared in the same year. *The Ball and the Cross* the best designed and most coherent, if not the greatest, of the novels came out in 1910, along with an important book of social criticism, *What's Wrong with the World*. Less thoroughly argued and grounded in theory than the post-war *The Outline of Sanity*, it marks a new stage in Chesterton's conflict with his society, dropping some of the lightness of touch and pure fun of *Heretics* and testifying to his sense of social crisis in the pre-1914 capitalist world, the imminence of its disintegration, and the need to 'repent and return', to earlier, pre-industrial conceptions of property and community.

The book is a milestone, too, in Chesterton's steady disillusionment with the Liberal Party, the conduct of parliamentary government, and the Establishment in general, which had been going on since 1906, and in his increasing interest in alternatives both to contemporary capitalism and to the various Socialist theories then current. The grounds for his disenchantment were partly a belief that corruption, collusion between both political parties – whose members often belonged to the same families and almost always to the same class – and the suppression of information, were combining to stifle freedom. Partly, too, it was the conviction shared with Belloc, who was to develop it in his *The Servile State*, that many of the social reforms of the Asquith Government, now regarded as the foundation of the Welfare State, meant insufferable interference in the lives of ordinary people, and were destructive of freedom and the family. Equivalent to the bread and circuses of ancient Rome, they tended to create a permanent proletariat who gave up liberty in exchange for a minimum of material security. They acted besides as a camouflage for the retention of power by the plutocracy and prevented the true solution of the social problem, a massive redistribution of property. As Chesterton's convictions on these points hardened in the crisis years before 1914, his writing took on a bitter tone absent before and not noticeable later.

The first of the collections of Father Brown stories, already published in magazines, appeared as *The Innocence of Father Brown* in 1911, together with the striking minor epic on King Alfred's struggle with the Danes, *The Ballad of the White Horse*. Father Brown was Chesterton's most popular, though obviously not his greatest literary achievement. The stories mark a sharp break with the ratiocinative methods of detection which were the staple of the detective story from its probable beginnings in Poe and which reached a climax in Conan Doyle. Father Brown operates instead by intuition informed by a theological knowledge of human nature. A few of the stories are outstanding narratives. Almost all have striking settings which illustrate Chesterton's taste in the visual. Generally they operate as vehicles, at a popular level, for his thought and distinctive view of life and confirm his interest, stated several times, in the possibilities of the detective story as a fictional form. *The Innocence of Father Brown* was followed by other collections, *The Wisdom of Father Brown* (1914), *The Secret of Father Brown* (1927) and *The Scandal of Father Brown* (1935). *The Man who knew too much* (1922), though less well known, is a collection completely different in flavour and with a detective most unlike Father Brown.

Manalive (1912), another fantasy novel, 'a hymn to life' in Maisie Ward's phrase, or rather a parable of the recovery of zest and delight in the gift of living, is interesting also as Chesterton's first fictional examination of questions of sanity and mental illness. The same year saw the appearance of a major collection of essays, *A Miscellany of Men*. Chesterton's work on Victorian literature was augmented in 1913 by a volume commissioned by the Home University Library, *The Victorian Age in Literature*. Full of vivid phrases and stimulating generalisation, it is a pioneering work in cultural history.

Observers had noticed for some years that Chesterton's rate of article and book production must be straining even his remarkable powers of work. The incessant flow of writing and public appearances contributed to stresses from about 1911 until his illness in 1914 in which his drinking, for the only time in his life, became careless. The main cause of his nervous strain, however, was almost certainly political disillusionment, reaching a climax in the Marconi Case (1912–13). It is unnecessary to rehearse the convoluted story recounted in detail by Maisie Ward,[14] of Lloyd George's and Rufus Isaac's dealings in shares of the Marconi Company. Though not actually dishonest, their conduct was certainly improper and the subsequent inquiry by the Government, of which they were both members, was a bland, whitewashing exercise. Chesterton's brother Cecil and Belloc, who in 1911 had founded a paper *The Eye Witness* to expose corruption and official secrecy, saw the Marconi episode as evidence of the manipulation of parliamentary forms by an oligarchy of financiers. Cecil Chesterton's attacks on Rufus Isaacs led to his trial on a charge of criminal libel which his brother attended.

There is an overheated quality about the Marconi Case, as about so much else in the period, such as the Irish crisis, the great waves of strikes, the Suffragette campaign, and the advocacy of violence over Ulster by the Tory Party. Cecil Chesterton's and Belloc's over-wrought reactions, typical of the time, coloured Gilbert Chesterton's mind. A deeply sensitive man, he found the sight of his brother in the dock traumatic. The onset of the war horrified him, although like thousands of others he believed it a crusade. He suffered a complete physical and nervous breakdown and almost died in 1914/15.

The Marconi Case had other deeply unfortunate consequences. Rufus Isaac's legal action against his brother, although, in fact, it led only to a £100 fine, confirmed the preoccupation with Jewish financiers Gilbert Chesterton had caught from Belloc. There are certain obvious points which might be made in what remains a painful and difficult subject. Neither Chesterton nor Belloc were racialists. Indeed their whole view of history was fundamentally opposed to racialist and historicist conceptions. They constantly ridiculed such expressions as 'Aryan', 'Nordic Man' and 'The Anglo-Saxon race' which were tolerated in serious writing at that time. Chesterton's attacks on Hitler and the Nazi movement in the last years of his life, were among the most vehement of any British journalist, as was recognised by Rabbi Wise, one of the leaders of American Jewry.[15] He himself rebutted the charge of anti-Semitism on more than one occasion. In fact, as he made clear in an important interview published in the *Jewish Chronicle* in 1911,[16] he supported the Zionist movement which was growing in the early years of the century and of his career. He developed this position in full in *The New Jerusalem* (1919), which records, among much else, a tour of Jewish settlements in Palestine, in the company of a friend, Dr Montague Eder.

However, in attacking individuals like Rufus Isaacs, or the Rand millionaires whom he and Belloc thought, not entirely without justification, had helped to cause the Boer War, he was thoughtless in his choice of language. Leo Hetzler remarks with some truth, but perhaps too much charity, that:

unfortunately Chesterton did on occasion carelessly collectivise such Jewish individuals simply as 'Jews'. This was due partly to carelessness, in view of his full and total position, partly to the habitually open way in which he expressed his opinion about every subject without giving heed to what connotations might be inferred, and partly to the strain he was undergoing in the years 1911–1914...[17]

This language, like much of the jocular references to Jews in popular literature up to the Second World War, reads far worse after the horrors of Hitler's final solution, an effect from which Chesterton may be acquitted.

Although a defence may be attempted along these lines, when all has been said, no one could or should attempt to deny that there are passages in Chesterton's writings which are painful to read, expressions of a crude anti-Jewish feeling, not very numerous indeed, but bewildering in a mind generally notably humane and sophisticated. So admirable and attractive in Chesterton that there is a strong temptation to gloss the subject over. Perhaps it is best simply to admit it without exaggerating its significance. It is far from being a dominant element in his work and other fine writers and artists were infected by what was, after all, one of the most insidious poisons of the European mind in this period. It is as well not to get the matter out of proportion. A critic who would, rightly, contend that we may admire D.H. Lawrence in spite of his, often hair-raising, political views should have little trouble with Chesterton's references to Jews which are small beer in comparison.

The Flying Inn (1914) containing Chesterton's most thorough analysis of Nietzscheanism was his last pre-war novel. After his recovery from his illness, Chesterton threw himself into pamphlet-writing in the Allied cause. He felt, sincerely, but too simply, that Prussia represented an attack on Christian and democratic values. However, the chief publication of the war years was, without doubt, his revisionist *A Short History of England* (1917), a deliberately provocative but suggestive attack on the Whig view of history. In answer to this prevailing orthodoxy, Chesterton tried to show England's post-medieval history not as a growth of liberty and wealth, but as a concentration of power and property in the hands of the few and the destruction of the sense of community.

Chesterton at the end of the First World War was filled with forebodings of future conflict, a warning which he repeated several times in the 1920s and 1930s and with a pain all the sharper for the death of his soldier brother, Cecil, shortly after the Armistice. He had edited Cecil's magazine, renamed the *New Witness*, during his brother's absence in France and felt it his duty to carry on both Cecil's political crusade and the paper, in some form or another. This decision was to be a drain on Chesterton's energy and resources for the remainder of his life, which it may have helped to shorten. His wife and many of his friends would have preferred him to have devoted himself to literature. His refusal to do this suggests how seriously he viewed the contemporary situation and how much he wished to influence it.

After some vicissitudes the magazine was re-founded as *G.K's Weekly* in 1925 and Chesterton edited it until his death eleven years later. He used it as a platform to crusade for the redistribution of land, for financial moves to create large numbers of small farmers and shopkeepers and for the strengthening of the family and the local community against the state and large capitalists. The Distributist League was founded to propagate this programme and to help support the magazine. Much of Chesterton's time was taken up in smoothing over the quarrels which occurred between the often prickly and occasionally cranky members of the League. Although during his lifetime it stirred some interest, the notion of Distributism sank into oblivion in the changed social and political climate after 1945, when the enormous extension of the Welfare State seemed the only answer to the economic and social problems of the mass of people. However, recently at least some of the ideas Chesterton promoted are being seriously discussed: as is witnessed by the immense acclaim given to Schumacher's book *Small is Beautiful* (1973), among others. It is difficult to offer a final verdict on the diligent and exhausting Distributist crusade of the 1920s and 1930s in the present unsettled economic climate but it would be wrong to dismiss it.

Chesterton travelled widely in the immediate post-war years and described what he saw in a number of books, *Irish Impressions* (1919), *The New Jerusalem* (1920) and *What I saw in America* (1922). All are acute and lively attempts to dispel British prejudices. He attacked what he saw as a mounting offensive against marriage and the family in *The Superstition of Divorce* (1920) and in *Eugenics and Other Evils* (1922). The latter book was an outstanding example of a campaign which began as early as 1901 with a denunciation of Professor Karl Pearson's advocacy of selected marriages to achieve racial purity. One of Chesterton's many services was his steady opposition to medical views which, although this is now forgotten, were widespread and respectable, at least until the rise of Hitler.

After contemplating the step for a number of years, Chesterton was received into the Catholic Church in 1922. Although this brought him personally much happiness, it was the conclusion and confirmation of long-established intellectual tendencies rather than a dramatic reversal of them. It cannot be said that his conversion is a vital date in the history of his work.

The interval between the closing of the *New Witness* and the opening of *G.K.'s Weekly* gave the opportunity for writing two of Chesterton's finest works, the engaging *St Francis of Assisi* (1923) and, perhaps his most important single book, *The Everlasting Man* (1925). The latter was written in response to H.G. Wells' *Outline of History*, itself a fine work of popularisation. Chesterton was concerned not to attack Wells, of whom he was personally fond, but to substitute for fantasies of scientific progress and inflated evolutionary ideology, a reading of history based on a better understanding of mankind's need of both the mythic and the rational.

Chesterton's growing political interests were reflected in *William Cobbett* (1925), an examination of a writer he plausibly regarded as the prophet of Distributism and *The Outline of Sanity* (1926), much more careful and programmatic than his earlier social criticism. It is possible that his interest in fiction declined somewhat. Collections of stories like *Tales of the Long Bow* (1925), *The Poet and the Lunatics* (1929) and *Four Faultless Felons* (1930) contain much that is both thoughtful and diverting but they cannot be compared with the pre-war novels. *The Return of Don Quixote* (1927), however, is the exception for which considerable claims might be made. Chesterton's later literary criticism, while not revolutionary as the Dickens and Browning studies had been, is still illuminating. *Robert Louis*

Stevenson (1927) is a plea for one of the writers he had most admired in his youth and whose reputation was going into relative decline. *Chaucer* (1932), although suffering from a somewhat partisan and simplistic view of the Middle Ages, remains a thoroughly enjoyable introduction to the subject. Chesterton made no claims to minute scholarship, but his critical books, in spite of his carelessness, occasional howlers, and refusal to engage closely with the text in a manner becoming more and more obligatory towards the end of his life, abound in illuminating phrases and exciting generalisation.

Collections of his periodical articles continued to appear for the remainder of his life, under such titles as *Generally speaking* (1928), *Come to think of It* (1930), *All is Grist* (1931), *All I survey* (1933), *Avowals and Denials* (1934), *As I was saying* (1936). While most readers would agree that these later essays show signs of fatigue and nobody would dream of resting Chesterton's reputation on them, the decline is far from uniform. There are many striking passages and individual pieces. The religious polemics, *The Thing* (1929) and *The Well and the Shallows* (1935) attacking the welter of confusions he discerned in contemporary Protestantism and the current intellectual chaos in general, have an astringency unlike most of Chesterton's controversial writing. They represent both a hardening of attitude and a fear of the future and suggest that he could have argued in an altogether harder, more stinging fashion, if he had so wished. (Curiously, but symptomatically, Belloc singled out one of these atypical polemics *The Thing* from his friend's writings as specially admirable).[18]

Perhaps the finest of the late books however, is *St Thomas Aquinas* (1933), the companion to *St Francis of Assisi*, which succeeds in rendering accessible the often abstruse thought and elusive personality of a figure who, unlike St Francis, has little in the way of romantic incidents or obvious charm to recommend him. The greatest Aquinas scholar of the time, Etienne Gilson, regarded it as incomparably the best work ever written on the subject.[19]

Chesterton's health had shown signs of deterioration from about 1934. The strain of overwork, of smoothing over internecine feuds among the Distributists and his distress over public events, which as an intimate friend said, left him heartbroken,[20] all contributed to undermine his strength. He died on 14 July 1936 at his home in Beaconsfield. The *Autobiography*, which he had completed in the last months of his life, was the first of a number of books to be published posthumously. These are mainly collections of articles from throughout his career, including much material of high quality, notably in *Lunacy and Letters*, *A Handful of Authors*, *The Common Man*, and *Chesterton on Shakespeare*.

Chesterton, although not exempt from sorrows and problems, enjoyed the rewards of his warmth and of his constant intellectual energy and curiosity. A friend remarked that 'It was his life-long beatitude to observe and ponder and conclude.'[21]

II

THE EDWARDIAN CULTURAL CRISIS

Chesterton's essay *Simplicity and Tolstoy* (1912)[1] is interesting for several reasons. Like much of his essay-writing published in book form, it contains evidence of revision and development of an original newspaper article. This habit of revision and partial re-writing belies, of course, the notion of a careless flow of language and ideas held even by many of his admirers as his commanding characteristic. He may have cared relatively little for literary form in some fields, especially perhaps in the novel. But the working-over of the essays, though not in itself proof of quality, is evidence that he was deliberate and careful in the expression of his thought; that he was concerned to correct imbalances, to develop points he made, and occasionally to bring his work up to date.

All these concerns are apparent in the Tolstoy essay of 1912, which is an amplification of a *Daily News* article of 1903[2] and of Chesterton's contribution to a booklet in the same year.[3] In the later version the tone of the writing is more serious and the figure of Tolstoy is used as the vehicle for a highly suggestive analysis of the tendencies of the times. The considered judgement of 1912 differs substantially from the perceptions of 1903. The earlier essays praise Tolstoy's teachings as an indication that the world is still young enough to experience enthusiasm, the only happiness possible or conceivable under the sun. Tolstoy is celebrated, along with Belloc and Shaw, for holding views on every subject consistent with one 'real solid and serious view of life.'[4] He is criticised for desiring to simplify life more than it is either possible or desirable to do.

In the later composite essay these points are developed into a view of the increasing ideological tendency of the twentieth century. Essentially, Chesterton declares, it is towards a great simplicity that the world is heading 'not deliberately but rather inevitably.'[5] Contemporary man's habit of speculation, his deep and continuous contemplation of things, necessarily produces a formula for understanding the world, for rendering its complexities down into a straightforward scheme. This contemplation is the only way in which the world can become comprehensible and as such is a natural habit in any intellectual man, rather than, as in the earlier essays, a portent peculiar to Tolstoy and a few others, a rare sign of life in a languid world. The sense of unity that contemplation produces is accompanied by a feeling of exhilaration. Often, too, the formula for understanding experience is 'sensational' in character. Neither exhilaration nor sensationalism, however, are, in themselves, a fair ground of complaint against the process of simplification. Both are features of its greatest manifestation, monotheism. They are, none the less, points where the mind is vulnerable, where danger may arise. If the simplification arrived at is unbalanced or fallacious, the natural constitution of the human mind gives it a terrible dynamic. The result is not a saving truth but a mad ideology.

To Chesterton the ideological nature of the twentieth century was, by 1912, its most salient feature:

> Few people will dispute that all the typical movements of our time are upon the road towards simplification. Each system seeks to be more fundamental than the other.[6]

The appetite for simplification explains the movement from the old classical and Renaissance idealisation of the human form through several phases, first Realism, a conception formed from the facts of natural history, of a faith to truth, however prosaic; then Impressionism, 'going yet deeper,' judging by the physical eye and preferring a momentary aspect glimpsed, however strange, to any categorisation and finally to Symbolism, which deserts both categorisation and sense impression, to arrive at truth through direct spiritual apprehension.

21

The essay of 1912 develops the notion of an historical process behind, and of the ambivalence and the dangers inherent within, the cultural movement towards simplification. In the two 'source' articles the historical consciousness is only faintly present. Chesterton is mainly concerned to show the startling novelty of 'a faith as fierce and practical as that of the Mahometans who swept across Africa and Europe shouting a single word.'[7] The additional material in *Simplicity and Tolstoy* relates mainly to the sense of a rebirth of the religious spirit, not as an isolated phenomenon or a stray survival but as 'one of the most thrilling and dramatic incidents in our modern civilisation.'[8] In 1903, Tolstoy had been a rare and startling event, 'something out of a dream..., in this iron-bound homogeneous and clockwork age.'[9] By 1912, Tolstoyanism is an apocalyptic cultural upheaval, marking some great change in the structure of thought and morals. Scepticism and 'schools of negation' having done their work and completed their cycle terminate in the 'stunning' and 'hypnotic' rebirth of religious ideology. Chesterton's final essay drops the rollicking and amusingly critical tone of the 'source' articles. In *Simplicity and Tolstoy* he is deeply impressed and deeply disturbed.

The revision of the Tolstoy material indicates the author's sense of having passed an historical dividing line. It is possible from other writings to date, fairly precisely, the point at which Chesterton's sense of the keynote quality of his time, of its cultural crisis, changed. The opening terms of his argument in *Heretics* (1905) represents a plea for an approach to contemporary literature through the history and evaluation of ideas. He attacks as a contemporary phenomenon of English life, a taste for indirection and blurring of issues. The refusal to think matters through has produced mediocrity in the arts and incompetence in politics. Without positive ideals and standards strong literary effects are impossible. Art may be theoretically 'unmoral'; the artist at liberty to produce what he likes. The result is 'a few roundels'. A notional freedom to wreck heaven and earth with an amoral energy results in Alfred Austin as Poet Laureate. The bondage of the men of old, dominated by their philosophy or steeped in their religion, comes to more than a 'freedom' devoid of will or sense of purpose. Politically, Chesterton refers to a constant harping on 'efficiency' 'practicality' or 'progress' at the expense of general theories of the good as the symptom and the cause of deadlock: 'Our affairs are hopelessly muddled by strong, silent men.'[10] The 'repudiation of big words and big visions' makes political discourse nugatory and political action, even the machinery of government itself, ineffective. *Heretics* is directed at the problem of a culture becoming stultified for lack of general ideas and clear thinking. It is a plea for the importance of ideology.

Within a very few years the climate it describes appeared to Chesterton to have altered radically. He began to put the accent elsewhere. In a *Daily News* article of 1910,[11] he remarked on the utter inconsistency of 'that old compromise of Queen Victoria', its muddle-headed determination to have all the good things at once: loyalty and liberty, Anglicanism and Agnosticism, Lord Tennyson and the Party-system. It was a very comfortable and cosy world but one whose intellectual framework had become untenable. In *The Victorian Age in Literature* (1913) he castigated the latter Victorians for the tired emptiness of their debates and discussions, their refusal to face fundamental questions, their disillusioned conviction that all ideas and issues were meaningless and jejune. It was an atmosphere of a spiritual autumn 'like one long afternoon in a rich house on a rainy day.'[12] In Chesterton's analysis the 'Victorian compromise' ended by falling between two stools, rejecting 'creative politics', citizenship or public values and equally, deeply felt spirituality. The features of that compromise, which coloured the intellectual scene in *Heretics*, a book intended to display the *unrealised* ideological element in contemporary writing rather than to discuss overt ideologies, have been relegated to the past.

Chesterton's initial perception, then, about the cultural crisis of his time was the need, inherited from the period 1870 to 1900, for simplification, for a discovery of essentials, a debate about ends, if intellectual stagnation was to be freshened. Within a few years he came to feel 'simplification' was taking place but in a heady and misdirected fashion. A watershed had been passed and the danger most apparent in *Heretics*, stultification, had by *Simplicity and Tolstoy*, if not before, become that of falling prey to perverse or misapplied simplification. The situation was complicated by the persistence into this changing climate of inherited habits of mind. The mental equipment they had inherited from the late-Victorians, their tendency to dodge issues, tolerate inconsistencies, avoid logical conclusions, above all their distaste for discussing general ideas prevented their recognising the effect of those ideas on their own minds.

Chesterton's first object in developing his controversial style, was to point out the forgotten importance of ideas, as a prelude to political action:

I revert to the doctrinal methods of the thirteenth century, inspired by the general hope of getting something done.[13]

His subsequent aim is an important modification of his first. Mental clarity, a re-awakened sense of the effect of ideas in a culture are not necessary now so much to break a deadlock. Rather they are a defence against an influx of ideology. Five years after *Heretics*, in *What's wrong with the World* (1910), his most elaborate piece of social and cultural analysis before 1914, Chesterton states as his main conclusion about culture that it stands in need of selection and rejection rather than expansion. The lethargy of a few years before has given way to a tumult:

Out of all this throng of theories [education] must somehow select a theory; out of all these thundering voices it must manage to hear a voice; out of all this awful and aching battle of blinding lights, without one shadow to give shape to them, it must manage somehow to trace and track a star.[14]

One obvious factor in Chesterton's change of priorities was, of course, his rapid disillusionment with the possibility of social, moral and intellectual change through the Liberal Party. The earlier essays belong to a period of high hopes and anticipations. A Liberal victory was obviously coming from the beginning of 1903. (Throughout that year the readers of Chesterton's *Daily News* articles amused themselves on the 'Letters Page' by speculating on who would be in the Liberal Cabinet). After 1906, there was no obvious solution to anticipate. It was no longer a matter simply of enlivening the cultural scene, whose problems came to appear more complex, intractable and dangerous.

Such an explanation, however, cannot be stretched to cover all the facts. Much more important was the effect of the rapid circulation of foreign philosophies after 1906. Orage's book on Nietzsche, *Friedrich Nietzsche, the Dionysian Spirit of the Age*, the first fairly accurate account of his thought in English dates from that year. No articles on Bergson were published in the seventeen periodicals listed in the *Readers' Guide to Periodical Literature* between 1905 and 1910. Between 1910 and 1914 there came a rush of over thirty.[15] Although Tolstoy had been a celebrity for many years, English interest in Tolstoyanism reached a climax between 1910 and the First World War.[16] Many examples to suggest an influx of foreign ideas after 1906, might be quoted.

Chesterton's changing attitude to simplification and to the importance of ideas represents a recognition of, and an agile response to this invasion which gathered force in the later Edwardian years. It represented an increased knowledge, due to fuller information and further reflection. It is interesting, for example, to compare the account given to Tolstoyanism in *Heretics* with that offered in *Simplicity and Tolstoy* seven years later. The *Heretics* essay ('Sandals and Simplicity'), treats the simplicity of Tolstoy's followers genially as a concern with the mere externals of diet and dress, a simplicity in things which do not matter coupled with a self-conscious over-elaboration of the things that do matter 'in philosophy, in loyalty, in spiritual acceptance, and spiritual rejection.'[17] Though the main criticism is serious, the tone of the essay is light and casual, relaxing into mild little jokes about 'grape-nuts' and raw tomatoes. Chesterton seems to feel he is describing a fad which could be cured by 'a little plain thinking'. In *Simplicity and Tolstoy*, he again makes the contrast between unselfconscious and studied simplicity but the manner of his approach to the problem is different. Chesterton recognises that he is dealing with a formidable ideology, typical of its time, which could overturn the world. He admits the power and appeal of Tolstoyanism, the magnificent and 'really honourable' confidence in human nature which ignores most men's account of their own motives. Its grandeur and terrifying consistency represent the revival, though in a perverted form, of a religious dynamic. Its Gospel literalness cannot be refuted by the 'facts of the world', but this 'simplification' runs counter to the complexity and ambivalence of human motives as they are, the vanity and self-advertisement and morbid sensibility of imperfect man:

> The command of Christ is impossible, but it is not insane; it is rather sanity preached to a planet of lunatics.[18]

The strange attractiveness of this short cut to a happy and harmonious world, of the 'sanity' of the Tolstoyan attack on family, patriotism, even on the instinct of sexuality, though utterly inhuman and destructive of civilised life, have a force which shows that ideas are, with the new century, coming into their own. The re-emergence of the religious spirit in the form of ideologies is a portent and Chesterton is clear both about the religious roots and the cultural importance of the phenomenon. Tolstoyanism is:

> one of the most thrilling and dramatic incidents in our modern civilisation. It represents a tribute to the Christian religion more sensational than the breaking of seals and the falling of stars.[19]

The apocalyptic images are appropriate since this is a messianic upheaval, the revenge of religious instincts suppressed or denied. This power makes such visions stunning and hypnotic. The most convinced rationalists must be dismayed and bewildered by the rebirth of such new forms of 'a strange and ancient vision'. The future is suddenly wrenched away from them and their schemes of thought, 'the immense sceptical cosmogonies of this age' vanish 'like dreams'. Forgotten levels of mind are stirred to a realisation that:

> the dark sayings handed down through eighteen centuries contain, in themselves, revolutions of which we have only just begun to dream.[20]

This crucial change in Chesterton's diagnosis of the intellectual climate of his early career cautions the student against taking 'The Edwardian Era', short as it was, as an undifferentiated unit or of believing that its controversies were conducted within the same ambience.

Between *Heretics*, the very title of which is playful, and *What's wrong with the World* or *Simplicity and Tolstoy* lies a greater seriousness, stemming from the recognition of new tensions, new dangers and possibilities. There is, too, a discernible shift in Chesterton's aim. At first he wished to activate a public who felt theories were jejune. A little later he felt the need to defend that same public against intoxicating, often unrecognised, theories which they possessed no equipment to criticise.

Accounts of Chesterton's reaction against the 1890s have tended rightly to stress his rejection of pessimism and solipsism, linking that rejection to his own emotional crisis recorded in *Autobiography*. From very early in his writing on the previous generation, it is worth noting that he remarked on provinciality, as well as apathy or pessimism, as a keynote of their culture. In 'A Neglected Originality,' a *Daily News* article of 1902, for example, he contrasted the poetry of such writers as Aubrey de Vere, or Roden Noel concerned with 'great problems and great struggles', the philosophical concerns of a strenuous period, with 'fin de siècle preciosity'. It is not the pessimism of the latter but its provinciality on which he dwells. He quotes at length and approvingly Roden Noel's remark that England has, more and more, as a nation, withdrawn itself 'from active participation in events of a cosmopolitan interest.'[21] Chesterton then comments that to such a man as Noel, the movement from ethics and politics toward a notion of beauty or an exaltation of technique in writing, as objects of intellectual concern, are a retreat into 'one fashionable *petite culture*'. Contemporary use of 'early Victorian' as a derogatory term is peculiarly inept since this was:

> the last period in our history which did anything or wanted to do anything, which had any theory of the present or any scheme for the future.[22]

The essay is interesting because it links the laziness or apathy which is Chesterton's constant theme with the secondary factor of ignorance or narrowness. Both are contributory to the nation's vulnerability to ideological invasion. In *The Victorian Age in Literature* (1913) he develops from hindsight, his perception of the 'odd provincialism' of the great Victorians. In a well-known passage he

27

touches on the inequalities, the lapses, in the work of the finest writers of the period. Carlyle, Dickens, Ruskin, even Arnold, with his ideal of a balanced culture, were 'lame giants'. Sweeping the intellectual sky at one moment, they 'suddenly shrivel to something indescribably small.'[23] The very vastness of their knowledge throws into stronger relief 'the abrupt abyss of what they do not know'. Most of the instances of this ignorance Chesterton quotes reflect an over-confident insularity, a contempt for the Irish, for contemporary European or English Catholicism, for example. These ill-founded, dismissive notions, invariably flavoured with a certain crankiness, reveal the 'freakish and unphilosophical' nature of a great civilisation, that it had too narrow a base, was too inward-looking:

> They were in a kind of pocket; they appealed to too narrow a public opinion. I am certain that no French or German man of the same genius made such remarks.[24]

In a subsequent essay, entitled 'From Meredith to Rupert Brooke' and published as a supplement to *The Victorian Age in Literature*, he instances the colouring of later Victorian thought by romantic racial theories as a primary and prominent fact about its perceptions, worth noting 'because it is not generally mentioned at all.'[25] It serves to contradict the false impression of an ever-expanding world and marks the great Victorian epoch as 'one of those many periods' when consciousness narrowed, 'visibly shrank and shrivelled'. It is at best romance, at worst irrationalism 'vague visions of barbaric migrations and massacres and enslavements.'[26] Victorian racialism represented a retreat from the universal and philosophical into the 'formless and partly imaginary'. It coloured the minds not only of its overt advocates such as Carlyle but remote cases like Arnold, the 'apostle of a cosmopolitan culture', or a 'liberal humanist', in one sense entirely international intellectual, George Meredith.

Even those who sought to correct the unevenness and eccentricity of Victorian culture by objectivity or understatement 'managed somehow to overstate their understatement.'[27] Arnold's attempt at French classical balance and critical detachment resulted in an unjust 'but not unthinkable' charge of priggishness. Pater's effort at an art criticism more detached than Ruskin's created an impression of artificiality. All in all 'it was very difficult to be classic in the later Victorian atmosphere.'[28] The 'loss of natural repose', of logic and clarity, the growth of an intellectual individualism, not only *outré* but positively seeking obscurity as a mode of expression, are the reverse side of the grandeur and the vision of the great Victorians.

These later and more elaborate characterisations of the age that had just ended are only hinted at in Chesterton's early writings. However, his analysis of the Edwardian vulnerability and the ideological invasion which took advantage of it rested on a funda-mental perception that the moral and intellectual equipment inherited from the later nineteenth century had been faulty and was now, in important respects, disintegrating. The Victorian com-promise, 'a balance of whims' having begun to lose its confidence and energy, its always latent irrationalism began to feed on increas-ingly sinister sources.

Other factors, particular to English culture, complicated the issue, hindering a recovery of democratic inspiration or a defence against the juggernaut ideologies or simplifications. One of these was the prevailing stuffiness of educated discourse around 1900, a pre-condition to understanding the intention and the shocking success of Chesterton's controversial style. He many 'times noted, with dis-taste, a flavour of 'serious' writing in his youth, its unfocused moral uplift:

> Perpetual talk about righteousness and unselfishness, about things that should elevate and things that cannot but degrade, about social purity and true Christian manhood, all poured out with fatal fluency and with very little reference to the real facts of anybody's soul or salary.[29]

This 'lukewarm torrent' was the harbinger of a religious crisis. It was the slush into which the Puritanism, which had moulded the national mind for two centuries, had melted. Moralistic verbiage was what remained when spirituality evaporated. Chesterton noted early in his career in the writers and the readers of 'quality' newspapers and journals 'an appetite for high-minded footling'. Irritating in itself, the typical 'public pronouncement' style was liable to abuse or corruption. It offered the stupid an opportunity to live above their moral income, counterfeiting an earnestness to which they had no right and gaining an automatic hearing for stale formulae and received opinion. For the dangerous idea it was an excellent camouflage. (Ivywood in *The Flying Inn* combines a Gladstonian oratorical manner with a passionate Nietzscheanism).

Much attention has been rightly given to Chesterton's style as an attempt to make the reader sit up, to see the familiar afresh. But, equally, it may be viewed as a reaction against linguistic bad habits, the verbal forms into which 'serious' or 'considered' writing for newspapers or journals had hardened. The moralising currency, the 'Victorian seriousness' literary critics now overvalue at the expense of Edwardian lightness, Chesterton saw, often, either as arrant nonsense, or a ponderous balancing of one statement against another, so that they cancelled out. In a characteristic *Daily News* article of 1911 on this subject, he remarked that a 'bonfire of rubbish' should not include anything, however alien or fantastic, which ever had a positive significance, such as the Lord's Day Observance Act or the Koran, but it ought to include masses of material from contemporary 'high-class quarterly magazines'. Things that never meant anything:

> the statesmanlike pronouncements, the wide outlooks and the well-considered conclusions, all the consciousness of the solemnity of the responsibility... all the realization of the reality of the tendency.[30]

Editors, leader-writers, pundits of all kinds adopt this style first, because it is easy. It was, Chesterton pointed out, far harder to write an amusing piece for a comic paper than a first leader for *The Times*, as anyone could prove who attempted both.[31] Secondly, moralistic penny-a-lining was favoured for its power to obscure discussion and make conclusions seem vulgar and crude by the type of mind that does not wish conclusions to be reached or if they have been reached to be investigated or challenged. The age of the demagogue has been superseded by that of 'the mystagogue or don' '... who has nothing to say and says it softly and impressively in an indistinct whisper.'[32] Chesterton had considerable fellow-feeling for his controversial opponent Bernard Shaw, much of it probably stemming from the consciousness of a shared enemy in the texture of contemporary educated discourse. Foremost among Shaw's services, in Chesterton's view, was that of having 'popularised philosophy', of having combined the intelligent with the intelligible. Faced with a corruption of language in journals into 'earnest' verbosity or a silence and sterility among academics, supposed to betoken intellectual authority, a clear concrete style such as Shaw's is invaluable. Chesterton's praise of his friend displays his own position and intentions regarding the popularising literary style and the cultural problem, both he and Shaw faced in evolving their different versions of it:

This plain pugnacious style of Shaw has greatly clarified all controversies. He has slain the polysyllable, that huge and slimy centipede which has sprawled over the valleys of England.[33]

The state of mind Chesterton diagnosed was not always polysyllabic in its expression but it was vague and vulnerable, marked, on the surface by a woolly moralism and, underlying this, an unrealised and dangerous hunger for simplification. Such a past frame of mind may be a real enough entity yet, of necessity, hard to reconstruct. Much of the evidence for the contradictions, stresses and dangers of the liberal mind may be found in the *Daily News*, during the years Chesterton wrote for it and this will be examined later. For the present, it is useful to look at a contemporary figure.

In *Autobiography*, Chesterton records his disquiet at finding himself on the same platform as J.A. Hobson, both opposed to Imperialism, but opposed to each other with every instinct, thought and predilection. Hobson's *A Modern Outlook: studies of English and American tendencies*, published in the same year (1910) as Chesterton's *What's wrong with the World* is a suggestive picture of the mental and moral equipment of an influential Liberal theorist; regarded, around 1910, as a more professional social analyst, more of an intellectual heavyweight altogether, than an entertainer such as Chesterton. It is possible to identify besides, in the most obvious features of Hobson's mind as revealed in his oddly-named book, recurrent themes of Chesterton's polemics at this time.

When one compares them with Chesterton's popular work in the *Daily News*, Hobson's reprinted pieces from the *Nation*, supposedly a higher quality journal of opinion, are disappointingly thin. But they are certainly closer to the contemporary intelligent, middle-class progressive 'consensus', views whose universal acceptability implies that they are obsolescent. Hobson displays the traits noted in his platform appearance by Chesterton. His is a nagging, carping, fundamentally unimaginative approach, seeking to deny or belittle the existence of great forces, unaware of the irrational ideological nature of the currents stirring the public through the new mass-circulation dailies. The movement towards war, for instance, is a mere sport for the upper classes:

> They are, however, willing to play the game up to a certain point, that is up to the point where it ceases to be a game and calls upon them to incur real sacrifices.[34]

Hobson may, perhaps, scarcely be blamed for failing to foresee the religious exaltation of the coming European War. Yet he discounts much more obvious facts close at hand such as the reserve power and susceptibilities of the newly-literate and the inevitability of them counting socially and politically. The national patriotic appeal can have no effect on these lower orders Hobson feels, since they read merely for entertainment:

> Will it induce the masses to abandon spectatorial football. . . ? Not a bit of it. They understand far too well what their *Daily Mail* is for.[35]

In fact, they can be ignored, left to their music-halls and Yellow Press. One wonders whether Hobson, like Asquith in these years, never opened a popular newspaper. For a writer on social and political issues, he is curiously blind to the energies, the depths of the mass-mind, its fears and fantasies with which Northcliffe and Pearson were in touch. Hobson is remarkably innocent too, about the power of moral exhortation and very ready with the lay-preacher's tone, a diluted Gladstonianism:

> A state which thus implicitly denies it is not strong enough or wise enough to stand upon right has, *ipso facto*, abandoned its moral claim upon the respect and obedience of the people. Its spiritual

foundations are sapped and an abandonment to such a policy of terror must in time extinguish any claim it may have upon the comity of nations.[36]

The substance of this particular comment, on a political trial in Spain, is defensible but the tone, glib and somewhat unctuous, is Hobson's practised manner, perilously close to the moralising penny-a-lining Chesterton mocked in 'Anti-Christ or The Reunion of Christendom', or in Ivywood's orations, and wished to throw on his pile of rubbish before the real issues of the day could be reached in an intelligent manner.

Not surprisingly, Hobson's view of 'Mr Chesterton and Mr Shaw' is mildly condescending. Their liveliness is incompatible with intellectual weight, of course. They are entertaining but without reticence or good taste and 'we do not feel how far they are capable of telling the truth, so intricate is the influence of combative humour.'[37] Oddly enough, he touches on one of the most important of Chesterton's early preoccupations, the current 'inability to grapple', the fact that there is 'no serious pertinacious endeavour to discover, state and contest the roots of any matter of dispute.'[38] The chapter 'A Plea for Controversy' catches one of Hobson's chief deficiencies, an inability or unwillingness to penetrate below the surface. He remains at the level of secondary symptoms. The 'vapid amenities', the shying away from 'the thrust and parry of living intellectual combat' are noted but the solution proposed is a slight modification of educational practice: intercollegiate public debates on the American model.

More revealing than the tone or the limitations evident in *A Modern Outlook*, its 'dated' quality, is the paradox that while stuffy and pernickety about the details of political and social life and shying away from mass-movements, myths or ideologies, Hobson is sentimental and uncritical about the foremost of these, the concept of evolution. He is gripped by Bergson's presentation of a myth, the vision of endless development in the physical and spiritual world. He speaks, with an unusual energy, of:

> the inability of scientific analysis to convey 'the urge of the world', the *élan de vie*, which is continually expressing itself in the emergence of new poems, incalculable from all knowledge of prior

conditions... a world of miracles, in the sense of results which no science can enable us to forecast and which differ, in quality, character, or human interest from anything that has occurred.[39]

The 'pretence', he remarks casually, elsewhere, that intellect can control human affairs is 'a great bluff'.[40] Both this statement and Hobson's intoxication about Bergsonian evolution, suggest a mind whose barely realised preferences are in conflict with, are undermining, its formal allegiances and habitual mannerisms. He epitomises those weaknesses in the Edwardian Liberal consciousness to which Chesterton addressed himself in his relationship with his *Daily News* readers.

Furthermore, Hobson's embracing of evolutionary rhetoric is a reminder of the joy which the myth of creative evolution, the *élan vital*, the life-force or its various surrogates was capable of bringing in the thirty years before 1914. Underlying a mass of disparate phenomena: the materialist cosmologies of Herbert Spencer[41] and Haeckel; the work of dominant academic philosophers (discussed below), Caird, Bradley and Green, of this, the golden age of British Hegelianism; the Imperialism of Kipling, as Halévy points out;[42] Socialism, as interpreted by leading publicists like Ramsay MacDonald[43]; the fuller impact of Nietzsche's writings after 1908 (to be touched on later); the rhetoric of Shaw's *Man and Superman* and Bergson's *L'Évolution créatrice* (1907) on the 'life-force'; and very many more beside, was a vast and tempting dream, a great collective aspiration. This was a spring from which major still-remembered figures and others, like Hobson, who have not stood the test of time so well, hurried to drink.

The particular phraseology or formulations of the myth varied. The impulse behind it was astonishingly simple, and satisfying to its devotees. Haeckel's *The Riddle of the Universe* (1899) so frequently mentioned in Chesterton's early writings, promised a vast, uniform, uninterrupted and eternal process of development linking organic and inorganic, matter and spirit, life and art. In this astonishingly popular book, Darwin became 'a catalyst in a transformation and sublimation of German traditions of romantic idealism.'[44] The Haeckel 'boom' around 1900, merely reinforced and popularised

well-established tendencies. The British Hegelians nominally reacting against materialism like Haeckel's had sought to re-establish
the claims of spirituality or 'the Absolute' within the same evolutionary myth. By 1900, they had been flourishing for almost thirty
years. Caird, virtually the founder of the school, was Master of Balliol
during Belloc's time there, and the target of several of the satirical
comments on 'German philosophy' in *Lambkin's Remains* and *Caliban's
Guide to Letters.*[45] In his view there were no antagonisms which could
not be reconciled. There must always be a higher unity within which
antagonistic tendencies were to find a place, a higher unity 'manifest-
ing itself in an organic process of development.'[46] This was especially
true of the spiritual life where there was no question of absolute truth
or falsehood but 'only how much truth has been brought to expression
and with what inadequacies or unexplained assumptions.'[47] The
dialectic would work on endlessly resolving all contradictions.

In its more sophisticated expression in the writings of T.H. Green,
this myth, or poetic image became a favourite mode of thought for a
large and very diverse group of intellectuals. R.G. Collingwood
remarks on the effects of Green's students on all branches of public
life, in figures as seemingly unconnected in their creeds as politicians
like Asquith and Milner, churchmen like Gore and Scott-Holland,
and social reformers like Toynbee:

> Through this effect on the minds of its pupils, the philosophy of
> Green's school might be found, from about 1880 to about 1900,
> penetrating and fertilizing every aspect of the national life.[48]

Given such a ramifying influence, it is worth inquiring what, in
simple terms and popular language, the chief preoccupations of
Green's philosophy were. They included a steady tendency, especially in the important *Introduction to Hume's Treatise on Human Nature*
(1877), to overthrow the view that reality exists as a fact, given to us in
experience. The simple data of sense can never be real. The best we
can have are the relations the mind makes and therefore the 'real
world' must be 'through and through a world made by mind'.[49] The
authenticity of our knowledge is guaranteed by the fact that we are
gradually growing to be the vehicle of, or to be completely identified
with, the eternal consciousness:

In the growth of our experience an animal organism which has a history in time, gradually becomes the vehicle for an eternally complete consciousness.[50]

'Imaginary objects' are objects constituted by us; 'Real objects' are constituted by our minds, when they are participating in the eternal consciousness. Green welcomed evolution as logically necessitating the existence of such an eternal consciousness.

Orage's summary of Nietzsche's views on the Superman, though it naturally stresses will as paramount in evolution, involves a similar blending of human particularity into an undefined and indefinable future being. Although the possibility of the Superman is the only justification for the lives of 'millions and millions of the mediocre, the dull and the unhappy':

the Superman is strictly indefinable. As man is not merely the tiger writ large, so the Superman is not merely man writ large. It is probable that the new faculties, new modes of consciousness will be needed, as the mystics have always declared.[51]

Deeper than the level of the various intellectual discourses of materialist evolution, spiritualising Hegelianism, Socialist, Bergsonian teachings and lastly, its most urgent form, the teachings of Nietzsche, lies an *emotional* craving. A.O. Lovejoy, long ago, drew attention to the metaphysical pathos of the term 'organic' as an explanation of its popularity with philosophers. Similarly it is reasonable to suggest beneath many seemingly conflicting creeds of the years 1880 to 1914 a metaphysical pathos, the yearning to break down existing division and conflict within the individual personality and in the community; to escape from unsatisfactory contradiction into a higher unity or a new identity. Connected with this is a reaction against the tyranny of fact, of individual phenomena; a wish to deny their physical reality. Whatever is unacceptable about the here and now may be blended and dissolved into an unknown entity, an Absolute, or a Superman, or some remote evolutionary goal. F.H. Bradley, perhaps the greatest of the Hegelians, in describing the *emotional* satisfaction of his teachings, offers a clue to the power of the myth in all its manifestations. In anything short of the Absolute, he says:

men are torn between the incompatible motives of self-assertion and self-sacrifice and infected by the self-contradictions of 'desire' which can satisfy itself only by destroying itself.[52]

In Orage's view, Nietzsche proposed to create a being who unlike man as we know him was:

> capable of *enjoying* life.... Only by the creation of such a race would the long and bloody toil of hundreds of centuries and countless generations be justified.[53]

The urgency of both Bradley's and Orage's versions of the myth is inescapable in such language. The yearning they express lies at the root of all the simplifications and ideologies. It provides a context in which the pattern may be seen behind the logomachies of evolutionary materialism and evolutionary spirituality, the right-wing views of Kipling and the Liberal views of Hobson, behind intellectual movements, in appearance, totally divorced and at odds. It is an emotional context revealing needs and urges which had in the past been satisfied by religion; needs for salvation, redemption, re-integration, healing of sickness and division in the mind. This emotional and religious root is the explanation of the power wielded by the myth of evolutionary transcendence. However perverted or in error it was, it touched powerful springs in the human mind. It really satisfied heartfelt needs.

In the forefront of that long controversial relationship with Shaw, deserving of a complete study to itself, was Chesterton's perception that the religious element was at the heart of Shaw's appeal and inspiration. (The most obvious place to verify such a suggestion would, of course, be *Man and Superman*, especially the 'Don Juan in Hell' section of Act III, but the 'conversions' of Dick Dudgeon in *The Devil's Disciple*, of Captain Brassbound, or of Blanco Posnet would also serve to confirm it. Such widely accepted features found here and elsewhere in Shaw's work as its impatience with life as it is lived, with man's sensual or romantic illusions, its violent rejection of a materialist, non-purposive universe, its assertion that true life is found in those ethical and spiritual strivings which serve the purpose of the 'Life Force' give weight to Chesterton's view of him). Shaw

37

was significant for his courage, intellectual consistency and for the distinction and clarity of his style which enabled him to popularise a new and exciting variant of the evolutionary myth of the period. But essentially, Chesterton saw him, like Tolstoy and the Tolstoy phenomenon, as the return of a buried religious impulse.

The rise of ideologies and simplifications was the filling of a vacuum left by the decay Chesterton observed in the Puritanism which had dominated English culture for three hundred years. 'G.B.S. who is the greatest of the modern Puritans and perhaps the last'[54] recaptures the dynamic of the great simplification historical Puritanism had been. This, as Chesterton pointed out, had been no mere negation or denial but a terrible obsession with the Absolute, 'a refusal to contemplate God or goodness with anything lighter or milder than the most fierce concentration of the intellect.'[55] As this 'mountainous ice which sparkled in the seventeenth century' melts into 'a weak and lukewarm torrent' of edifying clichés, so the urges which, however wrongly or destructively, it satisfied, seek fresh simplifications. Of these, Shavianism is one of the simplest and most comprehensible, because of its likeness in spirit to a known historical religious type. However, in Chesterton's view the whole hunt for ideological simplifications, expressed primarily but not exclusively, in the multiple variations of the evolutionary myth, made most sense when regarded as a religious crisis.

Chesterton's reading of the Edwardian cultural upheaval throws light on his controversial methods and on his relationship with his readers. His popularisation of ideas is not only a matter of expressing them in plain terms. It includes an effort to discuss their origin in the emotional life. What needs, he asks, are they intended to satisfy? Are these valid or false? The matter of the myth of evolutionary transcendence is such a case. Chesterton's account of its fallacy rests less on faults in the evidence offered within the various methodologies than in a fundamental emotional misunderstanding in the craving underlying all of them. This promises happiness but would, in fact, cut away the sources which, experience has shown, provide most men with such content as they enjoy. Chesterton denies the 'metaphysical pathos' of unity, 'the idea that unity is itself a good thing; that there is something high and spiritual about things being

38

blended and absorbed into each other.'[56] He asks the one essential question which strikes at the heart of the myth. Why should 'mere contact and coalescence' of themselves, be thought good at all? What they represent is rather 'a return to the chaos and unconsciousness that were before the earth was made'[57] than a new creation; an impatience with the problems of actuality, whether of one's own nature or of the world, and a wish to be rid of them even at the cost of disintegrating oneself or denying the whole of sense experience or objective fact. The aura of spiritual aspiration surrounding the concept of unity is spurious as is that surrounding the other agent for transcending the self, the Superman. Both notions satisfy a common, real emotion but it is not correctly described as aspiration. It is rather fastidiousness. In *Heretics*, Chesterton mentions a description by Nietzsche of his disgust at the common people with their common faces, common voices and common minds. This can be understood, as a momentary feeling, by 'anyone who has ever been sick on a steamer or tired on a crowded omnibus.'[58] It deserves the sympathy accorded to weak nerves but it cannot be regarded as a way into the future or an avenue to a higher life.

Chesterton's exploration of this potent modern myth involves an invitation to self-knowledge. To what concealed emotions is the image of a journey to a higher undefined life appealing? Why is it so pleasant for so many people, at a given time, to follow such a pattern of thought? The emotions involved may not be guilty. They may not be undeserving of sympathy. But they may have been misnamed. In the case of this, the central element of the modern ideological upheaval, what is involved is a flight from variety and definition in experience, from the thrust and multiplicity of men, events and objects, the demands of actuality. These are the difficulty of life but they are too, as he remarked in 1910, much of its reward:

> The varieties themselves, the reflection of man and woman in each other, as in two distinct mirrors; the wonder of man at nature as a strange thing at once above and below him; the quaint and solitary kingdom of childhood; the local affections and the colour of certain landscapes. . . these are the things that make life worth living.[59]

It is a question of a contrast between the 'few prigs on platforms' who are talking 'about oneness and absorption in the All.'[60] and the authentic experience of the 'living and labouring millions'.

Chesterton's view of the emotions underlying 'the Superman' is identical with those he attributes to the yearning to blend with 'the Absolute'. The satirical sketch 'How I found the Superman' (1908) was published shortly after the stir caused by handbooks on Nietzsche by Orage. Chesterton had known Orage personally, of course, for some years before the latter's eruption on to the London scene since he had accepted Orage's invitation to speak, without a fee, to the Leeds Art Club.[61] At the time of the Superman sketch, the period of the real beginning of the Nietzsche cult, he was involved, again at Orage's request, in the important debate on Socialism in the *New Age*. Quasi-Nietzschean imperatives of vital energy, will to power and hostility to religion were already rampant in political, social and military circles of the time. Nor, of course, was the Superman unheard of. Bernard Shaw's *Man and Superman* (1903), with its Nietzschean collection of aphorisms, *The Revolutionist's Handbook*, attacking conventional ethics, had already proclaimed the development of this higher being as the purpose of history. Orage's books, offered an already receptive public, a much more accurate version of Nietzsche than they had had before. *How I found the Superman* is a prelude to Chesterton's major consideration of the Nietzschean ideal *The Flying Inn*, to be dealt with later. Slight as the piece is, it neatly catches the essential points in Chesterton's approach to the myth of transcendence. The lack of definition, whose allure Orage exploits, ('Will the Superman be a man? Not a man as we know him' etc.) is ruthlessly parodied. Is the Superman good-looking? 'On his own plane', answers the proud father. Has he any hair? 'Well, not of course what we call hair ... but – ' ... Is it hair or feathers? 'Not feathers, as we understand feathers', answered Hagg in an awful voice.[62] Even more significant, perhaps, than the logical result of surrendering the known human form, is the fragility of 'the Universe's most magnificent birth'. The Superman cannot cope with common existence but 'lives quietly' in permanent darkness and dies with a 'small sad yelp' when the door is burst open; neurasthenic distaste for the vulgar demands of daily life as lived by 'ordinary' people, pressed to its natural conclusion.

Chesterton's relish for the ordinary experiences of the common man and his prolonged defence of and real admiration for popular culture may be shown to have been of immense advantage to him in his understanding of the spiritual and intellectual crisis of the new century. Both the fact, and partly the nature of that advantage may be seen by a comparison with the work of his friend and ally C.F.G Masterman. Both the lesser-known *In Peril of Change* (1905) and the celebrated *The Condition of England* (1909) offer confirmation of Chesterton's analysis of the cultural situation from a man of different temperament and intellectual range and substantially divergent outlook. It is possible to identify in Masterman most of the same perceptions and preoccupations as those, already touched on, in Chesterton's work during this period. *In Peril of Change* significantly subtitled *essays written in a time of tranquillity* although, of course, unlike *Heretics* of the same year both in style and in much of its subject matter, is like Chesterton's book in one vital way, that it is a study of a stagnant spiritual and moral condition. The great issues and causes, the 'manifest tremors and violence in the world of politics and religion' have died away into silence 'into the mere groundswell of past disturbance'. 'The thirty years of reaction', a phrase identical with Chesterton's characterisation of the later Victorian age, 'convinced that enough had been done, a little wearied with the tempests of Reform ... settled down to sleep.'[63] Under the weariness, the complacency, the 'certainties of an afternoon, golden and unending', however strange hardly-identified forces are at work. The English are 'a people on the verge of some vast disquietude, riddled with forces that are hastening the upheavals of the abyss.'[64] It is not a matter of outward modifications of the forms of society. If we were as sensitive to 'disturbance in the world of man's inner convictions' as to surface political events which merely reflect these we should know we were in the presence of 'growing and dying worlds'. Masterman, again like Chesterton, fixes on the religious vacuum as, perhaps, the most notable factor in the situation. He is at one with Chesterton in asserting that:

> the old religion, with its affirmations and denials, of Protestant and Puritan England and the civilisation definitely dependent

upon that particular outlook on the world is today visibly dis-integrating.[65]

The 'New Calvinism' of the natural sciences with its blind forces and destinies has not yet taken hold of the popular mind. What remains is a hiatus, in which old habits and institutions are maintained by inertia while their foundations are silently collapsing. Noncon-formist chapels are still being built in large numbers. Yet the doctrines preached within them grow increasingly diluted. The few survivals of an earlier time are secretly regarded as trivial and tedious, if not unintelligible, by the young. Along with the end of many pointless prohibitions and taboos, there is an increasing disposition to throw aside restraint, a loss of a sense of the distinct-ness of good and evil, of the absolute value of the human soul. The middle-class habit of Church-going, he pointed out a few years later, in *The Condition of England*, may still be maintained but:

> if the industrious householders of 'Holmlea', 'Belle Vue', 'Buona Vista', 'Sunnyhurst' and 'The Laurels' were ... deliberately to face their own convictions, the result might be surprising to the clergy.[66]

Masterman identifies two obvious points from which change will suddenly come, either from 'the outbreak of forces fermenting among the neglected populations' of the huge modern cities or from some great awakening of conscience, some new religious or spiritual movement for which the times, on the analogy of 'a former period of Imperial Peace', and later Roman Empire, are clearly ripe. Those interested in the soul's development, rather than material comfort, will welcome this.

While the points of similarity with Chesterton need hardly be laboured, what is striking is that Masterman's analysis virtually collapses at the point of diagnosis. Unlike Chesterton, he cannot make the leap towards propounding any kind of answer to the cultural and spiritual crisis, on the main features of which he and Chesterton agree. The gloom of *The Condition of England* has been noted by many readers. *In Peril of Change* is almost equally despon-dent. It is natural enough to suggest that this is a matter of temperament. Masterman's writings reflect the pessimism in which he revelled in conversation, in spite of, or somehow, because of which Chesterton found him very likeable. It is possible, however, to be more precise. The sadness of Masterman's writing stems from a disgust at the ordinary lives of ordinary people, the ugly or smug faces of men and women in the London streets, the impoverished minds which feed on the Yellow Press. One of the pieces in *In Peril of Change* roundly attacks Chesterton for his 'blasphemous contentment' and especially for actually liking the common man. To extol:

> the average decent citizen for his average decency, partakes of the nature of that sin for which there is no repentance though it be sought bitterly and with tears.[67]

To Masterman, ordinary people in themselves prove, on sight, the active existence of Cosmic Evil. He reproaches Chesterton for imagining that 'the good citizen...journeying through the tube, portly, double-chinned, reading *Bright Bits*'[68] has only to dance with joy to 'inaugurate the golden age'. If Chesterton feels that Surbiton is a city of enchantment or Penge and Poplar fairyland, then for him, clearly, 'the Devil is dead'. Love of popular life and culture are a blasphemy, even the Sin against the Holy Ghost.

Before dismissing Masterman's view as some curious personal malaise, it is as well to note its prevalence among other contemporary intellectuals, admittedly in a usually more restrained form. The emotion directly expressed by Masterman provides the cultural context for much of Chesterton's defence of myth, fable and the grotesque, of popular art forms and reflections of the mind of the common man, as will be shown later. Furthermore, Masterman's revulsion is not unmotivated. At the heart of his despair is the feeling that his culture is impotent. Literature, or the articulation of educated opinion has no role to play. Critics and novelists deserve Plato's sentence of expulsion. They are openly at war with the 'modern industrial ant-heap' and have nothing but a message of despair to offer to contemporary civilisation. Anyone who listened to them would throw up the struggle from inability, when the choice was offered, 'to fashion any intelligible goal of attainment.'[69] In fact, however, they are of no significance since literature is a luxury:

It influences a strictly limited class. It is produced by a still more limited class. is so little operative on the general life of the nation that its very claim to be considered in a survey of 'The Condition of England' is doubtful.[70]

Masterman hates a world of thoughts and feelings he assumes he cannot enter, whose needs and dangers he realises but cannot affect, although he was, paradoxically of course, a well-known public figure with a large audience.

As much as Chesterton, Masterman was a Fleet Street figure; for a time, in fact, Chesterton's colleague as literary editor of the *Daily News*. He shows no hope, however, in the potentialities of mass-communication, education or popularisation, no possibility of reaching the newly-literate masses:

> each a unit in a crowd that has drifted away from the realities of life in a complex artificial civilisation...rejoicing over hired sportsmen who play before him, the ingenuities of sedentary guessing competitions, the huge frivolity and ignorance of the world of the music hall and the Yellow Newspaper.[71]

That Chesterton felt neither the despair nor the distaste is an explanation of his altogether different role in the cultural crisis both he and Masterman foresaw. He did not despair of the power of reason and educated discourse to challenge the ideological forces which were about to enter on a stagnant scene, in peril of change. He did not share Masterman's distaste for those crowds in the city streets. Recording in *Autobiography* a conversation with Masterman, early in their acquaintance, he recalls that he felt an essential wrongness in the lives of the harassed people pouring through the passages of the Underground or living in houses 'like ill-drawn diagrams of Euclid'. But, he goes on to remark:

> I never doubted the human beings inside the houses were almost miraculous; like magic and talismanic dolls in whatever ugly dolls'-houses.[72]

Partly, no doubt, the difference between the two friends was temperamental. Masterman, from an innate sadness, saw symptoms of moral and social degeneration, the natural depravity of man aggravated by the work rhythms, living conditions and pastimes offered by expanding urban life, with its half-educated masses, half-baked ideas and trashy newspapers. Chesterton's buoyant and courageous nature found in those same 'ordinary' people signs of moral and spiritual health, hearty appetites, interests and affections, half-effaced but still persisting tastes and traditions from which national and individual life might renew itself. The struggle to reach the people in 'the ugly dolls'-houses' was abundantly worthwhile.

III

THE JOURNALISTIC ARENA

Writing on Chesterton has, no doubt rightly, dwelt on his personal crisis at the Slade School (*c.* 1892–4), his own emotional reaction against solipsism and decadence. He stressed himself, and much has been made by his critics, of his war against the influences of his boyhood and youth, the pessimism of the Wilde and Beardsley period. Lynette Hunter's recent, valuable study has sought to find a clue to most of his work in a quest, born of his own psychological tensions and private fears, for a mode of artistic expression tainted neither with Impressionism, nor with Rationalism. Frames of reference such as these, while helpful in exploring essential truths about Chesterton's personality and the sources of his inspiration have much less, necessarily, to offer in understanding the public dimension of his writing, the effects on his style of his working conditions, his colleagues, his specific relationship with a specific audience. His intellectual career was a series of debates, controversies and polemics as much as it was a private pilgrimage or a long introspection, It was a life in Fleet Street as well as a life of the mind. He rose to prominence and his style was formed in a period (1900–14), which, whether his own analysis of it is accepted, or not, was undoubtedly one of intense public debate in which, as has been suggested, novel theories, largely of continental origin, flooded into a vulnerable public consciousness. It was also one of change and stress in the newspaper world. Chesterton responded to movement and pressures in the world of ideas. He responded too, very largely in the context of

one paper, the *Daily News*, during his formative years, to pressures
from the expectations of his audience, from his relationship with his
editor, and from a contrast, deliberate on Gardiner's part and his
own, between his contributions to the paper and those of others. To
read Chesterton's essays in collections, or his writings in book form,
is to gain the impression of an individual thinking, perhaps using an
event or some statement by another as the occasion or starting point
of his reflections but, nevertheless, isolated; the thought abundantly
interesting, yet a deliberately formed, finished object. To read
Chesterton's articles in the *Daily News* is to be at once aware of the
processes of their making, the strategies, rewards and dangers of a
dialogue with particular readers at a particular time, the extent to
which the style is a reaction to public, external forces and factors at
work in a specific climate or ambience. It is proposed to examine
some aspects of these working conditions later.

In general terms, Chesterton's career gathered momentum amid
an often-noted jostling of rival political and social nostrums, itself
only one element of a time which stands foremost in English cultural
history as *the* epoch of discussion and popularisation. It is perhaps
arguable that only the pamphlet war of the 1640s showed a comparable engagement of the popular mind in disputes about rival views of
life, images of society or possible futures. 'Popular mind' is the
salient phrase. Attitudes to Chesterton and to some extent his
Edwardian cultural background, will inevitably be influenced by
attitudes to the popularisation of ideas. G.S. Fraser's account represents a sufficiently common and, I would suggest, erroneous view to
be worth noting. He complains that with the Edwardians the
'invigorating Victorian debate about high matters' lost its grand
style. Writers like Shaw, Belloc and Chesterton were too much
performers to be taken with the same moral seriousness as Arnold,
Newman, Ruskin or Carlyle:

> They expressed, to a popular audience, minority viewpoints in a
> highly personal way, whereas the Victorian sages had tried to
> articulate the uneasiness widely felt by a representative range of
> educated people.[1]

One detects here a complaint of decline in the quality of intellectual debate consequent upon reaching out to a much wider audience, without a recognition that such a reaching out was, in itself, of the utmost significance and value. This, of course, is to grant Fraser's initial position that there *was* a decline. An alteration in the style of discourse following a change in the audience addressed, is not, alone, synonymous with deterioration. Different tasks of communication required different idioms and serious thought does not have one literary means only of expressing itself.

A less categorical and final variant of the condemnation of popularisation is the attempt to 'rescue' Chesterton from the mundane trivia, the forgotten unimportant circumstances, as they are seen, in which, in fact, he forged his style and his persona. It is a prejudice which involves notions about art or thought from which Chesterton repeatedly dissociated himself; that they are the solemn, dignified products of 'high' culture and detached intelligence. The preconception is worth grappling with and overcoming since it is largely behind the impulse to view Chesterton, in isolation, as a moralist, philosopher or the hero of a personal intellectual or religious quest; offering pictures which, while not untrue, are certainly lacking in balance. It is felt that to remove Chesterton's working conditions and newspaper context is to separate him from the ephemeral, to enable his stature to be more fully realised. In fact, this doubtful increase in dignity is gained at the expense of an understanding of Chesterton's contribution to the cultural climate and the war of ideas in a most exciting period leading into, and throwing light on many of the preoccupations of our own. The 'timeless' quality of a style, of thought or art can blot out the tensions, pressures, contradictions, the making processes, knowledge of which is required for their fullest understanding and appreciation. The workshop as well as the finished product has its own legitimate interest.

Margaret Canovan in her recent and timely study of Chesterton's political views remarks that the British political spectrum of attitudes which seems rational, inevitable and all-embracing to the English has, in common with those of other pluralist societies, curious omissions to the eye of an outsider. It does not exhaust the range of intelligible attitudes. She notes, for example, that we entirely lack the popularist tradition so well established in the USA and within which, from a political point of view, she feels, Chesterton is best understood.[2] All English political attitudes, in her view, share a lack of egalitarianism, of that faith in the common sense of ordinary people which was one of Chesterton's constant themes. Whether entirely true or not about politics, Mrs Canovan's remarks certainly have some application to English cultural life, as Fraser's and many other writers' easy equation between popularisation of ideas and deterioration of intellectual discourse, suggest. The attempt to connect culture with the tastes, style and thinking of a minority has a long tradition behind it but it was a tendency against which Chesterton warred throughout his career.

A determining factor in Chesterton's career as a communicator and critic of ideas in a mass-circulation newspaper, with all its problems and rewards, was obviously his whole attitude to 'popular culture'. Hence, it is worth pausing briefly to look at this question. If Chesterton's work had no other significance, it would be interesting as *the* outstanding example, in its time, of the defence of popular culture, of the distinct sensibility, values and traditions revealed by cockney jokes, funeral-customs, festivals, views of theatre and music-hall, art forms like Punch and Judy, pub-life. If it is true, in political terms, that: against the dominant intellectual current he defended a view of human nature and the human condition that favoured the common man,[3] it is equally true in cultural terms. What, precisely, this involved is not so obvious. It is useful perhaps to suggest three lines along which a defence of popular culture might be made, three quite distinct meanings the phrase might have.

The first of these is the highly suspect admiration for an instinctive wisdom of 'the people' far superior than the mere reason of chattering intellectuals, a virile, healthy grip on life unspoiled by self-consciousness. A defence, in these terms, of the views and tastes of the common man, his moral attitudes and instinctive emotional or intellectual preferences has, for many, an undesirable flavour about it, involving an exaltation of emotion over reason, force over conscience, a tinge of the philistine, or even proto-Fascist, especially if the common-man's 'instincts' are to be interpreted for him by an élite. (Such a celebrated account of the spiritual origins of Fascism as Thomas Mann's *Doctor Faustus* locates some of its roots in a yearning for the old-time virtues and simplicities of 'the folk').[4]

A second possible emphasis is one which has become current in certain revaluations of the term 'culture' during the last twenty years, of which the work of Raymond Williams is an example. This stresses the creative response of the working class to the Industrial Revolution as their 'culture', rather than great individual artistic achievements. Middle-class culture is the basic individualist idea and the assumptions, habits or thoughts and intentions which proceed from it. Working-class culture is the 'collective democratic institution' expressed in the trade unions, the co-operative movement, 'or in a political party'. In its present stage of development, working-class culture is mainly social, creating institutions, rather than individual, creating works of art. In this context, however, it is a 'very remarkable achievement'.[5]

Chesterton's admiration of popular culture, although occasional superficial similarities to the first two views may be detected in it, was really quite distinct. It is true that, in his long journalistic career, he made enough breezy references to the 'healthy' instinctive views of the common man contrasted with the 'unhealthy' views of the intellectual minority to lend credibility to Pound's well-known remark that 'Chesterton *is* the mob'. It is true also that his sympathy with working-class institutions, especially trade unions, was warm and continuous, as witnessed later by his firm support, unpopular with the readers of *G.K.'s Weekly*, of the General Strike. But neither of these somewhat marginal aspects of his activities go to the root of his view of popular culture. It was altogether more nuanced, less emotional, than his casual remarks suggest. Nor was it evidenced for him, by working-class institutionalised response to the Industrial Revolution.

It rested, rather, on a sense that working-class culture, especially its values, assumptions and preferences in art and literature, were the remains of a wider, saner and more really civilised ground of response and creativity than the minority-educated culture of his own day. Popular tastes represented a residue of the appetites and emotional allegiances out of which past artistic achievement had grown. Work now enshrined in the pantheon of high culture had emerged from those appetites, and preferences; much more than it had or could ever have done from current high-brow aesthetic attitudes.

Chesterton was extremely cautious and qualified in his praise of this residue and not, in his most thorough and satisfactory statements on it, eager to draw an easy and simplistic contrast with the healthy 'instinctive' masses and the degenerate intellectual minority. The manifestations of popular culture might, as their detractors urged, be crude, uncouth, even trivial, but it was they, and not cultivated preferences in artistic treatment or subject matter which, because they were a fuller, subtler and saner comment on human life, were also the ground of the highest and most vital art. Two of the most important areas where popular taste preserved that of value which contemporary élite taste rejected, namely the realms of the grotesque and the fabulous, deserve a later and more detailed examination. For the moment, it is important to see in other specific early instances the connection Chesterton saw and tried to establish in the eyes of others between a mass, traditional range of attitudes and a wider, more humane view of existence, a deeper and more sensitive imagination.

Speaking of extravagant funeral displays among the London poor in 1908 he remarks that 'a thing may be a superstition and yet true'.[6] A tradition may preserve a core of validity, though transferred through a tarnished medium: such as liberty handed on through the eighteenth-century Whigs, or Catholicism through the fashionable eighteenth-century French clergy. By analogy 'therefore, when I say that the poor have the right tradition I do not necessarily mean that they are going on in exactly the right way.'[7] The wakes practised by the poor are psychologically sounder, carrying 'human nature over the open grave' than the current chilly fad of 'elegant stoics' that making a fuss about death is morbid or vulgar. But they are also, however dimly, connected with a wider and deeper cultural context:

> In the noise and heat of their houses of mourning is the smoke of the funeral baked meats of Hamlet and the dust and echo of the funeral games of Patroclus.[8]

The vulgar lower-class Christmas refined minds deplored was a living echo of 'that *antiqua pulchritudo* of which Augustine spoke. . . the old feasts and formalities of the childhood of the world',[9] for which refined minds, such as, in their various ways, William Morris, W.B. Yeats or George Moore, yearned.

This link between the deeper moral and emotional elements educated culture neglected, influenced Chesterton's attitude to contemporary popular phenomena. Working-class rhythms of work and play, that work should be expected to be laborious but that play should be freedom, seemed to him altogether a more defensible and universal response than the temporary upper-class converse that one played at work (diplomacy or finance) and took cricket seriously or the notion of professional educators like Froebel that play should be monitored and instructive. Popular jokes, as he pointed out at length in 1908, were often an elaborate art form, touching on subtle metaphysical and moral questions.[10] For him in 1907 the grave-digger in *Hamlet* was symbolic of the joy and endurance of poor men, the riotous and characteristic carol of satire out of the deep pit the poor dig, *their* response to suffering, a fuller and richer one, as Shakespeare had intuitively grasped, than that of the partial failure, the sophisticated Prince. A contemporary highbrow product, such as Maeterlinck's *Pelléas and Mélisande*, an example of the 'modern heresy of artistic monotone, ignored the need for, and value of the popular voice of tragedy.'[11]

Chesterton's somewhat unusual view of popular and of educated culture equipped him to accept and appreciate elements of the contemporary world, especially to deal with and handle the opportunities and problems of the wider literacy in ways which the attitudes of other commentators did not. It was not, for him, only a matter of the past achievements of the popular mind, folk versions of stories, such as those of Faust and Tannhäuser, without doubt superior to the products of the individual genius, Goethe or Wagner.[12] In the present, the music-hall, farce and melodrama to which crowds out at Hammersmith or Camberwell still flocked, possessed those festive, sensational elements which connected the theatre with its religious origin in ancient Greece. Middle-class intellectual plays, such as those of Ibsen had, for him in 1901 lost this authenticating dramatic quality.[13] Pulp literature, especially the

increasingly popular detective stories, represented a rudimentary
but real response to the romance of the new sprawling cities, a
great fact, to which the educated novel, often 'a babble of preciosity', had simply not reacted adequately.[14] (Chesterton's *liking*
for city-life, incidentally, his refusal to feel what Masterman called
'the burden of London',[15] the stock, diluted-romantic, sense of
'anonymous soulless streets' is everywhere evident in his early
writings, whether in essays like 'The Poetry of Cities' (1901) or as
the theme of major fiction such as *The Napoleon of Notting Hill*
(1904). He positively relished the little back-to-back houses, the
scraps of garden, the 'front rooms', and the life they nurtured and
defended, the variety, beauty and limited freedoms others could or
would not see. Social commentators like Hobson and Masterman,
in their descriptions of the burgeoning urban scene are largely
content to dismiss the dismal illiberal life of this or that hateful
district; all so like each other, as Masterman says, one hardly
knows where one is.[16] Chesterton, in 1912 by contrast sees 'each of
these glaring, gaping, new jerry-built boxes [as] the rickety stage
erected for the acting of a real miracle play,'[17] of the human family
and human death.

As well as his sense of the inalienable human dignity of their
inhabitants, the little boxes seemed to Chesterton to nourish an
'alternative culture'. It was opposed to educated and upper
middle-class values and attacked by State education, which as he
pointed out in a striking passage of *What's Wrong with the World*
attempted to eradicate the real values, attitudes and moral
achievements of the working class. Making the sons despise the
fathers, it substituted for a culture bred by work and experience, a
pallid, irrelevant imitation of that of the English public schools.[18]

In his own career then, he was ready to sympathise with and
exploit tastes, revealed in the newspapers, from which educated
opinion was divorced. In two of his most interesting early essays
related to this topic, 'The Defence of Useful Information' and 'The
Glass Walking Stick', he supported that popular appetite for
masses of bizarre facts, which seemed to many a mark of the barely
literate. It represented a worthwhile and valuable, though *other*,
response to experience, rather than an ignorant craving, as the

sophisticated assumed. It was a striking instance of the alternative culture, of which he, like his friend H.G. Wells, was aware:

The cultivated people go in for what is beautiful; but the uncultivated go in for what is interesting. For example, the more refined people concern themselves with literature – that is, with beautiful statements. But simple people concern themselves with scandal – that is, with interesting statements. Interest often exists apart from beauty; and interest is immeasurably better and more important than beauty.[19]

Behind Chesterton's relationship with the popular mind, as behind that of rival or kindred polemicists, lies the vast fact of the 1870 Education Act, the first generation of a new literacy in the 1890s and its exploitation by Northcliffe and Harmsworth. Chesterton's employment by the mass circulation *Daily News*, which printed a weekly essay by him (1901–13), was a move in the resulting contemporary battle of newspapers for readers, as well as of political creeds for adherents.

The foundation of the *Daily Mail* in 1896 and of the *Daily Express* in 1900 was culturally important for several reasons; for the arrival of the first, (with the partial exception of their short-lived but interesting forerunner, the *Star*, founded 1888, under T.P. O'Connor's editorship), cheap newspapers which tapped a lower-middle-class public; for a new emphasis on personalities rather than principles in politics; for the beginnings of the search for the lowest common denominator in public taste; as the origin of the division into papers of circulation and papers of opinion which subsequently became a leading feature of Fleet Street. It meant, too, that Chesterton appeared in the context of a newspaper revolution, as well as of a religious and intellectual crisis. Indeed, the changes in Fleet Street helped to make the intellectual crisis more urgent. The sudden arrival of new ideologies in an intellectually and morally stagnant culture threatened its stability and sanity. The advent of new technologies and methods of sale and management offered a vehicle, through a blurring of real issues and events, for diluted forms of these ideologies. This was a point Chesterton took up early in his career, in *Heretics*.[20] The chief characteristic of the 'Yellow Press' is a hypnotic beat of stale commonplace repetition. The large type and headlines of the *Daily Mail* are soothing, like the large alphabets used to teach children to read. The platitudinous 'timidity and mediocrity' are, however, the result of a 'worship of success and violence'. The dullness of ideas and language is bred of submission to a factitious 'trend of the time'. But this trend of the time is the product of those who do their thinking for themselves. Meanwhile the 'Yellow Press' is a perfect vehicle for a dulling of the masses into conformity to ideas which may well be indefensible or evil. Looking back on Northcliffe in 1927, Chesterton saw him as the merchant of fantasies:

> He had, at the best, all the healthy and hazy associations and prejudices which all his ten million readers had as much as he had; and he was by nature ignorant of the very idea of an idea.[21]

He lived not among things but among their 'vast shadows thrown upon a wall'. Much more serious than vulgarity, more even than the failure of mind to examine its own conventional terms, is the combination of a new power of communication with an almost complete intellectual incoherence. Northcliffe 'bought a pulpit from which ideas could have been given, when he had no ideas to give.'[22] Long before this, in his portrait of the leader-writer of a mass-circulation newspaper, Mr Hibbs in *The Flying Inn* (1914), it is the same characteristic on which he concentrates. Hibbs has no sense of truth or falsehood, right or wrong, no beliefs or firm opinions on any subject. His articles deliberately obfuscate every question with which they deal, moving away from the chief matter at issue, in any instance, to some entirely unrelated topic, on which, nevertheless, it is possible to appeal to the ill-assorted prejudices of his readers; a habit Chesterton describes as 'one of the worst tricks of modern journalism'.[23] He is shown in the act of devising one of his leaders, not from any conviction, but out of a complex of private motives, regard for the newspaper owner's 'hobby of spiritualism', and a desire to administer a mild and ineffectual check to a prominent member of 'The Other Party'.[24] The lack of connection in his ideas appeals to readers who, judged from their letters to the paper, are themselves almost incoherent, or gripped by personal obsessions. Such a lack of moral or intellectual purpose, combined with a new kind of power, is particularly dangerous. Chesterton was aware, long before such a study of that aspect of modern communications of D.J. Boorstin's *The Image*,[25] of the power of literacy and technology to create thickets of illusion between the mass-readership and the world, to rearrange life and events so that they do not have to be experienced. In the opening chapters of *The Ball and the Cross* (1910), he sketches the whole process of manufacturing and keeping up by the press around Turnbull's and MacIan's duel of a swirl of factitious public emotions, accompanied by reams of irrelevant 'comment' and 'opinion' under which its meaning and importance are buried. This grim picture of the 'new journalism' might be supplemented from other accounts in Chesterton's early essays.

Two forgotten squibs by Hilaire Belloc are worth some parenthetical notice at this point. *Caliban's Guide to Letters* (1903), most of which appeared in the *Speaker* which also took Chesterton's first connected series of articles, is, especially in conjunction with Belloc's other topical satire *Lambkin's Remains*, of three years before, an interesting clue to some of the deeper concerns of the *Speaker* group, Chesterton's first journalistic stable-mates. Although the periodical was founded to oppose the Boer War, Belloc's objects of attack in these two lampoons, are not individual political or military targets. They are rather aspects of the cultural malaise of England, the intellectual failure, as he sees it, behind cults such as Imperialism and events like the South African War. The presence of some similar concerns in Chesterton's early articles, together with a significantly different approach, is suggestive.

Briefly, the two Belloc pieces connect a moral and intellectual collapse within the Universities, the supposed guardians of culture, and the appearance of the new press. Both are aspects of the same problem. Lambkin and Caliban are literary men, representatives of a pompous and bankrupt world which hails their old men's platitudes as mature fruits of a lifetime, their doddering untruths as witty paradoxes. One a university don, the other a lay preacher with private means, they are both equally remote from actuality, and potter about without convictions or capacity for clear thought on any subject. (Caliban's political effect was 'immense' 'though he never acceded to the repeated request that he would stand on one side or the other'[26]). They share such characteristics as extreme laziness, blandness, an acceptance of received opinion, a vacuous gravity which imposes silence on those who would try to debate their teachings. When, for example, a 'young radical of sorts' challenges Caliban on the South African concentration camps, the latter:

> listened patiently, and at the end of the harangue said gently, 'Shall we join the ladies?' The rebuke was not lost.[27]

When questioned on another occasion, he replies 'with quiet dignity' that it is the first time he has heard the word of an English gentleman doubted.[28]

Both men share a contempt for foreigners. As Lambkin remarks:

> Our travels will not be without profit if they teach us to thank Heaven that our fathers preserved us from such a lot as theirs.[29]

Consequently they are pitifully ignorant of European culture.

More sinister is the taste, both men, although fusty and conventional in their styles of life, have for philosophies of ruthless will. This is shown as growing largely out of their vagueness about truth and falsehood, right and wrong. Lambkin in his lecture on 'Right' recommends an attitude which:

> transforms without metamorphosis and which says, 'Look at this, I have found truth!' but which dares not say, 'Look away from that, it is untrue'.[30]

It is a recognisable parody of the Hegelian preoccupation with development and reconciliation of opposites particularly notable in Caird, the Master of Balliol in Belloc's time. The preoccupation is connected with a growing antimonianism. Lambkin notes that:

> in a very interesting little book by Beeker it is even doubted whether what we call 'ethics' have any independent existence. This new attitude which we call 'moral anarchism' has lately cast great hold upon our young men and is full of interesting possibilities.[31]

There is, too, a strong suggestion in each man of an armchair toughness, an academic's sentimental liking for force. Dr Caliban writes monographs with titles like *The Effect of Greek Philosophy on*

European Thought, perhaps a snide reference to Caird's recent Gifford lectures on *The Evolution of Theology in the Greek Philosophers*. Yet he is delighted when he has discovered in Kipling 'a man who should *count*, who should tell', marking all the most brutal and cynical comments in Kipling's stories and reading them over and over with relish.[32] (Belloc, in a skit written in the political heat of the time, would not do justice to, and probably did not see the sublety and interest, the sheer creative force, modern critics have, rightly, discerned in Kipling's work).

Interestingly and, at first sight oddly, these two figures are intimately involved with the new phenomenon of the mass-circulation press. Caliban's ideas spread outwards. His 'political phrases' have passed into universal currency.[33] Lambkin, who in the view of a newspaper owner, was 'lost at Oxford and born for Fleet St.' has no difficulty in turning out leaders praising the Divinely ordained power of the Anglo-Saxon race.[34]

Light and ephemeral as Belloc's sketches are, they provide evidence for the existence, in a strikingly complete and coherent form, among the *Speaker* staff, of that diagnosis of the troubles of English culture which Chesterton was to develop and deepen. They suggest a precise target, a union of stuffiness, vagueness, and a vacuum of ideas, yielding to notions of an antinomian 'evolution' or 'development' and finally to a worship of power and will. This dereliction on the part of those who should have maintained intellectual standards is expressly connected to the power of the new press.

It is hardly possible to determine the degree to which Chesterton influenced this reading of events among his colleagues on the *Speaker*, was himself influenced by it, or was merely confirmed in views he already held. The question, in any event, is less important than his subsequent divergence from those colleagues. He was prepared wholeheartedly to embrace the popularising potentialities of a mass-circulation newspaper. For many years he thoroughly enjoyed the work involved and shaped his style towards it.

In this he was unlike the other contributors to the *Speaker*. Eccles and Phillimore soon went into academic life, eventually becoming university professors. Belloc regarded his journalistic employments with disrelish as somewhat demeaning tasks forced on him by the lack of a salary. He was an academic *manqué*, for whom the unexpected refusal of an Oxford fellowship was a permanent source of irritation. In spite of the abundance of his journalism, he never really succeeded in adapting his talents to the conditions of the newspaper revolution. He preferred to expound his serious opinions in the *Speaker*, the *Fortnightly Review*, the *Contemporary Review* or the *English Review*, 'quality' journals of opinion. There was nothing in his career corresponding to Chesterton's long and successful use of the new opportunities in the *Daily News*, although he occasionally wrote for that paper. Belloc's longest employment was with the Conservative daily, the *Morning Post*. This was a highly literate paper written by the educated for the educated, which failed eventually and preferred to fail rather than make any concessions to the new journalism. With even this appointment, however, he was unhappy, giving it up after three years.

As an attitude, that of Belloc and others like him, is intelligible. They were not prepared to compete on a level they despised and probably felt that in appealing to the educated minority who formed opinion, they would retain a significant influence. Chesterton's being drawn to sever his connection with the *Daily News*, largely, though not exclusively, through sympathy with Belloc's *political* attitudes, has tended to disguise the initial and long-standing difference between them on questions of culture and consequently of communication. Chesterton, as has been noted, evidently believed that a well-defined popular culture existed and was important. In the ignorance and contempt of the educated for that culture he saw one of the chief problems of the time. One of his most important tasks during the Edwardian period was to clarify and defend its achievements. While it is true, on the contrary, that Belloc was troubled by what he felt was a contemporary cultural deterioration, he saw it as due, as he remarked in a letter of 1906, to the low estimate put upon literature, 'especially by the governing public'. The solution to the problem was consequently the restoration of an intelligent and discriminating patronage by the ruling group:

> To judge our literature at the moment, posterity will think us perverted in our instincts, cowardly or wholly inept. They would

not think that, if what is best in our literature was sedulously fostered by what is best in society.[35]

The two men had a different frame of reference and consequently a different diagnosis of the cultural crisis of the period.

Chesterton's background diverged from those of the other contributors to the *Speaker*. Most of them, including the literary editor F.Y. Eccles, were former Oxford friends of Belloc, his collaborators in a book of *Essays in Liberalism* (1896). They were essentially a group of academics or men of academic background. Chesterton's not having been to a university propelled him, in that period and setting, towards an altogether different approach to mass journalism and one more congenial to his temperament. His comments on contemporary universities and his portraits of academics show a complete lack of the nostalgia which punctuated Belloc's acid and disappointed outbursts about dons. Chesterton simply did not regard the universities as culturally central. As he remarked in the well-known piece 'Oxford from Without' (1908):

> It is not a working way of managing education to be entirely content with the mere fact that you have, (to a degree unexampled in the world), given the luckiest boys the jolliest time.[36]

The essay good-naturedly demolishes the notion that universities, as then constructed, were places where men from different backgrounds exchanged experiences and ideas. Nobody could seriously pretend that they were, in that society, other than scenes for wealthy youths to enjoy themselves; all very human and pardonable if 'there were no such things in the world as danger and honour and intellectual responsibility.'[37] Beyond this criticism of isolated privilege, Chesterton had other objections to the intellectual life of universities, less purely related to past social circumstances. He doubted values which are still endorsed and claims which are still made. The life of the secluded scholar, the pursuit of 'ideas for their own sake', even academic objectivity, seemed to him of doubtful value, if not actually deleterious. A typical episode from the novels, such as Innocent Smith's threatening to shoot Dr Eames in *Manalive*, raises the question of theorising and speculation which do not affect and are not intended to affect the business of living. The internationally famous Shopenhauer scholar has delivered innumerable discourses on the worthlessness of human existence and effort from his sheltered throne since 'a don has only to continue any of his bad habits long enough to make them part of the British constitution.'[38] Smith's logical and pressing offer to murder the pessimist philosopher in order to put him out of his misery, an offer Eames energetically resists, calls in question the whole process of thinking without commitment, of teaching as a hobby views one does not ultimately hold and for which one abnegates responsibility but which, nevertheless, influence and disturb the young; a detached, almost frivolous attitude to ideas, which does not recognise they are what men will live and die for.

Chesterton questioned the value of 'academic objectivity' itself in the pursuit of a living truth or a truth to live by. He did not by this, of course, call in doubt intellectual honesty or scrupulous truthfulness but rather the academics' pretence, as he saw it, of emotional detachment, of being able to render equal justice to every side of a controversy. In history, the intellectual discipline he arguably cared most about, 'objectivity' and impartiality, he felt, clouded issues and prevented that natural engagement to one side or another in historical conflicts which would have given some life or meaning to the past. A number of early *Daily News* essays, such as 'A Plea for Partial Historians' (1902), and 'History versus Historians' (1908), strike at the root of this accepted academic attitude:

> The angry historian sees one side of the question. The calm historian sees nothing at all, not even the question itself.[39]

Lacking the university background of some of the other *Speaker* contributors, Chesterton may have lacked some of the specialist's confidence in specific areas, may, as has often been suggested, have leaned too heavily on Belloc for facts. In coping with the new journalism and the new ideologies, however, it was not a disadvantage to stand outside the cultural exclusiveness of an intelligentsia which, sharing very similar social and educational experiences, was very much at home with itself. Chesterton, unlike Belloc, simply did not consider universities *important* in the way in which his friend, in spite of his lampooning of dons, certainly did. He lacked, too, the sense of that particular 'standard of excellence' supposed to come from studying the best models, the Latin classics, Addison, or perhaps Swift, whom incidentally Belloc constantly re-read; the valuing of an understood convention of restraint, dignity, economy, correctness, clarity, weight, understated emotion, good taste. To an older generation of university critics nourished on these sources of 'good writing', and maintaining this convention, his style was glaringly defective. George Sampson's hostile account in *The Concise Cambridge History of English Literature* is representative. For Sampson, Chesterton is a 'journalist', writing for momentary effect, freakish, vague, elaborately silly. Belloc, with whose views Sampson certainly does not agree, is, nevertheless within the convention, a 'scholar', 'guarded by Latin restraint', who 'reposed upon tradition', a 'classic' where Chesterton is only a 'grotesque'.[40] In not reposing upon tradition in Sampson's sense, however, Chesterton was able to approach the new Fleet Street conditions with much less luggage, free to form a style suited to a different range of effects and to a different audience, many of whom the convention would have excluded. It is worth adding that this was a deliberate choice. Chesterton's relative lack of interest in the university world and its cultural influence was not the result of his being unable to share in them, had he so wished. Quite consistently with his views, he politely refused the offer of a newly founded Chair of English Literature at Birmingham which eventually went to Churton Collins.[41] (Collins, in Chesterton's view felt that literature was a dangerous occupation which one needed a licence to practise).

Chesterton's response to the opportunities and challenges of a newly enlarged, half-educated readership was, in spite of some disquiets, a thoroughly positive one. He was as aware as any educated man of the terrible dangers of the time contained in the blurring of issues by the mass-circulation dailies, while un-challenged, the ideologies moved in, to take over a defenceless culture, the role, already noted, of Hibbs towards Ivywood's Nietz-scheanism in *The Flying Inn*; the debauching of public taste by cynical and clever men. Hibbs, like Lambkin in Belloc's satire, is ex-university. He, too, is a manipulator of the popular mind.

Chesterton preferred, rather than 'maintaining standards', or closing ranks within the highly literate journals of opinion against the invading horde, to meet Hibbs or Northcliffe on their chosen ground. Unlike self-consciously cultivated men, he enjoyed the rough and tumble of Fleet Street as his biographers note, 'held it his proudest boast to be a journalist'[42] and exalted the ethical value of journalism as a means of communication, and of corporate effort, above that of a narrow literary life. In an early piece 'A Word for the Mere Journalist, 1902' he offers the definitive statement of his relish for the career he embraced:

> The poet writing his name upon a score of little pages in the silence of his study may or may not have an intellectual right to despise the journalist: but I greatly doubt whether he would not be morally better if he saw the great lights burning on through darkness into the dawn and heard the printing wheels weaving the destinies of another day.[43]

Chesterton's often-noted liking for the colour and conviviality of Fleet Street is less important in this statement than two other factors; a serious and defensible preference for an ethic of corporate effort, of team work, over an individualist one based on intellectual discipline in the pursuit of truth or art; and, secondly, a wish to work on a large and effective scale 'to weave destinies', rather than indulge in the isolated pleasures of pure thought. He saw his business not only as thinking, as the investigation of ideas, but even more, as their communication. This impulse goes far to explain his laborious years as the editor of *G.K.'s Weekly*, in the much more financially constrained post-1918 Fleet Street.

A recognition of the importance of Chesterton's chosen role, and a giving of due weight to its implications, are hindered by the disposition, already touched on, of critics, such as Hugh Kenner and Marshall McLuhan, to separate Chesterton from his day-to-day interests. We should, in Kenner's view, forget the accident of his having been an Edwardian journalist and imagine him at the medieval Sorbonne instead of dissipating his energies. In McLuhan's opinion the journalistic context is devoid of significance. Chesterton is rather a metaphysical moralist. These are understandable and pardonable pleas for the recognition of Chesterton's stature, but cannot be allowed to stand. Chesterton *was* an Edwardian journalist. He was not a medieval theologian at the Sorbonne. If he had been, he would have been a different Chesterton, whose style would have been formed under utterly different pressures and conventions.

Another obstacle to grasping the significance of Chesterton's working conditions lies in a misreading of them, traditional, as it seems, in Chesterton criticism. This stems, I would suggest, mainly from the personal reminiscences of his old friend E.C. Bentley, on whom Maycock and other commentators have relied. In Bentley's view Chesterton, though he liked to think of himself as a journalist, could not really be called one, at least in modern terms. He was never set a task, wrote in his own way, under his own signature, on topics of his own choosing, 'in a manner which was distasteful to large numbers of his paper's public,'[44] and knew nothing of team work. It is reasonable to point out, however, that Bentley's memoir was written long after the events of Chesterton's early career. He blurs together the later Chesterton of the well-developed public image with the young journalist making his way on the *Daily News*, under a particular editor who certainly regarded Chesterton as part of a team he managed. Also, it is hard to avoid the impression that Bentley's feeling in his somewhat disappointed later life, that his own had been a hard furrow to plough, coloured his view of his friend's career and made it seem a great deal easier than it was. It was all very well for Chesterton to think there was a romance of Fleet Street, but:

> very little of it came within my own experience, if only because I never found there was time for it, if the work in hand was to be done to my satisfaction, to say nothing of other peoples.[45]

Two stumbling blocks, more than others, probably hinder further knowledge and appreciation of Chesterton's work. One is a preoccupation with certain off-colour remarks about Jews. The other, more pervasive and relating to his role as a journalist, is that he was too much of a performer, a 'personality merchant' to be consistent with intellectual integrity. Besides, the performance has dated. It would be better, perhaps, to avoid the embarrassment of trying to deny or to minimise either point; to admit that Chesterton's style was a performance, related to the needs of a career in journalism at a particular time; to accept too that tastes, at least for the present, are different. Granting this, what were the positive aspects of that specific presentation? To just what tastes was the style geared and what tasks did it enable Chesterton to accomplish?

In dealing with these matters, we are the prisoners of certain intellectual and aesthetic preconceptions, the historical relativity of which we refuse to recognise. Largely, these amount to little more than a preference for one superficial social manner rather than another. We prefer an appearance of earnestness, even of agonising, in fiction or criticism. It is important to recognise the existence of two distinct postures within Edwardian literature. The first is much the best known and has been given most attention by academic literary critics. It is exemplified by such writers as James, Conrad and Ford Madox Ford, who stressed the high claims of the novel form, the demands it was entitled to make on readers who must not expect mere entertainment, and the value of a highly finished, stylistically and morally strenuous art. The second Edwardian literary stance, now much less studied, but probably more important at the time, was that of the essayists, polemicists and propagandists, notably Wells, Shaw, Belloc and Chesterton. In much of their writing the convention is one of ease. Pains might be taken but they should not be seen to be taken; an attitude which has a rare capacity to grate on us. Little more than manner is involved, since an appearance of graceful negligence might co-exist with great seriousness while an air of dogged application concealed triviality or the need to 'publish or perish'. James Purcell has offered one of the best generalised accounts of this aspect of literary climate of the years 1900 to 1910, and its difference from our own. He notes the Edwardians' preference for 'wit' both in the limited comic sense and Pope's much broader one. Edwardian readers valued:

> panache, brio, the ability to aphorise one's experience of life under the stylistic convention of maintaining an improvisatory conversation with one's intellectual peers.[46]

A difference in literary or social manner involved a difference in a writer's strategy. As Purcell puts it:

> If a writer like Chesterton had the requisite intellectual personality and productivity, he set out not to write a bestseller or Great English Novel/Poem, but to build a loyal repeat-buying public. He became a recognisable brand name, an image; one knew his initials or his in-group nickname.[47]

One might add the vital point that Chesterton built up his persona and his hold on his public by carefully controlled techniques of provocation, by adopting an unexpected stance towards the conventional seriousness of the *Daily News* 'house-style'.

Popularisation of ideas through mass-circulation newspapers, the building up of a persona to catch the public eye, the very fertility with which Chesterton wrote, are all matters of complaint to scholars who expect to receive a small sum each month, whether they have spent it in writing or in meditation. It is no discredit to Chesterton that his serious wish to act on the culture of his time, to disseminate, or to criticise thought, went into harness with an honourable ambition, in a young married man, to earn money or to build a career. Neither desire, according to the standards of public etiquette of his time, was inconsistent with deliberately giving pleasure to oneself and others as an entertainer or performer. Hence a *Daily News* article might contain a serious philosophical point in one paragraph, a joke about his size or having been run away with by a hansom cab in the next. Nor is the element of innocent design on the part of Chesterton or his employers in the *Daily News* in any way reprehensible. In *Autobiography* Chesterton is quite candid about his strategy:

> I wrote on a nonconformist organ like the old *Daily News* and told them all about French cafés and Catholic cathedrals; and they loved it, because they had never heard of them before.[48]

The light-hearted tone of this familiar passage should not prevent us from realising that Chesterton had an intelligible and consistent journalistic method. Rather than the common plan of studying the market and writing for it, Chesterton preferred the more risky but potentially more rewarding scheme of stimulating and provoking readers by challenging their settled pattern of tastes and values. The *Daily News* essays contain echoes of abundant, often indignant correspondence.

In the situation of a paper facing a battle for readers against a new rival, the *Daily Mail*, the employment of a journalist such as Chesterton was clearly part of a series of manoevres such as the cutting of the *Daily News*'s price. Both were calculated risks on the part of George Cadbury and A.G. Gardiner and the result was substantially successful. Although the *Daily News* could never equal the *Daily Mail*'s readership of 800,000 it more than held its own, steadily increasing its circulation from a low point of 56,000, in 1900, just before Chesterton's employment to 400,000 by 1909,[49] a marked and interesting contrast with the *Standard* which plummeted from a position of second most popular daily paper to virtual oblivion during these years.

The relationship between Chesterton and his readers was obviously a delicate one. It involved knowing how to keep up a controversy, to surprise, shock or to challenge what seemed the natural order of things in art, history, culture and religion. And yet this had to be done while remaining on speaking terms with them. The problem was partly one of managing a difficult relationship, partly one of devising a literary manner which would educate without offending, of treading a line between the provocative and the insulting. The reward was substantial. Chesterton, as he estimated himself, reached more readers at this time than at any other. Even more important he was continually preaching to the unconverted and to the vulnerable. As his brother remarked in 1908:

> Thousands of peaceful semi-Tolstoian Nonconformists have for six years, been compelled to listen every Saturday morning to a fiery apostle preaching ... War, Drink and Catholicism.[50]

As a summary of what Chesterton was 'preaching' this is, of course, and is intended to be, light-hearted nonsense, but it does underline the disparity between the writer and his readers. This, probably, was not an anomaly but more like a device, accepted and endorsed by the owner and editor of the *Daily News* and by Chesterton himself, and justified by its success.

In reaching a substantial body of readers whom Margaret Canovan has described as 'members of the Nonconformist middle class, teetotal, semi-pacifist believers in progress and enlightenment,'[51] Chesterton was probing the consciousness of a susceptible, inwardly confused group, the weakening of whose traditional dogmatic religious beliefs left them peculiarly open to the new ideological invasion. Historical generalisations involving the intellectual and moral condition of whole sections of a community are obviously difficult but here the judgement of several historians is confirmed by contemporary evidence. (This is, I would suggest, quite markedly the case in some of the day-to-day particulars, to be examined later, of the *Daily News*, as it printed Chesterton's articles). A malaise among the liberal, Nonconformist middle class, an uncertain hold by many of them on their own inherited values, the fissiparous nature of the Liberal Party at this time, its tendency to break into cliques and segments with little in common, the changing and often incompatible definitions of Liberalism; above all, the loss of confidence, even the boredom with the Liberal truisms noticed by many observers; all these are themes of many generally accepted analyses of the period. Bryce,[52] Hobson, Masterman and other contemporary witnesses record not merely political stumbling or loss of purpose, but a deeper spiritual uncertainty; not merely a fear that Peace, Retrenchment and Reform were no longer the obvious answers politically but that the whole description of man offered by traditional Liberalism was inaccurate and outmoded. The increasing awareness of the force of the herd instinct (witnessed by Trotter's important studies);[53] and the growing interest in political violence reflected, among much else, in spreading influence of Georges Sorel, are often noted. The long-standing and deepening attraction of philosophies of evolution towards the unknown Absolute, or irrationalism and the assertion of the Will, or alternatively of its total abnegation form the staple of writing on the period immediately preceding the First World War.[54] Alan O'Day has remarked, in a recent collection of essays by historians on the period, that although none of them agree with the *details* of the picture of disintegration painted in George Dangerfield's

The Strange Death of Liberal England, most of them 'do provide substantial support for his brushwork – the central thesis that the Edwardian age was one of severe testing and crisis for Liberalism.'[55] Some recent historical writing has, perhaps as a useful corrective, been inclined to stress the 'stability and continuity' of Edwardian ideas and institutions but this tendency towards revisionism has by no means carried the field. O'Day remarks of the collection he edits that:

> here reassessment of traditional themes and the inclusion of new material has led the majority of contributors to points of view which stress conflict and are more congenial to the Dangerfield thesis.[56]

It is, of course, worth noting as he does, the resilience and toughness with which the Edwardians approached their problems and the fact, above all, that the story was broken off:

> The events of 1914 cut short abruptly the brief attempt at regeneration made by the vigorous Edwardian generation.[57]

It is perfectly possible and not inherently unreasonable to assert that Chesterton must have been aware of the tensions of a threatened Liberalism. Such an assertion only gains value if it can be sustained in particular instances. How did Chesterton's awareness affect his journalistic style and concerns?

In 1914, shortly after Chesterton had left the *Daily News,* Ford Madox Ford Hueffer wrote, in *Outlook,* an amusing summing up of Gardiner's paper and the curious *mélange* of attitudes, the odd cast of mind for which it catered. Since that Edwardian Liberal mind was soon to be engulfed by the First World War, and its attendant upheavals, both moral and political, Hueffer's piece has, retrospectively, the quality of its epitaph. It is also an excellent introduction to the scene on which Chesterton's most important series of essays made their appearance. For Hueffer, writing social commentaries for the *Daily News* must have been 'of the queerest things in this queer world, the queerest of all.'[58] It would not be a disagreeable occupation since it would be so funny, but it would be an 'obstacle race', a 'tip-toeing amid the egg-shells' a holding of one's breath amid the avalanches. One would, for instance, have to be 'extremely anti-Romanist' to please the Nonconformist readers and, at the same time, 'pretty fairly Papist' to please Asquith's Irish allies and 'the tolerant'. One would have to swing backwards and forwards through a spectrum of inconsistent attitudes:

> rejoice in the triumphs of Fabianism, Labour, Syndicalism, Anarchism and strong government by turns.[59]

The paper's readers, however, liked in the things of the intellect an air of impartiality and had a curious appetite for theoretical novelty:

> You might uphold the sanctity of marriage, or praise a book extolling Free Love à la P.B. Shelley; for in the *Daily News* public there are many mansions.[60]

You might, in fact, praise any writer, except Kipling, and the more he was one of 'les jeaunes' the more the readers would like it. Most significantly, perhaps, Hueffer saw the paper as bearing the stamp of its editor's personality:

> Its delicate treading; its bright niceness; its feeling of unreality – all these things were due to Mr A.G. Gardiner.[61]

Any account of Chesterton's work in the context of the *Daily News* must obviously start with his and Gardiner's relationship. One preliminary puzzle is that twelve years of close association (1901–13) between Chesterton and Gardiner left so little trace in *Autobiography*. There is only one polite but cursory reference to the *Daily News*'s well-read and sympathetic editor'.[62] In fact, it seems clear, this indicates that the break between the two men, when it came, was peculiarly painful. (From other sources, it may be suggested that it took place at a time of, and perhaps contributed to, a period of uncharacteristic irritation and heavy drinking on Chesterton's part during which he broke his arm).[63] Stephen Koss, author of the latest and standard biography of Gardiner, is in no doubt of the closeness of their working relationship:

> Gardiner loved him dearly – Chesterton was godfather to his youngest child, Gilbert – despite certain painful incidents that punctured their professional relations.[64]

The liking was founded on Gardiner's relish, in spite of the difference in their habits, for Chesterton's ebullience and lack of self-consciousness.

It was a relationship particularly interesting for two reasons. First, because the divergent elements of Gardiner's nature may, without being fanciful, be seen to epitomise the contradictions of the paper he edited, perhaps the contradictions of a dissolving Liberalism. Secondly, because the way in which he assigned a role to Chesterton, contributed to Chesterton's persona, his literary identity, hence to his success but also, eventually, to the strains which ended their association.

An underlying factor both in Gardiner's editorship and his various strategies, including the employment and the role assigned to Chesterton, was a new economic toughness in Fleet Street conditions. The price of creating a new political organ had become prohibitive by 1900. The result was a series of 'take-over bids' and a struggle between parties and factions for control over the editorial policy of papers, persisting through Gardiner's career with 'profoundly unsettling effects in Fleet St.'[65] The relationship between press and politicians was closer than at any time before or since. Together with the kaleidoscope of ideas becoming available on every topic and the political and social change and tension, these Fleet Street conditions made for instability in the expression of opinion in newspapers. The specific factors which accompanied Chesterton's rise to prominence on the *Daily News* ended after 1918, in a wholesale amalgamation of newspapers and a growth of syndicates. In this difficult climate Gardiner was a strikingly effective editor whose increase in the circulation of his paper was an even more impressive achievement. He had been a relatively unknown provincial journalist from Blackburn, born in 1865, a self-made and self-educated man from a disadvantaged background. Perhaps because his father had been a drunkard, he was a strict temperance reformer and very acceptable on that ground to George Cadbury, the paper's owner. His first act at the *Daily News* was to outlaw not only betting advertisements and 'tips' but any form of racing news. In Halévy's view the new regime at the paper was puritan as well as radical.[66] The manoeuvre, which certainly strengthened the hold of the *Daily*

News on its traditional Nonconformist readers, was accompanied by several more positive steps, bolder typography, columns of table talk, regular features on 'News from the Provinces', 'Life and Labour', a great increase in the space devoted to literature, and a sparking off of interest by an artful throwing of ideas and personalities, of whom Chesterton was one, into collision. Gardiner, fortunately for this last element of his strategy, was pleasant and accessible, gifted, in E.C. Bentley's view, with 'a faculty for getting on good terms with all men, great and small',[67] adroit in the management of an extremely talented but contentious group of contributors:

It is doubtful whether anyone else could have maintained reasonable harmony among so many prima donnas.[68]

Rather as Asquith is said to have done in his Cabinet, Gardiner sought to balance one individual against another, allowing nobody to become dominant in an overall effect which he orchestrated:

He could not allow the leader page or, for that matter, the literary department to be dominated by writers of any particular school or obsession.[69]

He valued his colleagues not merely for their abilities but 'for the way in which they promised to fit into the general operations.' Chesterton must, then, be fully understood as part of a team under Gardiner's firm but tactful management.

A more personal undercurrent in the relationship is provided by the inescapable suggestion that Chesterton, or at least Chesterton as Gardiner saw him, appealed to a suppressed side of the editor's nature. Gardiner was, as Koss remarks, a combination of antithetical qualities,[70] a man who evolved two identities for himself, the combative declaratory political writer and the gentle and discursive 'Alpha of the Plough' whose pieces on favourite old books, cricket matches, 'On Being Tidy', 'On Talking to Oneself' and other examples of 'intimate triviality', were used by schoolmasters in the 1920s and 1930s to teach boys to write graceful essays. It is possible to detect other suppressed traits of Gardiner's identity. A strenuous advocate of international understanding and peace at almost any price with Imperial Germany, he greatly enjoyed writing reports on boxing matches, under a pseudonym. A strict teetotaller, he relished and exaggerated Chesterton's drinking. (Curiously enough when invited to address the Darwen Literary Club, he had chosen to speak on Falstaff. Chesterton was, for him, a Falstaffian figure).

Gardiner's sketch of his friend and leading contributor in a book of pen-portraits, *Prophets, Priests and Kings* (1908), is highly suggestive of what he valued Chesterton for, the roles which he assigned to him and his work. Repeatedly in his short essay, Gardiner emphasises the point that Chesterton is 'not of our time', he is 'a legend', something out of a fairy-tale. Unlike most of us, who are creatures of our own age and circumstances, Chesterton has escaped the 'temporal tyranny'. But not by becoming a rebel. Rather he is elemental, primitive:

> One imagines him drinking deep draughts from the horn of Skrymir, or exchanging jests with Falstaff at the Boar's Head in Eastcheap.[71]

He has the 'freshness and directness of a child's vision'. He sees the world 'as a child sees its first rainbow.' Life for him is a book of coloured pictures and this is what gives him his 'kinship with children.' Most of us on reaching maturity find existence stale and unprofitable, but Chesterton has never 'come into the light of common day.' He 'is free from the tyranny of things.' He 'rambles along without a thought of where he is going.' His writing is 'blithe improvisation', without relation to conscious literature:

> He is like a child shouting with glee at the sight of the flowers and the sunshine.[72]

Perhaps, one day, he will tire of Fleet Street, don a giant suit of mail and ride off into the greenwood.

Without dabbling in amateur psychological analysis, one may infer that for Gardiner, Chesterton was a harmless surrogate indulgence in styles of behaviour which the plain-living, high-thinking editor of 'the largest-selling Liberal newspaper in the world' could not have permitted himself. Interestingly, he did not evolve his second persona of 'Alpha of the Plough' until three years after he had parted company with Chesterton. Whatever speculations one may entertain about the recesses of Gardiner's personality, however, his portrait of Chesterton clearly implies that this is how he saw his role in the *Daily News* and the appeal he was intended to have for its readers. To some extent, literature itself was in the 'Alpha of the Plough' columns and Gardiner's other non-political writings marked out as a form of relaxation, of fantasy, a liberation of the spirit from the moral demands of the adult world.

If Chesterton was an ebullient child, his antics could be indulged as harmless and delightful excursions from workaday existence. He would have that freedom of speculation noted by Hueffer as characteristic of the *Daily News*. It is easy to say that Gardiner made Chesterton play a part, the diminishing one of a resident *enfant terrible*. Certainly there is force in Chesterton's complaint in 1911[73] that other contributors were allowed to make serious and telling points about the deficiencies of official Liberalism, while he was not. (It was, of course, his ultimate insistence on expressing views hostile to the Liberal 'party-line' which led to his leaving the *Daily News*). He was, presumably, outside his assigned role and ceasing to be ebullient, childlike, etc. The deficiencies of the situation seem so obvious that it is hard to see why it continued for twelve, highly successful years.

The truth is, perhaps, more complex. Chesterton needed a public who could be startled, whose plainness, stuffiness and irrational prejudices and shibboleths, he could shake and question. But his ideal was not, like that of Wilde and some of the minor 1890s figures, *épater les bourgeois*. He had to stand in a certain relationship with his public which included elements of shock and calculated affront, but which included too, affection, trust and a certain accepted freedom. A great deal about such a role would depend on how he played it. It might have been a foolish exhibition, a prolonged comic 'act' or it might, as it indeed was, be a careful blend of the amusing and serious, the disarming and the sometimes devastating. What gave depth and humanity to his relationship with his readers was, I would suggest, his sense of their vulnerability; that under outward social manners and verbal conventions, they were, generally speaking, intellectually and morally confused people, caught uneasily between conflicting emotions and impulses, like Gardiner himself, between the remnants of a Nonconformist culture which was rapidly losing its rationale and, as has been suggested, an onrush of dangerous new ideas.

The evidence for these suggestions must be found by looking at Chesterton in action in greater detail, and, choosing examples from one year only, by seeing his essays in context, responding and provoking response in this dissolving Liberal world. Throughout 1903, Chesterton was anxious to reassure his readers as to his fundamental seriousness, that despite his 'youth', (he was in fact nearly thirty) and a style different from the kind of discourses to which they were used, he meant what he said. On 18 July for example, he remarked that:

> the great characteristic of the English is that they are sanguine and dreamy. Someone is sure to call this paradoxical or something, but I beseech him to believe that I am not disposed to play the clown on the subject of poverty, at any rate.

On 10 October, he protested that:

> I fancy that certain people for whom I entertain a very particular regard thought the article I wrote last week undesirably frivolous... that I do not in these and similar compositions mean what I say... I do think my own opinions funny but I think them absolutely true.

On 17 October, he responded to the rebuke of being an 'ignorant and presumptuous young man', by stating that all his generation were ignorant and presumptuous, in the sense that, without being scholars, they presumed to argue and have opinions. On 4 July, he had, again reacting to comments on his 'youth', agreed that he was young but that:

> even youth has, as well as dangers, advantages, and one of these is that it tends to know which way the world is going.

This painstaking guarding of himself against being thought 'scintillating', or an entertainer suggests from the first a tension between the role assigned to Chesterton and that which he intended to assume.

At the same time, he refused to capitulate and take on the accepted 'serious' tone. What emerges from a study of the *Daily News* is a clearer picture of that 'seriousness' which Chesterton saw it as his task to breach. A new light is thrown on the style of writing he developed, from a contrast which, it is likely, was designed by Gardiner's editorial policy of balance and variety. Week by week, the reader is bound to compare Chesterton's work with the now, perhaps mercifully, forgotten writing of 'Verax'. The *Daily News*'s second major essayist during this period, 'Verax', the 'truth-teller' may have been designed as a 'straight-man' to Chesterton's comic turn. He became more like a target, epitomising the tone and the ideas against which Chesterton was campaigning. On 4 July 1903, their two articles dealt with the subject of discussion. 'Verax' felt 'Converse' (his subject for the day) was an activity which 'setting up no jarring discord with intelligence or conscience is a source of pure, restful recuperative enjoyment.' The subjects of conversation 'are not of much moment', provided they are 'uninfected by bad or improper feeling of any kind.' Intelligence, wit, information 'can all be spared if true, manly, honest sympathy do a real good trade between the hearts of the talkers.' This sentimental and anti-intellec-tual attitude is in marked contrast to Chesterton's piece two pages earlier:

I believe this age wants philosophical arguments, arguments about fundamentals, more than anything.

On 24 October, 'Verax', in a piece entitled 'Luggage Labels' argued that religious or philosophical ideas about life are of little sig-nificance:

The mental picture does not necessarily correspond with the actual reality; is, in fact, only a help to the imagination.

Accepting one set of labels, one scheme of ideas, rather than another is irrelevant, since reality 'transcends not only our powers of com-prehension but contradicts our very laws of thought.' In any case, men whose 'attitude of heart was right' would 'receive the light of life' whatever they thought or believed.

Chesterton's essay of the same day, 'A Plea for Philosophical Uniforms' is, in effect, a plea for 'Luggage Labels':

It is precisely by these external differences that we learn the most essential differences.... The superficial symbols of a man generally betray him.

Ideas are real and concrete, involving sundering divisions between men on the aims and conduct of life, naturally requiring 'physical rituals' which express these fundamental philosophical differences. Only a month before, (19 September), Chesterton had discussed the origin of religious wars, in connection with the current massacres in Macedonia by the Turks which the *Daily News* was reporting throughout the year.

The origin of such wars lies in 'the nature and definition of religion', which 'our Liberalism tends to forget.' It is a passionate conviction or philosophy about the nature of life, not a matter of 'right-mindedness'. A man from another period or place may be 'as good as any of us – self-restrained, aspiring, magnanimous, sincere' but may, from firm intellectual conviction, practise human sacrifice:

It will altogether depend on the nature of his philosophy. And that is how the case stands at the root of the horrors of the Near East.

The Turks really have, in spite of many virtues, a different view of the value of human life. Our opposition to them is, and must be, based on the fact that they think and act 'against everything for which we stand'. Such a stress on the importance of ideas and the divisions they cause went very much against the grain of many *Daily News* readers and contributors. On 22 September, a correspondent reported a visit to Syed Ali Bigrami, Professor of Arabic at Cambridge, who reassured him that the views in 'Mr Chesterton's article' were unfounded:

I left Professor Bigrami feeling that Islam has much more to say for itself than most of us had realised.

The problem Chesterton faced was that the prevailing sentimentality and dislike of logical distinctions and definite beliefs, of which 'Verax' was representative, the harping on 'good, manly feeling' and 'propriety' did, in fact, accompany *undiscussed* ideas, the consequences of which were scarcely suspected.

On 5 September, for instance, 'Verax' in an article on the relationship between evolution and truth, proclaimed that 'the purpose of Nature, as revealed by Evolution, is not the discovery of truth but the maintenance of life.' Nature selects types whose 'illusions or delusions' keep 'painful or hampering truths' at bay. If we saw the world as it really is, 'with our present organisation we could not live.' It is very strange to find a writer who, if he accepts such a statement, must also accept the impossibility of knowledge and the complete relativity of morals, yet (on 18 July) inveigh against the habit of smoking ciagrettes, 'In our time, from what one sees and from all one hears and reads, the extent to which narcotics and opiates are indulged in is truly alarming', or on 4 July attack vivisection. What are the use of medical discoveries which 'produce no glow of high ennobling emotion?' Chesterton, perhaps not surprisingly, was very much taken up during the year with expressing a contrasting view of the relationship between objective fact and evolution. On 17 March, he protested against 'philosophers of evolution' who have inaugurated a custom of setting forth 'hypothetical civilisations', or unknown states of being as definite ideals, 'of saying that we ought or shall be another kind of race, another kind of creature.' We want, presumably, a new kind of man, 'possibly a man with two heads'.

In its context, in the day-by-day columns of the paper, Chesterton's insistence on the reality and value of the external world and his physical pleasure in it, seem less a private psychological concern, as it is treated in many studies, and more like one voice setting itself deliberately against a chorus. Evolutionary development towards the Superman may not be impossible, he says, (22 August) but:

> nothing will induce me to say that a child or a brass band or a baked potato are bad because there are not other things that would be good.

Chesterton's frequent reference to ordinary physical pleasures, food and drink, family life, the 'brass band and baked potato' element of existence is more like a polemical device than a personal indulgence, as it may look out of context. It is designed to explode a tone of mincing uplift, of moralising preciosity which divorced the mind from reality; as when, on 18 July, 'Verax' discussed 'Our Nerves.' Those of us who suffer from 'Nerves', he is convinced, need:

a life of true enjoyment, of real worth, a return to the Fountain of Living Waters, which, if we read Jeremiah aright, meant a return to common sense, wise policy, simple faith and plain duty.

Chesterton's alternative suggestion of a visit to the pub is not altogether flippant. There is, he feels, a certain kind of refinement in which the mind loses hold of the anchor of instinct, and the humility which accompanies a sense of the appetites and needs common to all men. This has two evil consequences; a tendency to be lost in a world of ideas which so long as they sounded 'ennobling', could be any kind of poison; and secondly, a disposition to exaggerate the social and intellectual gap between oneself and gross, earthy 'ordinary' men. The contrast of tone between Chesterton and the other contributors to the *Daily News* is marked enough to seem designed. The edition of 8 August has a finical and patronising piece by 'Verax' on 'Faulty Pronunciation', following one on 'Incorrect Spelling' of the week before. It carries, also, an article by Chesterton praising Hampstead Heath because it is beautiful:

but it is more than that; it is vulgar. It is the real playground of the poor who have the vast, beautiful, and incontestable superiority to the rich, that they do not think their fellow creatures spoil the face of their mother earth.

The essence of Chesterton's power in these week-by-week polemics lay elsewhere, however. While it was enjoyable and timely to praise drink and baked potatoes on a paper whose other contributors were attempting to sound like arch lay preachers, Chesterton's chief advantage was his early understanding of the transitional nature of the cultural background against which he was writing. His achievement was to see through the mask of refinement and the moralising manner to the dimly visible oncoming forces. The *Daily News* of 1903 contained an odd mixture of relics of a decayed Nonconformist culture, isolated fragments of prejudice, and a high-minded tone, no longer supported by any coherent system of thought, together with

79

foreshadowings of what became some of the most evil attitudes of the twentieth century: attitudes the prevailing 'seriousness' showed no power to detect.

On the one hand, the *Daily News* reported with horror (17 April) the use of a Tractarian 'Mass Book' by an Anglican clergyman in the London Docks or, (15 September), discussed the 'propriety' of mixed family bathing. A more sinister set of notions, pointing to the future rather than the past, was already present before the unsuspecting eyes of its readers. They show in the ready ear given to fatalistic scientific theories; those, for example, morally bracketing people by the size or shape of their heads (such as Chesterton attacked a little later in his essay 'The Criminal Head'), or even by the colour of hair or eyes. On 14 March, the paper gave a respectful report to a lecture by Professor Karl Pearson at the Royal Institute, 'Character Reading by External Signs' and quoted its views seriously:

> Statistics for which schoolmasters were responsible showed that boys with fair eyes were more conscientious than boys with dark eyes, but they, on the same basis of calculation, drop the idea that curly hair meant crooked ways.

There is too, a recurring anti-intellectualism, showing particularly in the repetition, in and out of season, without argument, but with an air of stating the obvious, of some variation of the remark that thought does not count, only action. On 17 November, for instance, Chesterton's column appeared next to a long and highly favourable review of a book, *Humanism* by one R.C. Schiller, which asserted that the primary face of life was not ratiocination but 'living', that ideas were never more than working hypotheses 'designed for the practical ends of human life.' Chesterton's essay of the same day is an attack on the anti-intellectual cult of the 'practical man', the idolising of the 'rough sanity and determination' of the businessman who does not trouble himself with theories, as if the same cast of mind which made a profit from bacon could manage the War Office.

Along with determinism in an evolutionary framework, or in terms of physical characteristics, there appeared a pronounced taste for historical and racial, even goegraphical determinism. 'Verax' on 22 August was convinced that:

geographically it is only within a belt of about twenty degrees of latitude, from about 35 to 55 that all great civilisations, world empires, great genius have developed. If we go much over that boundary on the one side, we reach the Esquimaux, if on the other, we get to the West Indies. Deeds of high emprise are to be expected from neither.

Throughout the year, Chesterton's recurrent targets were 'Historical Inevitability' and 'national fates' and 'destinies' unconnected with human will and choice; as (on 7 November), the 'absurd distinction between living and dying nations':

It is surely obvious that no people and no institution has ever steadily advanced along one line, growing or decaying.

The various forms of fatalism and pseudo-science were, however, less sinister than the ready reception given to the principle of eugenics, against which Chesterton many years later, was to write a major book. What is disconcerting then, as now, is not the existence of individual cranks but the response of the ostensibly sane to their ideas. On August 15th, the *Daily News* reviewed *Essays in Buff* by a certain Walter Scott, under the heading of 'A Plea for the Body'. In this work the author urged:

the control of the future race by means of selection and improvement, the choking and sterilization of the unfit. He is amazed that such work has not yet been undertaken by some patriotic government.

The reviewer takes the book quite seriously, makes no attempt to condemn or even criticise the ideas offered, any more than if they had been gardening hints. He remarks that Scott is clearly 'in deadly earnest' but shows 'a pretty talent for writing.' In spite of the subject, one must admit that it is handled with every attention to good taste and the avoidance of impropriety:

The droll lucidity and ingenuousness of the writer removes any suggestion of irreverent intention.

Chesterton's sense of what was going on is, perhaps, most in evidence if one contrasts his article at the end of the year, ('The Feast of Christmas Day,' 26 December) with the sermons carefully reported at length on the 'Religious News' page. (Of these an effusion by the Bishop of London on 'the chimes of church bells in early childhood' is entirely typical). Chesterton dismisses worries about 'ritualism' in Church services. The centre of gravity has shifted to other matters. He recalls 'Mafeking night', the first evidence of a public upsurge based on the effect of the new mass-circulation press:

> We need not trouble to guess what ritual religion would sweep over England if Christmas faded. A ritual religion did sweep over England in the last few years... then men blew through horns at night like savages hooting at an idol.... The immortal beast that is in all of us cried out against God. If we let go the old superstition of Charity, do not let us fancy there will not be new philosophies to step into its place; vast, shapeless and inhuman philosophies.

The 'serious' tone offered no protection against such outright evil. The tendency of writer after writer on the *Daily News* to fall, almost automatically into a manner of vague edification, divorced from moral or intellectual perception, makes it easier to understand Chesterton's blend of prophecy with casual flippancy, his disregard of his own dignity in writing. There was too much false dignity about. Silliness, in such an atmosphere, may be a weapon more subversive of pomposity and sentimentality than wit, which gives them the benefit of an intellectual criticism. The 'showing off' and clowning of Chesterton's early performance are a deliberate contrast to those of too many others on the paper. They represent, too, the giving up of a literary manner which has become a confidence trick, an invitation to trust a writer as sincere since he is not afraid to show an ordinary degree of 'silliness' and inconsequentiality. They are, besides, an invitation to the reader to climb off the pedestal, shed the mantle of a false air of responsibility. Gardiner's picture of Chesterton as 'a child', though irritating in expression does suggest the pleasure he gave by demolishing the regulation sanctimonious manner.

Of that manner there is an excellent instance in 'Verax's' the *Speaker* on Fairy-tales. 'Verax' recommended fairy stories not because they are, as Chesterton had said, morally true, but because they cannot be taken for reality and produce:

the flabbiness of resolution, the aversion from everyday work and duty, the result of too much novel reading. . . . The minds of the young should be employed on bright, airy nothings. In this way they are powerfully helped in getting that strength which enables them to deal with the gaunt realities of after life.

This difference about the significance of fairy stories supplies a clue to another aspect of what was wrong with much serious contemporary writing on men and affairs. It was not simply the trick of moralising without intelligence. It was the much deeper problem of intellect cut off from what Chesterton saw as its roots in the popular imagination and the imagination of childhood; the cultural split to which he addressed himself in his studies of myth and of the grotesque.

Chesterton was opposed to 'Verax's' standard contemporary view of adulthood as a time for the putting away of childish illusion and for taking on an air of dignity which masked deep-rooted ideological follies. His insistence on an organic relationship between childish and adult identity, a connection between the dreams, aspirations and fantasies of the one and of the other is, of course, one of the initial perceptions of novels such as *The Napoleon of Notting Hill* and *The Flying Inn*. On a lighter note, and typical of his deflating humour, he protested in an essay, not in fact in the *Daily News*, but in *The Venture Annual*, belonging nevertheless to the same year 1903, against the picture of children as essentially different from those of adults. Like poor people, they are not another species, as educated middle class seem to imagine. As we become 'separated from what is really natural' we tend to talk of both 'as if they were goblins':

Children are simply human beings who are allowed to do what everyone really desires to do...when seriously wronged to emit prolonged screams for several minutes.[74]

He did not do this when reading 'Verax' or his kind, but, one suspects, he did indulge in a little, quite understandable nose-thumbing.

Passing comments such as those quoted from other contributors to the *Daily News* are open to the criticism that they are mere flotsam and jetsam of a vanished world, ephemeral fragments. But it could be seriously maintained that if such a thing as an atmosphere in opinion or ideas exists or may be ascertained, these trifles give more of a hint of it than the considered views of Chesterton's intellectual equals. The major controversies with Shaw or Wells are instructive, but it is almost more important to be aware of the enemy without a name, the score of little rebuttals, overt and implied, of multitudes of 'Verax's, the continued pressure of his work against their current, which helped to form the substance and the manner of his writing.

IV

SYMBOL IN *THE FLYING INN*

Interesting as was his newspaper writing, Chesterton's most sensitive accounts of the ideological invasion, took place in his fiction, through the mediums of image and of the analysis of character. It was here he did his subtlest thinking. In the next two chapters it is proposed to look first at the way in which he worked within one novel, *The Flying Inn* (1914) to probe Nietzscheanism and then to explore the changing emphasis within his involvement with one image, that of Don Quixote, (an image which, incidentally supplies *The Flying Inn* with a wider context), an image which, more importantly, was the vehicle of much of his understanding of historical processes.

Chesterton's most satisfactory examination of Nietzscheanism is found not in his journalism, but in his novel *The Flying Inn*, where, concerned less with polemic and more with understanding and pity, he reveals its origins in the individual personality and its potential effects of the national culture. *The Flying Inn* deals ostensibly with the consequences of a successful attempt by Lord Ivywood, a puritanical aristocrat and influential politician, to carry through Parliament a measure to close the inns of England. In fact, the novel is a diagnosis of the social and spiritual state of the country. Ivywood gains ideological support for his designs both from a general sympathy with Islam and from the teachings of Misyra Ammon, a 'prophet' whose ridiculous career is also traced. Received with indifference by the poor in the opening scene, Ammon is taken up first by the middle class, and, with increasing warmth, by the leaders of society and finance. Taking advantage of a legal technicality in Ivywood's Act of Parliament, the Dickensian landlord Humphrey Pump, and the Irish rebel and adventurer Captain Dalroy, whose love for Joan Brett supplies the book's romantic interest, move across country with Pump's inn-sign and a supply of liquor. This they preserve in their flying inn, thereby saving a vital English institution from ideological attack. Their travels, and the incidents, anecdotes and songs with which the novel abounds offer a picture of English society in crisis. The book displays the vulnerability of the upper and middle classes to any half-baked exotic notions which appeal to their snobbery, the venality of institutions like Parliament, popular journalism and the press, the dottiness of much supposedly intellectual writing. What appear to be digressions are, as will be seen, closely related to the intellectual themes of the novel. Dorian Wimpole might serve as a preliminary instance. At first sight, he is a stock, if amusing, figure of the affected aesthete, a sort of Bunthorne. He writes pretentious poems which develop the notes of the bird songs into dialogues and soliloquies of feathered philosophers. (These works, which recall the well-known Persian poet Attar's *Bird-Parliament*, connect with the modish orientalising touched on elsewhere in the novel).

Wimpole, who leaves his chauffeur for hours at a time without food, embodies the isolation of a supposedly cultivated élite from common needs, ordinary people and their lives, which helps to create the world of 'indirectness and insincerity' in which Ivywood carries through his scheme. The poet's awakening from his moral blindness in a striking scene in the Smoking Room of the House of Commons is also, as several critics have noted, the moment when Ivywood's plans pass over into complete fanaticism or obsession. This moment suggests, among much else, the possibility of awakening and repentance even in the most unlikely figure, the precious and affected 'poet of the Birds'. A summary of the plot of *The Flying Inn* gives even less of a sense of its spirit and meaning than it does with most novels. The flow of incident and extravagant action, as Pump and Dalroy are chased across country with their inn-sign gives the book a surface life and colour but its unity is essentially intellectual.

A question which should be asked about *The Flying Inn* is whether enough attention has been paid to Chesterton's *art*. To read Chesterton as an artist one has, of course, to cut through his own disclaimers and constant self-deprecation, one of the thickets of Chesterton criticism. This, and a certain loss of control in some of the later work, has lead to a neglect of this feature of his writing. Even some of his admirers, as we have seen, feel that he is better presented as an aphorist or in selections. *The Flying Inn*, by this view, would be regarded mainly as an excellent quarry, a rambling fantasy, interspersed with comic songs, jokes and arguments. It is an angry book, we are told. Perhaps, then, it is simply a vehicle for working off Chesterton's irritation at some of his pet hates; teetotalism, vegetarianism, modern art, bureaucracy, and the political corruption which came, for a while, almost to obsess him after the Marconi affair (1912).

Such an account denies *The Flying Inn*, the close attention it deserves. It may be seen as a coherent work whose strategies and devices provide Chesterton with an opportunity to tackle a single issue on many levels, social, political, philosophical and religious. The book is a surprise to those who see paradox as Chesterton's sole important device. The first impression is one of sheer variety and then one senses, I feel, the power of an organising principle. *The Flying Inn* possesses a design not unworthy of the author of *The Man who was Thursday*.

There is a mixture of styles in the novel which might seem to indicate an unevenness of tone. On the one side it touches the 'real world,' caricatured but basically recognisable; the 'scholarship' of the *Hibbert Journal*, Lord Ivywood's parliamentary manner, Hibbs' editorials, the House of Commons section, all these belong to a fairly simple but effective category of parody. The exaggeration has a sombre edge to it. Chesterton has detected a touch of evil in various cultural and social phenomena and wishes to show their madness. This intention and this style have no apparent connection with the Turkish fantasy, with Misyra Ammon and his obsessive insistence that everything of worth in English culture is Islamic. Christopher Hollis seems to have a point, at first sight, in remarking that 'the notion of a Turkish army invading Britain was so bizarre as to be hardly worth suggesting even as a joke.'[1] Between these extremes of satire and of fantasy, there is a multiplicity of material, landscapes, conversational exchanges, symbolism, elements of sentiment and humour, which seems to justify Hollis's comment that it is not a tightly constructed book.[2] Is it, in fact, simply a very entertaining bag of tricks?

The Flying Inn seems to rest on two central propositions: the loss of natural good, consequent on the loss of individuality and the distinctiveness of things; secondly, the need for the acceptance and the right use of inevitable suffering. These propositions go far deeper than the fable of the book and are the cement which holds it together. It is a philosophical novel whose many devices seem part of a desire to explore rather than to expound.

It is interesting that Misyra Ammon should first present his philosophy on the beach to a seaside audience. He is at first merely one of a number of assorted eccentrics, 'a new exhibit in the now familiar museum of cranks and quacks',[3] along with an evangelist, a militant atheist, and a man with a ring of carrots around his hat. Chesterton is at pains to suggest initially the intellectual feebleness of a 'philosophy' which is later to become so formidable. It does not draw its power from intellectual causes. Misyra always argues with the same laborious silliness throughout the book; a flow of consistent fatuity, mildly amusing at first, gradually becoming more and more oppressively boring. The contrast between the pungency of the interplay and argument between Pump, Dalroy and Dorian and Misyra's steady drivel is marked enough to suggest a deliberate strategy on Chesterton's part.

A clue to his intention is, perhaps, the mood of Lady Joan as she listens, somewhat receptively, to Misyra's speech in this first scene. She is 'one of those people in whom a real sense of humour is always at issue with a certain tendency to boredom or melancholia.'[4] This hint of a choice between humour and melancholy is a central thread in the book. When Chesterton, after portraying Lord Ivywood's fanaticism at great length, finally provides the explanation for it, it is clear that Ivywood has made a fundamentally wrong choice in this very matter; the right method of coping with sadness. When he was twenty he fell in love with a fisher-girl in a German coast town where he was studying. It came to nothing since he could not have entered diplomacy with such a wife. The answer he found for his grief on the banks of the Rhine was a proud fatalism:

> Things came over me but for which I might have been crying stinking fish to this day. I thought of how many holy or lovely nooks that river had left behind and gone on.[5]

Ivywood's explanation turns on his manner of dealing with sorrow; one in which Chesterton, most significantly, makes him evoke both modern philosophy and ancient eastern wisdom:

> Doesn't Nietzsche say somewhere that the delight in destiny is the mark of the hero? We are mistaken if we think that the heroes and saints of Islam say 'Kismet' with bowed heads and in sorrow. They say 'Kismet' with a shout of joy.[6]

Ivywood is made both a devotee of Islam and a Nietzschean 'superman'.

It appears that this is an important clue to Chesterton's intention in the elaborate Turkish fantasy of *The Flying Inn*. The nominal target of the book is the Islamic prohibition of alcohol, but its real enemy is the Nietzschean *amor fati*, a vision both powerful and seductive. Zarathustra's answer to human unhappiness is two-fold; to transcend human limitation and to accept what is fated with joy:

> I walk among men as among the fragments of the future – the future which I envisage.... To redeem those who lived in the past and to recreate all 'it was' into a 'thus I willed it'.[7]

Ivywood accepts the past as part of the pattern of his destiny:

> There is a kind of freedom that consists in never rebelling against Nature and I think they understand it better in the Orient than we do in the West.[8]

Like Zarathustra he sees men in the present as raw material for a future which he envisages. Arguing about the nature of art with Dorian Wimpole, he denies that there is any limit to humanity. Like Nietzsche's Superman he sees the answer to the pain of life in transcending the man of the present in the name of the future:

> I would walk where no man has walked and find something
> beyond tears and laughter.... I will think what was unthinkable
> until I thought it; I will love what never lived until I loved it – I
> will be lonely as the first man.[9]

Chesterton has caught the very essence of Nietzsche's Zarathustra;
the impatience with the present, with the particularities of man as he
is; the longing for the unknown future as the only balm for the pain of
the present. The habitual and genial looseness of reference, ('Nietzsche says somewhere'), should not disguise this grasp not only of the
spirit, but of the poignant eloquence of Zarathustra.

> Alas, where shall I climb now with my longing: From all moun-
> tains I look out for fatherlands and motherlands. But home I
> found nowhere.... Thus I now love only my *childrens' land*, yet
> undiscovered, in the farthest sea.[10]

In Misyra Ammon's early harangue on the beach the only note of
real force is this very one of homeless wandering, of impatience with
particular places in one's urgent quest:

> What does it matter where we come from, if we carry a message
> from Paradise? With a great galloping of horses we carry it, and
> have no time to stop in places.[11]

The attempt on Chesterton's part to connect Nietzsche's morality
with that of Islam is an important part of his critique of *amor fati*.
Although it may, and has, laid him open to a charge of having a view
of civilisation too centred on Europe, it serves a useful purpose. The
morality of the Superman, in spite of a superficial novelty, is a
familiar and tried one. Substantially, it has formed the basis of many
Eastern civilisations, of which Islam is only the latest. Chesterton is
ready enough to grant its power and impressiveness. As in the later
essay 'On the Simplicity of Asia' or in the poem 'To a Turk', he
allows its followers courage and a certain moral honesty. The figure
of Oman Pasha in *The Flying Inn* is a hint of this. More significantly,
the sheer dedication of Ivywood is constantly stressed. When he is
attempting to have his Act of Parliament amended Joan admired
him as she had never admired him before.... For she felt God's wind

from nowhere which is called the Will; and is man's only excuse on this earth.'[12]

It is a formidable philosophy because, as Ivywood has found, it goes far to answer the inevitable pain of life. As a temptation it possesses a certain dignity.

In spite of Chesterton's reputation for a rollicking optimism, there can be no doubt of his appreciation of sorrow and mysterious darkness in things. A view of life which offered to probe these depths was, for him, a serious view. *The Flying Inn*, then, engages a dangerous intellectual enemy, with every device of Chesterton's subtle mind.

He presses the attack on the question, especially, of individuality. The reason for making Misyra expound his views on the beach with other cranks is to emphasise the silliness of those views. They draw their power over men not from their intellectual appeal, but because they are a complete answer to life. Ivywood admits that some of the Prophet's arguments are crude and fanciful but he feels that it is a view of things which squares with his needs. The factor that renders Misyra's views so wearisome is that very completeness he admires. They reduce all facts to aspects of the same ideology. Misyra is in possession of thousands of pieces of information which he ingeniously threads together but he drains every one of them of its integral quality:

> In every case what he knew was a fragmentary fact. In every case what he did not know was the truth behind the truth behind the fact. What he did not know was the atmosphere. What he did not know was the tradition.[13]

Such a philosophy has an appeal because, in blending all things into one, it relieves one of the burden of personality. To Dalroy the Moorish interior decoration of Ivywood House is 'gorgeous and flamboyant, yet featureless and stiff' and 'like rows and rows of brightly coloured corridors empty and going on for ever.'[14] Ivywood himself finds a deep meaning and value in this endlessly repeated pattern. Speaking with a fervour Joan has never heard from him before, as in a dream, he explains its power over him, the melting sense of the loss of individual identity:

It has the power over me of making me feel that I were myself absent and distant. When I see that greenish-yellow enamel there let into the white, I feel that I were standing thousands of leagues from where I stand.[15]

His political programme, involving a blending of East and West, of Cross and Crescent into 'Croscent' is a kind of constantly developing syncretism, absorbing everything in the name of an unknown future. As in politics, so in art he deliberately seeks the destruction of personal identity, to reach like the Nietzschean Superman, a transcendence of his present self. In personal terms the effect is both disastrous and ludicrous. In a scene of horrifying comedy, Joan finds the women in Ivywood House losing their identities under his influence, repeating, as if hypnotised, the phrases he has used to woo *her*:

'Girls! Women! Do you know what this place is? Do you know why it is all doors within doors and lattice behind lattice? . . . From the distant and slowly darkening music room Enid Wimpole's song came thin and clear:
Less than the dust beneath thy chariot wheel
Less than the rust that never stained thy sword
'Do you know what we are?' demanded Joan Brett again. 'We are a harem.'[16]

Her reaction to this creeping loss of personality is violently to assert her own individuality:

I will not wait and expand. I will not be evolved. I will not develop into something that is not me.[17]

The objects of satire in the book are, on second examination, not simply personal dislikes. Their common denominator is this very denial of the distinction in things, of their solid quiddity. Hibbs' editorials, for example, are the quintessence of the diplomatic manner, each remark so carefully qualified that the whole means nothing:

People who knew him had no difficulty in believing that what he said was the right thing, the tactful thing, the thing that should save the situation; but they had great difficulty in discovering what it was.[18]

He dismisses, as has been noted, the important part of a question to pass on to an entirely irrelevant point, 'following some timid and elusive train of associations of his own.'[19] The 'Higher Criticism' of the Bible, as practised by the *Hibbert Journal*, another target, involves the denial of something concrete, an intransigent fact, in the name of something nebulous, modern psychology or our alleged higher moral level, as in the comment on the Marriage Feast at Cana:

> Authorities as final as Pink and Toscher have now shown with an emphasis that no emancipated mind is entitled to question, that the Aqua-Vinic thaumaturgy at Cana is wholly inconsistent with the psychology of the 'master of the feast' as modern research has analysed it.[20]

Deliberate mystification and *non sequitur* are used to dissolve the existence of events. The question whether they did or did not happen becomes completely obscured.

Ivywood's parliamentary manner involves casting everything, however morally dubious, into the same verbally beautiful form. He is able to take any statement, however objectionable, tendentious or self-contradicting and present it as a sustained piece of moralising in the Gladstone tradition. As the early use of this technique in the Peace Conference on Olive Island shows, it is a method of blurring meaning and distinction. Allowing the Turks to keep the Christian women they have kidnapped becomes avoiding a 'new disturbance of whatever amicable or domestic ties have been formed during this disturbed time.'[21] *The Flying Inn*, then, is more than an amusing attack on the Prohibition Movement. It is a study of an intellectual nightmare. The modern philosophy of Nietzsche with its Superman, eternal recurrence and *amor fati*, is, for Chesterton simply the ancient fatalism of the East, the cure for suffering which blends all in one, and destroys personality. Having diagnosed the sickness on many levels, he sets about to propound the cure.

The first element of the remedy, a familiar one in Chesterton's thought, is embodied in the Tory landlord of *The Flying Inn*, Humphrey Pump. It involves a sense of the value of minute particulars, objects, memories, places and traditions. Almost everything in Pump's house is individual, made by himself and 'slightly different from the same thing in anyone else's house.'[22] He knows nature in particular, bird, fish, leaf and berry, and for him the landscape is enriched by a sediment of personal and inherited associations:

His mind was a rich soil of subconscious memories and traditions and he had a curious kind of gossip so allusive as to almost amount to reticence.[23]

A.L. Maycock has pointed out how central in Chesterton is the belief that 'you do not get nearer to the ultimate mysteries by reaching out for the abstract and the infinite',[24] since it is the tangible thing that is closest to the spiritual. In *Pump* he suggests the value of the material world not only as a means of spiritual insight, but simply as a method of maintaining human health and balance.

In the Irish Radical Dalroy, Chesterton suggests the complementary half of the cure. Flamboyant and moody where Pump is dogged, he is shown throughout most of the book as a man coping with a frankly expressed unhappiness stemming from thwarted love and military defeat. He neither represses nor denies this feeling but seeks such fun as may come his way. One simply has to be tough about unhappiness. Ivywood's friends, he feels, with their talk of Universal Joy, expect what nature has never promised:

I don't know whether God means a man to have happiness in that All in All and Utterly Utter sense of happiness. But God does mean man to have a little fun.[25]

In effect the remedy involves an acceptance of the distinctive qualities of things, of particular objects and traditions and of one's own personality. In each case they are accepted for what they are now rather than in the hope that they may be transmuted into what they are not.

If *The Flying Inn* could be reduced to an intellectual thesis in the terms indicated it might possess a limited interest. It would, however, lack most of the suggestiveness which it does in fact possess, and which it draws from poetry and symbol. Ian Boyd has wisely stressed the importance of allegory in Chesterton's philosophical novels. Their meaning is never a series of abstract moral statements:

A parallel argument can indeed be constructed which expresses partly the truth which is expressed imaginatively by the allegory, but the allegory is in no way a translation of a discursive argument into symbolic terms.[26]

The art of Chesterton in *The Flying Inn* is more than the coherence already suggested. When the book has been defended from the charge of being a mere rambling extravaganza, its inner quality may still be missed.

One clue to this is the interaction between Pump and Dalroy. Allies against Ivywood's attempt to close down the inns of England, they are far from identical. Many of the novels most entertaining pages record the arguments between them. Dalroy is much the more articulate. Both, however, are made to have a contribution to offer to the other. Dalroy's is largely on the level of political argument. He challenges such clichés as that hoary one about the English having a genius for compromise. In fact, they are a sentimental people who 'go by associations. . . . You won't have one thing without the other that goes with it. And you can't imagine a village without a squire and parson.'[27]

Any revolution is in fact a compromise. One has to decide what to keep and what to reject: a practicality alien to the artistic English temperament.

On this level of verbal argument Dalroy dominates the partnership and his role is clearly to act as a leaven. Pump's contribution Chesterton expresses not on an intellectual plane but in an image, 'The Hole in Heaven'. After their initial escape with the inn-sign, he leads Dalroy to a forgotten childhood hiding-place, a hollow in the sand covered by the furze:

> Dalroy was staring about him at the cavern of his old picnics, so forgotten and so startlingly familiar. He seemed to have lost all thought of singing anything and to be simply groping in the dark house of his own boyhood.[28]

'The Hole in Heaven' seems to symbolise the awareness of the roots of one's own personality in childhood, the persistence throughout life of one's fears and fantasies; a salutary knowledge:

He suddenly understood he had grown bigger; bigger in a bodily sense. He had doubts about any other.[29]

Humphrey Pump's conservatism, although faulty on the social and political level, has its own positive side in a certain moral rootedness, a sense of the coherence of one's own personality throughout life. It goes beyond the words of political programmes, however admirable. The relationship between Pump and Dalroy has something of the quality of the debating club, of that atmosphere of amicable but incisive interchange between strong characters which is so common a feature of Chesterton's work and which goes far to remove the slur of writing as a propagandist levelled at him by George Orwell.[30]

The journey across country in a two-man crusade, perhaps a vague reminiscence of *Don Quixote*, and the use of the inn-sign as a comic catalyst, are probably too obvious as symbols to require much comment. More interesting, because more ambiguous and mysterious are the turret-room of Ivywood House and the nearby tunnel. Ivywood has been having the interior of the family home redecorated in an oriental style. He has the end of a long suite of rooms boarded up:

I want it to be like that. I want this to be the end of the house. I want this to be the end of the world.[31]

The 'new architecture' ends in an exquisite panelled turret-room, in which five windows of Saracenic design look out on a landscape of 'bronze and copper and purple',[32] empty of every living thing.

On one level the room clearly symbolises the abstraction from the unsatisfactory material world of the present which it is Ivywood's dream to create. The suite of rooms formerly ended in a staircase which lead to a ruined medieval chapel, so that there is a connection, too, of a wish to sever connection with the past. The steps also lead to the unsuccessful tunnel, dug by an eccentric ancestor to launch an amphibious railway into the sea. The need to board that off is a need to erase whatever derogates from one's dignity. Supermen cannot afford humour and so Ivywood remarks: 'The scandal and joking about the unsuccessful tunnel... did us no good in the country.'[33] However, Chesterton suggests, this is a highly artificial paradise. It is penetrated by a questing and irreverent dog, Quoodle. The staircase, in the unfinished panelling leads the tipsy Hibbs down into a deserted garden where he is touched first by a *natural* pleasure in 'one fungus that was white with brown spots',[34] and then, in spite of his diplomacy, made to stumble face downward in the grass. The past and the sense of human limitation cannot be excluded.

Nor is there any reason why they should be. Chesterton implies, through Dalroy, that there is a natural good in things which has the power to absorb human follies:

> 'It is man's futility that makes us feel he must be a god. And I think of this tunnel; and how the poor old lunatic walked about on this grass, watching it being built, the soul in him on fire with the future. And he saw the whole world changed and the seas thronged with his new shipping; and now' and Dalroy's voice changed and broke – 'now there is good pasture for the donkey and it is very quiet here.'[35]

What the tunnel embodies is what is ultimately hostile to the Nietzschean vision. It is symbolically appropriate that from it emerge the forces which crush the Turkish army at the end of *The Flying Inn*; an apt linking together of the many levels of the book.

V

THE RESTORATION OF THE PAST

Among readers not very well acquainted with his work, no subject is more likely to be misunderstood than Chesterton's 'Medievalism'. They might grant that he was resolute in opposing 'historicisms' and notions of Historical Inevitability prevalent throughout his career and in defending the freedom of societies and individuals to will the terms on which they lived. But the hostile critic might then ask if he was not concerned merely to substitute one set of myths for another, to replace fantasies of the inevitable rise or fall of nations, races or cultures, of evolutionary transcendence, of the ascent to the Super-man or the Absolute by day-dreams of some impossible restoration of long-past conditions as distorted by his own romantic fancy.

In fact Chesterton's sense of the past is a complex and evolving appreciation of its many lights and shades, acknowledging half-tones, embracing the moral and psychological difficulties of writing history in general, understanding and assessing his own emotional predilections, in particular. It is an intellectual exploration, sus-tained by an increasing self-knowledge, thoughtful and, in a sense, morally impressive. His generalised ponderings on historical methods, on the shape and nature of former periods, on historical myths, on the problems, dangers, and rewards of attempts to recapture the qualities of another age, all are informed by self-scrutiny, by an unusual readiness to test his own motives, evaluate his cherished fancies. He does not tread softly on his own dreams and does not ask his reader to do so. Clearly the common notion of a sentimental celebration of the Middle Ages, a propagandistic romance of some never-never Age of Faith, is a simple travesty of Chesterton's subtle views. It is proposed to examine some aspects of his historical sense in the light of a figure which, it seems, haunted him, and became the vehicle of his changing views, a figure, above all, of central importance in that war of values which forms the substance of much of his writing, that of Don Quixote.

One of Chesterton's very earliest essays, *The Divine Parody of Don Quixote* (1901), sketches some of the ambivalence which he saw in the story, an image, he felt, of the condition of man and the nature of life:

> The battle between the idealism of Don Quixote and the realism of the innkeeper is a battle so hot and ceaseless that we know they must both be right.[1]

The 'doubt and turmoil and bewildering responsibility of life' arise from the vast amount of good in the world; from the fact that different truths and different goods or aspects of the good are in conflict. There are 'too many truths that contradict each other, too many loves that hate each other.'[2] *Don Quixote* is the perfect image of a 'maddening and perplexing world in which we are all right'; not an unweeded garden but a garden choked with its own abundance of neglected flowers.

Chesterton, significantly, insists on an unresolved tension between Don Quixote and Sancho Panza; a reading which contrasts markedly with that of common opinion later expressed in a standard critical work such as Salvador De Madariaga's study.[3] Unlike De Madariaga, Chesterton denies that the Knight Errant is ever defeated and in order to support this thesis, is forced into the somewhat dubious position of preferring Part I of *Don Quixote* to Part II. The point at issue, however, is not Chesterton's stimulating but probably partial and dubious reading of Cervantes' novel but his philosophic understanding of a myth which he felt represented a fundamental truth about man and life. Dichotomy, tension, stress and unresolved contradiction which he attributed to *Don Quixote*, he strikingly and, at this stage, happily, accepted in life ('a sobering thought but assuredly not a depressing one').[4] Although he never found the thought simply depressing, he gradually developed an awareness of the ironies and sadnesses inherent in the myth.

The importance of *Don Quixote* and the Don Quixote myth in Chesterton's writing, from this very early stage, is two-fold; as an image of life, certainly, but, more particularly, as an historical testimony. *Don Quixote* is important to us because the Middle Ages are important to us. Its pathos and irony depend on this fact.

> For the core of the truth is that we have the follies of Don Quixote in our very blood; we are by, irrevocable generation, children of the Middle Ages. Adventure and ceremony, chivalry and idolatry, fantastic pride and fantastic humility lie at the very root of our institutions and in the inmost chamber of our imagination.[5]

Clearly the connection between Chesterton's version of the Don Quixote theme and his sense of history, notably his view of the Middle Ages, the period which by common consent he most emphasised, is significant. It is an important, perhaps somewhat neglected, ingredient in his scheme of values.

A reasonable case may be made for Chesterton's historical work as, simply, an overdue corrective to the prevalent 'Whig view of history' or the notion of the rise of Anglo-Saxon race widespread in his youth. This is the line which, for example, W.H. Auden plausibly takes in the introduction to his *Selection* from Chesterton's writing; Chesterton's was a prejudice which answered a prejudice; a biased view which combated earlier biased views. However, such a defence, or rather excuse, severely limits the value and interest of the work it purports to defend. Also, it closes the subject. As Auden observes:

> The literary problem about any controversial writing is that, once it has won its battle, its interest to the average reader is apt to decline. Controversy always involves polemical exaggerations and it is this of which, once we have forgotten the exaggerations on the other side, we shall be most critical.[6]

This would be true only if Chesterton's writing were simply and solely a polemical exercise. In a sense, however, Auden has, by an extremely damaging and unnecessary admission, given over the game half-played. There is much in Chesterton's historical values which the term 'polemical' simply will not cover. Its moral discriminations are altogether more subtle and complex than it suggests.

Chesterton's view of historical writing was not, of course, one which favoured a scientific impartiality. For this, in 1909, as at other times, he expressed little sympathy.

> It appears to avoid the dangers of describing great men by the bright and simple solution of not describing men at all. By this method the historian looks down on all movements of men as if they were ants.[7]

Chesterton regarded history as pointless unless it removed a man from his local circumstances and enlarged experience by imagination. In this sense it was romantic. In aim, at least, he felt that the historian's task was not to provide evidence for a thesis but to challenge provinciality, especially that of a mushroom technological civilisation:

> The whole object of history is to make us realize that humanity could be great and glorious, under conditions quite different and even contrary to our own.[8]

An inability to see man 'divine and democratic' under the disguises of the ages, the 'trappings and externals erected for an age and a fashion',[9] is a kind of learned ignorance or pedantry; and something worse, a narrow, groundless prejudice of the same kind as any other prejudice.

> If the Dark Ages must be as dark as they look, why are the black men not so black as they are painted.[10]

History is a recovery of a blurred sense of human nature, of the scale of man's achievement and degradation, of the qualities which the modern man shares with those of the remotest periods. It is unnecessary to have the specially learned to teach us these since they are the intimate facts of a common psychology we can ignore for a while but never really set aside. The inner subjective sense or meaning of a past experience is what is really significant and really difficult to reconstruct, as opposed to producing or repeating terminological expressions of vague import such as the notorious term 'totem' which once bedevilled the study of anthropology and comparative mythology. Such expressions are of no help to the historian unless they have precise emotional significance, to be grasped, if at all, through imaginative sympathy and a shared humanity. It is, he remarks in *The Everlasting Man*, among other things his longest and most sustained piece of historical writing, a study which has hardly got off the ground,[11] 'psychological history', 'history from the inside', 'the consideration of what things meant in the mind of a man, especially an ordinary man, as distinct from what is defined or deduced from official forms or political pronouncements.[11] The feeling of the Roman legion for the eagle or the primitive man for the 'totem', are historical riddles, hinted at by art, which sometimes transcends the current limits of historical study.

Chesterton's stress on the 'elemental outlook' as the real object of the historians quest explains and justifies the value he gives to fable, story and myth. It is the royal road to historical understanding, the most important element in Chesterton's method. As much as Huizinga he sees man as *homo ludens* and *The Everlasting Man*, is, in one aspect, almost an analysis of the role taken by the spirit of play in the growth of cultures. Play enters myth through the pleasure of story-telling and fuels technology through the pleasure of dexterity within a game with rules.

Granted the general importance of myth and fable in his view of human history, there is a particular significance in the recurring Quixote pattern in Chesterton's work. It was, for him, a rich myth, capable of different emphases, which might serve to bring together, and into focus, many intricate elements of his evolving vision. The pattern is found in its most straightforward and explicit form in *The Napoleon of Notting Hill*, almost contemporary with the early essay on Cervantes.

The Napoleon of Notting Hill (1904) grew, as its dedicatory poem reminds us, out of Chesterton's own childhood fantasies of the defence of a Kensington street near his home from invaders by the seizure of a gigantic water-tower, an incident actually used in the novel. Many commentators have noticed the recently ended Boer War as part of the book's context. This awakened Chesterton to his sympathy with small nations and with small units in general, the family, the local community, as against larger powers, whether political or financial, of the modern world. It is in such local associations that men most discover a patriotism or loyalty that has meaning. A few streets are more than a Socialist world state or an empire on which the sun never sets. The novel grows also from an opposition, touched on in its delightful first chapter, to prophecies that the future will develop inevitably from a continuation of present trends and to the view, shared by Fabians and Imperialists, that, just as inevitably, power will pass to larger and larger units. (This latter view is found in Wells's much-discussed *Anticipations* of the previous year). *The Napoleon of Notting Hill* expresses, also, that feeling for the value of limits in art and thought which, Chesterton explained later in his *Autobiography*, was one of his earliest intimations and which remained a central thread in his thought.

The novel is set in 1984, in a world which has embraced the doctrine of evolution under the rule of a hierarchy of civil servants, a little like the Socialism of Ramsay MacDonald or Sidney Webb. England is part of a vast empire or world-state which has swallowed smaller nations like the Nicaragua whose deposed President we meet early in the book. (It is interesting to recall, as throwing light on Chesterton's linking of Fabianism and Imperialism, that Shaw, a Fabian Socialist, supported the crushing of the Boers on the ground that their republics were too small to be economically viable). The novel's action really begins when Auberon Quin is chosen by lot as King, according to the accepted procedure. The elevation of the one member of the civil service noted for his bizarre humour and eccentric attitudes disrupts the settled, tedious order of things. Quin decides to restore local autonomy accompanied by medieval pageantry to the different districts of London. His scheme is taken up with enthusiasm by Adam Wayne, the Provost of Notting Hill, whose resistance to the destruction of Pump Street as part of a large urban development, becomes a kind of Thermopylae in which Notting Hill fights off the armies of the entire city. Notting Hill itself now becomes an imperial power, until the other districts, catching the patriotic spirit, rebel against its hegemony which they combine to overthrow.

The book is a study of all those human needs which a comfortable, well-run conglomerate, Fabian or Imperialist would not satisfy. The grey ennui and predictability of such a world leaves out that hunger for the fantastic and whimsical incarnated in the prankster Quin. Its routines of administration in which 'efficiency' and 'public order' mask the reality of control by business interests (a theory developed later in Belloc's *The Servile State*) thwarts man's hunger for his own home, street or district which Adam Wayne embodies. Apart from its many other aspects, some of which will be examined later, it embodies Chesterton's early view of the Quixote myth with great clarity.

The relationship of Adam Wayne and Auberon Quin, in the novel, may be viewed as a study of the origin of adventure; a picture of the necessary tension, perhaps even a 'dialectic', between the fanatic and the humorist, the two halves of a man's brain. Quin's role in disrupting the settled order of things in a bureaucratic world of rational self-interest, represents a liberation of the instinct of play, a healthy appetite to be wilful, a freedom from imaginary general rules and a dreary consensus of 'all thinking people'. To this natural assertion of the right to choose, Wayne adds the sense of honour, that abiding by the consequences of one's choice which as Chesterton remarks in 'A Defence of Rash Vows, in *The Defendant*, validates and enhances both human dignity and the enjoyment of the game itself. From the reaction between play and honour, the game and the rules of the game, grows first a sense of enhanced life, that feeling of adventure for which *The Iliad* was only a poor substitute; then the creation of what is virtually a new civilisation, the 'Empire of Notting Hill'.

The sense of this basic dichotomy, or tension between opposing and equally essential forces in the mind of man, helps to explain Chesterton's interest in the 'Quixote myth'. It is worth noting, however, that the notion of the fruitful conflict between the two halves of a man's brain was present in his work before that conflict assumed an identifiably Cervantic tinge. The feeling of a war in the mind of man preceded Chesterton's interest in *Don Quixote* and was modified by it.

In its very simplest form, perhaps, it is found in a *Daily News* article of the year before *The Napoleon of Notting Hill*. Here the two colliding impulses are delight and fear; the desire to 'dance and kick about in the sunlight'[12] and the need to institute rules and so create morality; essentially, to will and to restraint of will. This is not, of course, really the Cervantic polarity, nor are Quin and Wayne necessarily best seen as Sancho Panza and Don Quixote. For one thing, they are simple, primal, perhaps eternal forces, humorist and fanatic. There is none of that nuance, that influence of one upon the other, the subtle interplay and shifting of identity, which as De Madariaga has noted,[13] is so vital an element in the relationship of Cervantes' great pair. There is nothing ambiguous about Wayne and Quin. They are four-square and final. Although the great game, high romance or epic of the Empire of Notting Hill, organically connected, as he admitted to Chesterton's boyhood fantasies,[14] crashes to final ruin, this is not because of any inner contradiction in the two who launch it on its career. The reason for its collapse seems to be the tendency of the spirit of play to become institutionalised, for the game to wear out, to ossify, to lose its initial joyful impulse. (This wearing out of play was a phenomenon noted by Chesterton much later in *The Everlasting Man*, when analysing the corruption of paganism).[15] But in *The Napoleon of Notting Hill* the conclusion to be drawn is not a sad one. In this work which he had to write, if he was to write anything else, he celebrates rather than scrutinises his childhood dreams and reveries. Play and honour remain in their primal energy, once they have, as the opening of the novel shows, been re-awakened in the world. They are free to start on a fresh cycle of adventures, conquering and creating new worlds.

As a study of the act of recapturing the past, *The Napoleon of Notting Hill*, exciting and enjoyable on so many levels, has a similar simplicity. It embodies, as a fable, a feeling of historical openness. Deeply anti-determinist, *The Napoleon of Notting Hill* sustains a thorough attack on the idea that any line of development is inevitable in human history. From the preliminary chapter on mankind's delight in playing 'cheat the prophet', Chesterton gently but very effectively mocks the notion that the future may be predicted on the basis of current trends, that a particular set of circumstances represents an irreversible development, and, most important, that the past, as an alternative, can never be recalled. Such a feeling is only the product of a subjective boredom. In the bureaucratic despotism with which the novel opens 'that vague and somewhat depressed reliance upon things happening as they have always happened which is with all Londoners a mood, had become an assumed condition.'[16] *The Napoleon of Notting Hill* is, among much else, an exhilarated celebration of the rediscovery of choice. The adventure ends in high tragedy, but not in futility. The sense of choice in human life and history is not defeated. There is, in effect, none of the Cervantic pathos which comes of knowing that 'there are no birds in the nests of yesteryear.'

Adam Wayne's childhood fantasies and daydreams of heroism and chivalry provide the substance of the Notting Hill saga. Once they are tapped they gush forth and change the substance of life around them. And it requires little to tap them. Auberon Quin's perversity is enough to break the spell of boredom and resignation to things as they are and will be, to recall a 'medieval' chivalric world and, more significantly, a forgotten and by 'reasonable people', undervalued and denigrated childhood imaginative life. And it is clear that to Chesterton the theme had a deep personal importance. His imaginative life, his daydreams were the same as Wayne's, a reason perhaps for the exuberance of the novel. The images of childhood were being proved valid and asserted against the march of commonsense, reason and progress, so-called. *The Napoleon of Notting Hill* is not a self-indulgent but it is a self-fulfilling book. There is in it a whole-hearted enjoyment, by the writer, of the pattern, the type of architecture, of his own mind; of that element Chesterton felt was the original quality in any man of imagination, 'the sort of world which he would wish to make or in which he would wish to wonder.'[17] His enjoyment of the flora and fauna of his own mind was never again to be so simple, or so full-blooded. That imagery which was the landscape of his own fantasy, and which approximated to or had affinity with his vision of the medieval world, would never be as easy to recapture and body forth. It is with an increasing sense of the complexity, the inextricable mixture of victory and defeat, the self-contradictions, and curious inherent sadness, hard to define but nevertheless deep, that the influence of Cervantes begins to make itself felt, in a new way, on his vision. Its most notable effect, I would suggest, was on his view of the dichotomy between the humorist and the fanatic. In *The Napoleon of Notting Hill*, these two are stable, almost archetypal, and clearly defined. When the Quixote motif appears, after 1911, the relationship is more subtle. The humorist and fanatic are overlapping, interacting, and at times changing places. Wayne's defeat ends with a ringing affirmation, and summing-up of his career:

> 'As the tree falleth so shall it lie', he said. Men have called that a gloomy text. It is the essence of all exultation. I am doing now what I have done all my life, what is the only happiness. What is the only universality. I am clinging to something.[18]

Drawing strength from the fantasies of childhood, and acquiring dignity through the finality of moral choice and one's loyalty to it, the vision remains, even though defeated. After 1911, there is a delicate melancholy, a sense of the ambivalence and complexity of human nature. The vision is not so easily recaptured and affirmed, because of an essential sadness in things, a limitation of man's personality, mutual incomprehension, lack of self-knowledge. Yet the vision remains, always there and able to be revived in the most unlikely circumstances. The sense of childhood fantasy still stirs uneasily beneath the bonds of adult weariness and fatalism. The spirit of Don Quixote, of a lost medieval world, can, in spite of the odds, burst forth disrupting historical trends and the compromise of modernity. After 1911 there is a subtle interplay between that sense of pathos and that abiding vision.

There is a certain significance in choosing 1911, rather than the perhaps expected date 1912 as the watershed, the point when the dichotomy and the vision became in some fuller sense, 'Cervantic'. It was the latter year which, after all, saw the production of Chesterton's extraordinary heroic poem 'The Ballad of Lepanto'. Maisie Ward's account suggests that the poem was inspired by a mood of excitement, that it was born out of controversy:

> In the spring of 1912 he had taken part in a debate at Leeds affirming that all wars were religious wars. Father O'Connor supported him with a magnificent description of the battle of Lepanto. Obviously it seized Gilbert's mind powerfully, for

while he was still staying with Father O'Connor he had begun to jot down lines and by October of that year the poem was published.[19]

However, there does seem to be evidence that the inception of 'Lepanto', probably, after the Father Brown stories, Chesterton's best known single piece of writing, was by no means so sudden as Maisie Ward here implies. It is of some importance, both to the account of Chesterton's intellectual development, and arguably, to a correct understanding of a particular nuance in 'Lepanto', to be aware of the parallels between it and a *Daily News* article on Cervantes, 'The True Romance', published the previous year. This short piece raises the odd point that Cervantes, whose own life was a course of wildly romantic incidents, should 'have ridiculed romance and pointed out the grave improbability of people having any adventures.'[20] The major portion of the essay, however, is a description of the battle of Lepanto, in which Cervantes took an active part. 'The True Romance' closely follows the sequence of events recorded in the poem a year later. There are clear indications that Chesterton's approach to the subject, particular expressions he used in 'Lepanto' and, most significantly, the actual subject of the poem, and a dichotomy within it, of Don John of Austria and Cervantes, of crusader and humorist, were all present in his mind a year before the debate in Leeds. Like 'Lepanto', 'The True Romance' records a Europe 'as it is now, in one of its recurring periods of division and disease.... The whole civilisation was bitter and trivial and was apparently tumbling to pieces.'[21] Like 'Lepanto', it mentions the 'sombre fanaticism' and 'sinister enthusiasms' of the Northern nations. In the poem this becomes:

> The North is full of tangled things and texts and
>   aching eyes,
> And dead is all the innocence of anger and surprise
> And Christian killeth Christian in a narrow dusty room.[22]

Against the futilities and torments of emergent Protestantism the essay juxtaposes the 'equally sombre statecraft and secrecy of the Southern Nations'. Philip II is described in 'The True Romance' as 'morbid, mean and lethargic; a man of stagnant mysteries, as he looks in those fishy, pasty-faced portraits which still endure.'[23]

In 'Lepanto' this atmosphere is evoked in the unforgettable picture of the King's closet:

> The walls are hung with velvet that is black and
>   soft as sin
> And little dwarfs creep out of it and little dwarfs
>   creep in,[24]

and a reference to Philip's face like 'a fungus of leprous white and grey'[25] which forcibly recalls the earlier description. The hopelessness and decay of European civilisation and ideals which both the essay and the poem describe make the triumph of the Turkish onslaught seem a forgone conclusion. In 'The True Romance' the Turkish ships are 'like genii summoned out of that Eastern sea by the seal of Solomon, robed in the purple of twilight or the green of the deep'.[26] In 'Lepanto', the 'seal of Solomon' makes another appearance to summon literal genii who 'rise in green robes roaring from the green hells of the sea',[27] to give 'worship to Mahound'.

The essay mentions specially two points taken up in the poem: Don John's earlier exploits on the coast of North Africa, and the rescue, after the battle, of thousands of Christian galley-slaves. The second forms the subject of an extended passage in 'Lepanto.' In 'The True Romance' there is also a hint of another and more important element in 'Lepanto', a likening of the Turkish power to the tyrannies of the ancient world. There is an identity of feeling between 'that enormous outside world of Asia and Africa that has always felt slavery to be a natural and even a monotonous thing,[28] and the fleets and armies of Xerxes which 'seemed stronger than the gods'. In 'Lepanto' the galley-slaves are

> countless, voiceless, hopeless as those fallen
> or fleeing on
> Before the high King's horses in the granite
> of Babylon.[29]

What, perhaps, confirms the view of 'The True Romance' as the germ or seed of the poem published a year later is the way in which they both conclude. In each the battle ends with the figure of Cervantes smiling. In the first version it is a 'sad, crooked smile. For he had a face capable of expressing both pity and amusement.'[30] In the second:

> He sees across a weary land a straggling road in
> Spain
> Up which a lean and foolish knight forever rides in
> vain
> And smiles, but not as Sultans smile, and settles
> back the blade ...[31]

These corroborative details not only suggest the existence of the themes and images of 'Lepanto' in Chesterton's mind well before the Leeds debate; they clarify their meaning. 'Lepanto' is not solely or even mainly a ringing song of victory. In spite of its exhilarated tone and those pounding rhythms which men remembered in the trenches of war years 1914 to 1918, it has a subtle resonance. There are elements of defeat as well as victory. The smile of Cervantes is counterpointed with the crusader glory of Don John. The spirit which saves a beleagured Europe tilts at windmills. The wildly improbable revival of chivalry in a world grown cold and weary is touching and vulnerable as well as triumphant. But Cervantes' smile is set, also, in a deliberate opposition to the smile of the Sultan with which 'Lepanto' opens. The 'Soldan of Byzantium' smiles a smile of calm assurance, because, like Xerxes in 'The True Romance', the sea is covered with his ships. The Cervantic smile, by contrast, comes not from a simple sense of power, but from a complex awareness, a consciousness of half-tones, of human limitations, of defeat in victory, of victory in defeat.

It is possible to make two generalisations about the 'Quixote myth' in Chesterton's work. First, that it was particularly important to him, expressing some specially vital quality about experience, the defence of values and the recovery of the past, during the years 1911 to 1914. This short period saw not merely 'Lepanto', but two other works strongly coloured by the 'Quixote myth'. The first is, of course, *The Flying Inn* (1914). It appears, also, that *The Return of Don Quixote*, although not completed and published until 1927, had been planned and probably largely written before Chesterton's serious illness, coinciding with the outbreak of war. Secondly, the 'Quixote period' was, as biographers agree, both a crisis and a watershed in Chesterton's life. His distress at the Marconi scandal and what he felt it revealed of political corruption, his disillusionment with the Liberals, and various personal distresses, combined to produce considerable emotional and physical strain culminating in the complete breakdown of his health. This context throws considerable light on the 'Quixote theme'. Dichotomy existed in Chesterton's thought before he became interested in Don Quixote. He had even recognised affinities between his own preoccupation with the humorist and the fanatic and 'the Divine Parody' of Cervantes' novel. It is arguable that now, in a time of unhappiness and loss of political confidence, he moved away from the clear cut model of *The Napoleon of Notting Hill* to one which more clearly expressed a sense of limitations, pathos and self-delusion; a version of the vision which conveyed its elusive quality.

The Flying Inn is probably better understood in this light. Christopher Hollis's view already mentioned that 'the notion of a Turkish army invading Britain was so bizarre as to be hardly worth suggesting even as a joke',[32] and his remark that the novel was not a tightly constructed one are, at first sight, plausible and would probably be echoed by most readers. Two answers to this verdict might be made. The first, already offered in Chapter IV[33] of this study, might be that *The Flying Inn* is a highly coherent philosophical novel resting on two propositions: the loss of natural good consequent on the loss of individuality and the distinctiveness of things; secondly, on the need for the acceptance and right use of inevitable suffering. There is an identification between the ancient fatalism of the East, and the teachings of Nietzsche, beginning to be known in England through the Orage circle, and voiced by Lord Ivywood in the novel.

The second answer to Hollis's complaint relates to the first, but differs somewhat in emphasis. It would involve seeing *The Flying Inn* against Chesterton's interest in the 'Quixote myth' and the Cervantic tone in those immediately pre-war years. The Turkish invasion of England is pictured in the novel less in military terms than as a moral and religious assault, an ideological war against, superficially wine-drinking, but fundamentally, against the sense of identity and individuality in people and in things. It implies, as shown earlier, the blending of all things into one, the transcending of a limited, contradictory and fallible human nature, to achieve an unknown but presumably higher type of humanity. Lord Ivywood, the 'Superman' is also a Sultan with a 'harem' of doting female admirers. The novel's strategy merges explicitly Nietzschean material with something ancient and eastern found, as Chesterton suggests, in the Islam of 'Lepanto':

> We have set the seal of Solomon on all things under
> sun,
> Of knowledge and of sorrow and endurance of things
> done.

Nietzschean '*amor fati*' is in Chesterton's view the old enemy 'Kismet' and the battle is as it was at Lepanto.

The appeal of Ivywood's Nietzscheanism, like that of Islam originally, is one of simplicity. There is a heroic straightforwardness about them both, an ending of the problems, contradictions, and most important, the sorrows of being merely human. The conflict is basically that of 'Lepanto', the smile of the Sultan, opposed to the sad, crooked smile of Cervantes. One of Ivywood's opponents in *The Flying Inn* remarks of him:

> I may say that what everyone says is that he has no humour. But that is not my complaint at all. I think my complaint is that he has no pathos. That is he does not feel human limitations.[34]

It is, *The Flying Inn* suggests, more difficult to be merely human than to be a Superman. (Chesterton sees, as a connected truth, that Europe was more complex and mysterious than Asia. In the 'mysterious East' things, including man, are much what they seem). The novel ends by contrasting complex, arduous, real human life, which accepts that happiness is bound to be limited and imperfect, (a chord struck elsewhere), with the 'happiness that lasts', in this world, which can only be that of madness, to which Ivywood, like his prototype Nietzsche has succumbed.

What this suggests is that the 'Cervantic' quality of *The Flying Inn* .lies much more in this necessary sense of human limitations under- lying the philosophical conflict of values, as Chesterton saw it, between Europe and the East, than it does in the wanderings of Pump and Dalroy around England with their inn-sign, or even in what is often a subtle interaction between them; both of which have their analogies with *Don Quixote*. These secondary features, the comic quest and the relationship of the two adventurers, in whom two different, complementary strands of man's mind are dominant, are nevertheless of some importance. The quest is specifically fore- shadowed in Chesterton's earlier description of Cervantes' adventures:

> And in all this still horror of heat and sleep, the one unconquered European, still leaping at every outlet of adventure or escape; climbing a wall as he might a Christian apple-tree, or calling for his rights as he might in a Christian inn.[35]

Pump and Dalroy struggle against a dead repose, which blends all individuality into one, a fatalism accepted as the price of coping with the sadness and limitation of human life. The inn-sign they defend is a symbol of the ordinary companionship, the necessarily limited happiness of the individual, retaining the burden of free-will and his own personality. As Dalroy remarks, to ask for 'Utter Trust' or 'Universal Joy' as the supporters of Ivywood's syncretism do, is to ask for what nature never promised. In any case

> they don't look any more cheerful than anybody else; and the next thing they do is start smashing a thousand good jokes and good stories and good songs and good friendships by pulling down 'The Old Ship'.[36]

In the quest and in the relationship of Dalroy and Pump, however, more than this is implied. As well as the defence of something threatened, there is the recovery of something lost, the 'faint renewal of that laughter that has slept since the Middle Ages.'[37]

The lost vision has two distinct elements. It is social, a pattern glimpsed in the medieval centuries and subsequently lost in the oppressiveness and corruption attacked in *The Flying Inn*, before its very basis, in a right conception of human nature, was itself attacked by an alien ideology. The vision is also personal as we have seen in Chapter IV, seen in childhood, and lost in the compromises and defeats of one's adult years.

If we place all those features of the novel, examined in Chapter IV specifically in relation to Nietzsche, against this much wider context of the Quixote myth, as a means of historical understanding, and a fable of peculiar and developing importance to Chesterton, they gain in depth and in pathos.

The leading symbols of *The Flying Inn* suggest the nature of this vision and hint at the method of recovery. The tunnel, built by Ivywood's eccentric ancestor to launch railway trains into the sea, (a fact that Superman is anxious to forget), is as Dalroy declares, a pattern of all the futile, arrogant dreams men have tried to impose on the world. Unfinished, it testifies to man's finiteness. Significantly, it is the route by which the Turkish army is taken in the rear and Ivywood is defeated; the element in life, in effect, that he has refused to recognise. The bricked-off staircase in his home, leading to the ruined medieval chapel, symbolises the past which England, and even more his own philosophy of unending transformation, has repudiated. More important even than the tunnel or the staircase, however, is the 'hole in heaven', the childhood retreat, where Dalroy had played as a boy and where Pump leads him to take refuge at the opening of their flight,[38] and whose significance has already been discussed.

What the 'hole in heaven' seems to suggest is a lost time, not of happiness, but of intensity and significance. Remembering it is an act of linking one's present with one's past, an act of integration; the very opposite of Ivywood's Nietzschean repudiation of past selves and past societies.

What the Quixote image has hitherto suggested in Chesterton's work throws considerable light on his views of human psychology, history and religion. It is a mark of the richness of the image that it should be capable of such a varied suggestiveness, a diversity of meaning which justifies Chesterton's early belief in its importance in western culture. At the heart of the myth is, perhaps, that element which mythographers such as Mircea Eliade have seen as central in religious experience, the notion of restoration, or re-integration. ·Subtly in 'Lepanto' and *The Flying Inn* it touches on this theme in society, on the return to a lost state, on the defence of Christian values such as free-will, and of individuality against that fatalism which simplifies the complex truths of the human condition. It is a defence of justice and human dignity against that hierarchy of slaves and sultans or 'Supermen' which is more straightforward and also more 'natural' than Christianity. Both fatalism and slavery are simpler and easier to understand than a faith, which, as Chesterton suggests, is full of tensions, compromises, reconciliations of different instincts and needs. But the figure of Quixote has another source of appeal. Its comedy and poignance imply that the crusaders and the crusade have their ludicrous elements. It is not a matter of their not taking themselves seriously, or being taken seriously by Chesterton. Rather it is that they are finite and fallible, and unlike the forces to which they are opposed, they know this from the outset, or come to know it. The Don Quixote myth and the 'Cervantic tone' function in Chesterton's quest for the past as an 'earth' connecting the quest to sanity, humour, humility, and a sense of fallability. They are admirable vehicles for a faith which is not a fanaticism, an over-simplification or a fad.

The Return of Don Quixote represents the culmination of Chesterton's use of the myth. This novel was serialised in *G.K.'s Weekly* from December 1925 to November 1926, thus spanning the period of the General Strike. Chesterton, although very much preferring the distribution of property to Socialism as a solution to the economic collapse he felt was coming, felt much sympathy with the plight of the working classes, and, to some extent, with trades unions as the only practical means of defence left to them. The novel, though planned and partly written much earlier, reflects something of his social concern and of the crisis period during which it appeared. It is exceptional among the rather relaxed later novels for its tight construction, the care with which it is written and the subtlety of its implications. Leaving behind the clear polarities and relatively simple black and white conflicts of Chesterton's earlier handling of political themes, the book recognises a far more difficult and complex social and political situation than the pre-1914 novels had seemed to acknowledge. Above all, *The Return of Don Quixote* shows, on the political level, that the salvation of the community cannot lie in a simple reproduction of the external trappings, manners and institutions of the past, in this case the medieval world Chesterton admired, unless such a return were to be rooted in the moral and spiritual values, and conception of society which underlay the picturesque surface. Unless it had such a root, the return would be a mere archaistic dalliance, a romantic indulgence at best, at worst, the means of reinforcing the very tyranny it had been intended to cure.

The novel shows how such a misconceived return is launched by a group of fanatical artists and scholars and then manipulated from behind the scenes by politicians who, aware that the existing order which they have controlled is breaking up, are delighted to be provided with new stage-machinery, novel slogans and catch-phrases, with which to conceal their operations. The result is not a medieval but, although Chesterton does not use the term, a crypto-Fascist society.

The book's action originates in the emotions generated by Olive Ashley's amateur play, while most of its imagery relates to her search for a lost illumination colour. The play fires the obsessive scholar Michael Herne, whose passion for the medieval world is, unknown to him, an expression of his love for Rosamund Severn. In the midst of a crisis somewhat like the General Strike these aristo-cratic dilettantes, partly through the collusion of politicians like Lord Eden, seize power and establish their Utopia.

As several critics have pointed out, *The Return of Don Quixote* recapitulates in more subtle form, conflicts and collisions of per-sonality and principle found in several former books. The contrast between the idealist Herne and the easy-going, detached Murrel recalls the polarity between Adam Wayne and Auberon Quin in *The Napoleon of Notting Hill*. The clash between Herne and the trade-unionist Braintree recalls the division between the religious idealist and romantic reactionary MacIan and the rationalism and

Socialism of Turnbull in *The Ball and the Cross*. However, no straightforward dichotomy adequately describes the complex of contrasts found in *The Return of Don Quixote*. Ultimately, the image of a good society and a worthwhile life is made up of the fragments of truth or the different visions of characters who collide with each other.

After the 'League of the Lion' under Herne's leadership has taken power, it becomes obvious that the workers, under their leader, Braintree, have no faith in the pseudo-medieval vision. After they have been defeated, Braintree, put on trial for sedition, displays his contempt for the medieval camouflage and the realities it disguises. Politically, it is neither Herne nor Braintree who has the power to heal the failure of communication between men. This results, in some degree from the complexity of a modern industrial society, but its chief cause is innate human sinfulness. Murrel's ironic sense of human limitation and *his* sympathy for the poor, based on the realisation of a shared humanity, rather than on romantic fancies or political theory, equips him to deal with issues which he refuses to oversimplify. After Herne, accepting the justice of Braintree's reproach, relinquishes his power, it is Murrel who, with Herne as his Sancho Panza, goes forth as a righter of wrongs. Clearly, this is to be done piecemeal, with wisdom and humility. Chesterton has given over his earlier anticipations of and perhaps his wish for, the wholesale 'disintegration of the capitalist order'. In *The Return of Don Quixote* which, in conception at least, appears to follow immediately after *The Flying Inn*, the emphasis moves away from a concern with philosophical truth. The Quixote myth is applied, instead, to a particular English context. In that context the themes of restoration, both general and personal, touched on previously, receive their fullest development. *The Return of Don Quixote* becomes nothing less than a judgement on the nature of historical processes.

The 'quixotic adventure' of the novel is a search by James Murrel for a particular kind of red pigment, one of 'Hendry's Old Illumination Colours', which had been successful imitations of medieval paints. Hendry, a friend of William Morris, and one of the pre-Raphaelite circle, had kept a small shop in the Haymarket, before being driven into bankruptcy in the manipulations of chain stores; a point of departure for a familiar Chesterton attack on big business.

To Olive Ashley, the pigment used by her father had an intense significance, as part of an aesthetic education which provided her with a whole scheme of values and sympathies, among which is a romantic conservatism:

> All those things that for so many people are called culture and come at the end of education had been there for her before the beginning. Certain pointed shapes, certain shining colours were things that existed first and set a standard for this fallen world and it was that which she was clumsily trying to express when she set her thoughts against all notions of progress and reform.[39]

Olive, not specially talented artistically, tries to express her vision in mediocre verse dramas about Richard the Lionheart and in laborious imitations of 'the flat jewellery of medieval illumination'. What is suggested in her character is the strength and weakness of the whole tradition of aesthetic admiration of the Middle Ages, neo-Gothic or Pre-Raphaelite. Painstaking and precious, it attempts to capture the essence of the lost age through a concentration on externals of costume, manners, and architecture. Born of a deep sense of the beautiful, it encourages a disdain for the 'ugly present', and a turning away from progress as such, neither of which Chesterton endorses. Nevertheless, like the Pre-Raphaelite movement, Olive's vision is an aspect of the truth. Although the aesthetic approach alone is inadequate, it bears witness to the fact that a quality of beauty existed in the chosen period, and has since been lost. Although it is snobbish, humourless and not particularly intelligent in its expression, it acts as the faithful guardian of a fragment of something, which, including what it cherishes, included much more besides: as Olive treasures the drawing of an angel's wing in the mysterious red pigment, once part of a much larger design by her father. *The Return of Don Quixote* is concerned not to repudiate that aesthetic and romantic interest in the Middle Ages which reached its climax in William Morris and the Pre-Raphaelites but to suggest its limitations, to show why it remained at the level of day-dreams or escapist fantasy; how in spite of its sincerity and a real love of a real beauty it was not more fruitful.

The novel might best be considered as a welding together or a synthesis of scattered elements or aspects of some larger truth, all parts of a lost design for living, a forgotten past, but all distorted and tending to become false in their isolation. Olive's somewhat naive, but genuine, medieval enthusiasm and high Toryism, become in Mr Almeric Wister, 'the art expert', a smug attitude of distaste for the 'modern' and the 'masses' which covers a lack of any creative capacity and of human sympathy: 'Democracy, of course, is not favourable to authority. And I very much fear that democracy is not favourable to art'.[40] Chesterton has lightly but accurately sketched a prevailing danger of the merely aesthetic approach which suggests how a whole tradition, real enough in its origin, may have become sterile.

A second route to the past, or way in which it may be restored is through scholarship. Michael Herne, the librarian of Seawood House, is a dedicated research worker, soaked in his subject, and lost to all else. He does not notice when a practical joker removes his ladder, leaving him stranded high among the shelves, but goes on feverishly reading and making notes. As in Olive, Chesterton suggests a somewhat naive person, isolated from ordinary human life and contacts, whose purity and simplicity are touched with the fey and the cranky:

> His wan blue eyes were a shade wider apart than other men's; increasing an effect of having one eye off. It was indeed rather a weird effect, as if his eye were somewhere else. . .[41]

Herne's lanky physique, and frantic reading of old chronicles which fire him to resurrect the world of which they tell, might lead one to suspect that he is a straightforward imitation of Cervantes' Knight of the Sorrowful Countenance. This is true enough on one level. In fact, however, the essence of the Quixote myth is not found in him. He is not the focus of the quest; a somewhat surprising but a challenging and interesting strategy on Chesterton's part. What Herne implies is rather another aspect of the problem of restoring the past. Fairly bluntly, Chesterton shows that there is an imbalance about him. He does not see how, in practical politics, romantic medievalism can be exploited by selfish and corrupt politicians to retain power; or how idealism without common sense and moderation can produce ideological warfare. Yet, like Olive's passion for beauty, his scholarship is real and fired with an imagination which is 'buried under his mountains of material and alone enabling him to support them.'[42] He can be kindled into a passion for the past. When, under the influence of Olive's pageant at the start of the novel, his interest shifts from Hittite archaeology to the study of the Middle Ages, his qualities of 'real eloquence, logic and living enthusiasm'[43] are engaged. He is able to fire the minds of others with his dream. It gives him a decisiveness, a quality of knowing what he wants. (Chesterton remarks that the qualities of intellectual energy, and the clash of debate have taken refuge in the byways of scholarship since there is no place for them in the flat, stale world of politics). Herne is inspiring, and dangerous, and his medievalism is plausible, Chesterton shows, against the moral vacuousness of modern intellectual life. As an example of this emptiness, there is a sketch of the career of Julian Archer, a creation of the media, in modern parlance: 'one of those men who seem to be in a great many places at once; and to be very important for some reason which it is difficult to specifiy.'[44] Ubiquitous and photogenic, his career a tissue of self-advertisement and loudly asserted clichés, he incarnates that void which, almost anything, probably, would serve to fill.

Herne appeals most to practical people starved of aims and ideals whose representative in *The Return of Don Quixote* is Rosamund Severn. Rosamund hungers for simplification and action. Hers is a temperament shared by many modern young people who bring their qualities of hard work and efficiency to the support of any cause, however cranky, which promises to give a meaning to their lives. When such a type is found in such a setting, it is likely to be 'very conscientious and very unscrupulous'.[45] Perhaps it hardly needs saying that here, as with Olive and Herne, Chesterton is sketching an angle of vision, or a cast of mind capable of being of service to the truth. Rosamund's practicality becomes unscrupulous only through her lack of spiritual depth and of a critical faculty concerning her enthusiasms which are likely to be intellectually unsupported and eccentric.

The scheme of *The Return of Don Quixote* embraces in John Braintree, the trade unionist, another element of the lost truth. His passion for justice and his integrity enable him to brush aside the patronising airs of a group of cultivated nonentities to whom Olive, somewhat fatuously, has introduced him in the hope that he will catch their tone, and have his sharp edges smoothed down. Intellectually he is more than equal to them and is able to penetrate below political slogans and camouflage to the essential nature of the quarrel. His candour evokes a similar candour in them and what is revealed is the clash of values fought in 'Lepanto' and *The Flying Inn* between freedom and that slavery which is so simple, so rational, so fatally defensible:

> In the lull after his more stormy retort, men with quieter voices began to ask him more sensible questions; often conceding many of his claims, often falling back on more fundamental objections. Murrel almost started as he heard the low and gutteral drawl of old Eden, in whom so many diplomatic and parliamentary secrets were buttoned up and who hardly ever talked at all, saying to Braintree: 'Don't you think there's something to be said for the Ancients – Aristotle and all that, don't you know. Perhaps there really must be a class always working for us in the cellar.'[46]

Intellectually well able to fight the battle Chesterton had described elsewhere, against this old enemy or insidious temptation of the European intellect, Braintree is deficient in other ways. Unlike the easy-going aristocrat Murrel, he has no bond of sympathy with the working class he leads. He likes neither their pubs nor their jokes. To that extent, like those of Olive and Herne, his perception, although impressive as far as it goes, can only be partial.

Ian Boyd has dealt carefully and at length with the political themes and content of *The Return of Don Quixote*[47], showing Chesterton's sophistication, the novel's criticism of simplistic or doctrinaire policies, its awareness of how medievalism and romantic politics might be manipulated. On the political level it is, quite arguably, a distributist or syndicalist novel. In philosophical or religious terms, it is a novel of truth fragmented, in which a quest is shown, conducted haltingly on many levels, which must be fused in one vision if it is to succeed. While in no way contradicting Boyd's analysis of the symbolism of Chesterton's 'best and most interesting novel', it does appear that certain elements in *The Return of Don Quixote* are made clearer by seeing it in terms of a long-standing interest in the Quixote myth. As a novel, it is much more than an endorsement of a particular political programme. Although it is surely right, as Boyd does, to show that it can be read with pleasure and profit, as a brilliantly constructed work of art, by those who have no sympathy with Chesterton's religion, it is in the religious framework, after all, that the quest finds its fulfilment. It is here that the scattered elements of the synthesis are gathered together.

As one might expect from the earlier incarnations of the Quixote spirit in Chesterton's work, it is Murrel who is its ultimate representative, not the idealist Herne, in whom it makes a temporary home. Murrel finds the missing illumination colour, and rescues Hendry from the hands of his wealthy oppressors who plan to have him certified as insane. Along with his lackadaisical, detached attitude, he possesses a human sympathy, a realism, a sense of humour and limitation, and ultimately of humility which the other characters lack. (In a revealing remark he sees himself as a leper who, as in the Middle Ages, can only approach the Church through a grate). Murrel's act of courage and chivalry in rescuing Hendry have a liberating, even a purifying effect on him:

> as if the real story lay rather in front than behind him; as if the unexpected liberation of the poor old crank. . . were but a symbol of the liberation of many things and the opening of a brighter world.[48]

This, rather than the self-conscious medievalising is the true recovery of the past, the book's 'Lepanto'. It is Murrel who smiles the smile of Cervantes.

As Chesterton's early essay on Don Quixote had remarked, the problem of the world was that there are 'too many truths that contradict each other, too many loves that hate each other.' *The Return of Don Quixote* is the image of such a world, except that here a resolution is found. Perhaps the central image of the whole novel is that grotesque fragment of medieval sculpture, from the old abbey, a dragon's head of which nobody seems to know the significance. Admired as picturesque during the Gothic revival, it was:

incongruously poised upon a more modern pedestal, probably by the rather hazy romanticism of some gentleman a hundred years ago who thought that a subsequent accumulation of moss and moonlight might turn it into a suitable subject for the ingenious author of Marmion.[49]

It symbolises the true medieval world, ignored, patronised, romanticised, dimly and partly perceived, distorted and yet a vision yearned for, in various ways, by the leading characters in *The Return of Don Quixote*. Chesterton gives to Olive Ashley, at the end of the novel, a final verdict on both the medieval revival's quest for colour, beauty and chivalry and, significantly, Braintree's search for justice. Both impulses have proved abortive since they have not gone to the root of the matter:

> We have only the dragon left. A hundred times I've looked up at that dragon and hated it and never understood it. Upright and high above that horror stood St Michael or St Margaret, subduing and conquering it; but it is the conqueror that has vanished. We have no notion of what it would really be like; we haven't tried to imagine what image really stood there. There burned in this court a great bonfire of visionary passion which in the spirit could be seen for miles and men lived in the warmth of it; the positive passion and possession, the thing worth having in itself.[50]

It is the only possible end to Don Quixote's quest.

VI

CHESTERTON AND ADVENTURE

In the two previous chapters, we have examined Chesterton's insights into the nature of the ideological invasion and something of its effect on the personalities of individuals. Of almost greater importance, however, and complementary to his view of these emergent forces and their personal consequences, is his assessment of the vulnerability of the culture on which their attack was made. The nature of the attacker and the weaknesses of the victim are inextricably connected. Three important subjects, adventure, myth and the grotesque provided Chesterton with much of the staple of his early and most innovative writing. This was partly, it is suggested, because he felt they were matters most misinterpreted or neglected by educated readers, a neglect or misinterpretation eloquent of the narrow basis, the ignorance or a curious strain of melancholy, all of which weakened the mandarin culture of his time.

Adventure, although perhaps the most straightforward of these topics, has been somewhat neglected, or apologetically treated by Chesterton criticism, given the degree to which Chesterton himself emphasised it. It is certainly clear enough that adventure is both a leading concept and a principal field of interest in Chesterton's work. Both the experience itself and the ideas which were its support and its consequence were of supreme importance to him. In his views on literature the presence or absence of the sense of adventure was a factor he tended to stress again and again. The impulse behind the very early essay 'A Defence of Penny Dreadfuls' in *The Defendant* reappears, in spite of some shifts of emphasis, almost thirty years later, in Chesterton's agreeable summing up of the reading habits of a lifetime 'On Philosophy versus Fiction'. At no point in his involvement with the theme was there any suspicion of that whimsical self-conscious intellectual slumming of the kind which used to be called 'camp', whose characteristics Chesterton sketched before the name in the 'Hammock school' with its preference for 'a rich badness' in poetry, in *The Napoleon of Notting Hill*. His interest, on the contrary, was serious. He felt that much 'highbrow' literature throughout his career had lost or was neglecting what was possibly its most important source of satisfaction. But adventure was more than this. It was, he felt, an essential element in personal life. The sense of adventure was necessary to happiness both social and moral and adventures themselves were, in some sense, a normal and reasonable expectation for the individual in his own life.

'Adventure' in various aspects, in ideas, in moral choices and in its simplest sense of exciting incident and high romance, is a factor hard to overestimate in Chesterton's world view. One's approach to the subject might well be biographical, an examination of its significance in his personality and philosophy through his own utterances on the subject. An understanding of the meaning of adventure in Chesterton's work is probably enhanced, however, by setting it in a wider context. Edwardian writing is, substantially, a literature of adventure. Reflecting the social effects of the Education Act of 1870, like the Fleet Street world already discussed, it is a literature with a strong element of popularisation, in the sense of discussing choice between different ways of life, both public and private, of debate between 'public figures' on matters both practical and ideological. An important factor in an understanding of Chesterton's early career is, as we have seen, the growth and change of English newspapers in the 1890s in response to:

> the white collared lower middle class expanding rapidly in numbers under the stimulus of commercial development. It was an ignorant public but an eager and inquisitive one, keen to better itself and looking for the knowledge that would enable it to do so.[1]

Although at least one moving utterance suggests that Chesterton thought himself partly a victim of his own public persona,[2] of the 'media', he really drew much of his stimulus from his relation to an expanding readership, a public which was the pre-condition of the Edwardian 'war of ideas'. This was the audience at which the styles of Wells, Shaw, Chesterton, and many others, were pitched and helps to explain a common element in all of their controversial prose, of the crisp, entertaining Edwardian debating manner with its preference for first principles, not too heavily encumbered with statistics, for logic and for clear distinctions. Recent literary criticism has tended to see the whole period as 'dated', as much further away than the Victorians. In one highly influential interpretation:

> we tend to look at the period 1880–1914 as a kind of interregnum. It is not the period of the masters, of Coleridge or of George Eliot. Nor is it yet the period of our contemporaries, of writers who address themselves, in our kind of language, to the common problems that we recognise.[3]

There does seem a very strong objection to Raymond Williams' view of William Morris as the last of a line of great Victorians whose 'energy, expansion and readiness to generalize' are radically different from our own age of 'critical specialism'. Surely energy and expansiveness are much more the marks of Shaw, Wells and Chesterton than, for example, of George Eliot. Edwardian debate was essentially hopeful. It assumed, much more than the pessimistic Victorian prophets, Carlyle, Ruskin or even Matthew Arnold, that it was really possible to change one's life by rational argument and deliberate action, even to choose one's frame of reference. Chesterton felt himself living in a time which had recovered a sense of fighting for fundamentals, of expanding and diverging possibilities, of adventure. His view of his immediate predecessors emphasised, as we have seen, an inexorable inevitability, a lack of challenge, imagination and vigour in their debates and pronouncements. The later Victorians were tired men.

> The magnificent emancipation evaporated; the mean calculation remained. One could still calculate in clear statistical tables how many men lived, how many men died. One must not ask how they lived; for that is politics. One must not ask how they died for that is

religion. And religion and politics were ruled out of all the later Victorian debating clubs; even including the debating club at Westminster. What kind of third thing they were discussing, which was neither religion nor politics, I do not know. I have tried the experiment of reading through a vast number of their records and reviews and discussions; and still I do not know.[4]

Opposed both to the Socialism of Shaw and the Imperialism of Kipling, he still felt them far better than such deadness. At least in their literary expressions they were fresh and challenging. Chesterton's impatience with the dullness of his predecessors may be paralleled by Shaw's persistent lampooning of the stuffed-shirt Lord Morley, Gladstone's biographer, or Wells' caricature of a 'representative organ of British culture' 'The Sacred Grove' in *Tono-Bungay*.

While it seems valid to use the term 'adventure' to describe this freshness, this opening-out to possibilities of choice and discovery of right action, it is the more usual sense of the term that is specially applicable to Chesterton's work. It is also much more controversial. 'War of ideas', even 'popularisation' sound respectable enough. But 'the romances, the sword sticks, the handsom cabs, the anarchists'[5] which even a powerful defender of his work feels obliged to mention apologetically, surely they are best passed over in silence, a facet of the Chesterton world for which no intellectual defence is possible. Embarrassingly for this point of view, it is an inescapable fact that Chesterton revelled in adventure, in strong yarns, romantic settings, stirring events.

In his delight in adventure in this sense too, he was at one with the pre-1914 reading public. It is hardly necessary to mention that this was the heyday of the spy story, the detective novel, the historical romance, the age of Stanley Weyman, William le Queux, Rider Haggard, G.A. Henty, Conan Doyle, Seton Merriman. More significantly, writing such as that of Kipling and Conrad offered in a refined form the satisfactions of the adventure stories found on the railway bookstalls: tense narrative; romantic events, settings and characterisations. Chesterton deplored the division between 'highbrow' and 'low-brow' reading matter and defended the latter but in some ways the division was less marked than it has subsequently become. And here lies a difficulty in discussing Chesterton's own variant of adventure. Recent critical frames of reference hardly allow respectability to a kind of fictional satisfaction which it never occurred to the Edwardians to question. 'But Edwardian readers who were looking for an adult view of their world would turn probably, neither to Kipling nor to Conrad,'[6] a reputable textbook has suggested. Instead they would read E.M. Forster. This use of the word 'adult' implicitly denies the worthwhileness of the subject. Chesterton's exploration of the nature of adventure, is, by this showing, unimportant, if not a blemish: another aspect of a kind of childishness prevalent among many of his contemporaries.

Whatever the general objections to a kind of prescriptive criticism which defines some sorts of fictional concerns as 'adult' and some as 'childish', there can be little doubt that it serves the reader ill with Chesterton. It offers a truncated version of his work. Chesterton can and should, of course, be considered as a psychologist, social critic, and aphorist. Undoubtedly though, he was a writer of adventure fiction. He wrote, and repeatedly went on record as the defender of, a kind of fiction modern criticism almost lacks a vocabulary to discuss. Well-equipped to examine irony, ambiguity or symbolism, contemporary criticism shows much less understanding of narrative or the management of pace or excitement in literature.[7] The reasons for this are complex but it is probably as true as any historical generalisation that the post-1918 rejection of the saga of Empire building extended to the whole notion of adventure which came to seem part of a set of discredited values; a reaction which gathered force just as English Literature was becoming a recognised academic discipline and which established the frame of reference within which critical work was done.

While Chesterton's early rise to prominence was associated with pro-Boer agitation during the South African War and he remained the trenchant critic of Imperialism in its pre-1914 zenith, it is interesting to note that he felt himself in odd company at times, on this very question of adventure:

Some of the Liberal specialists, of the more frigid Cambridge type, did faintly irritate me.... They seemed so very negative and their criticism was a sort of nagging.... I disliked Imperialism; and yet I almost liked it by the time Hobson had finished speaking against it.... I may be wrong; anyhow, I missed something, as he picked holes in the British Empire until it consisted entirely of holes tied together with red tape. And then Cunninghame Graham began to speak; and I realised what was wanting. He painted a picture, an historical picture like a pageant of Empires.[8]

Chesterton's description of an attack of malaise while listening to J. A. Hobson at an anti-Imperialist meeting might perhaps be dismissed as the attitude of an incurable romantic who preferred the 'pageant of Empires' to facts and figures. But to label is not to understand. Chesterton's temperamental preference for romantic adventure is a notable characteristic of his psychological and literary landscape. Much more interest and significant, I would suggest, than the mere taste itself, was what he did intellectually with his temperamental preference, his own working out of the true nature of adventure.

The impatience with Hobson stems from an instinctive feeling that an essential element, the colour, the vitality, the spice of life, a certain quality of generous response, of sheer excitement was missing from his make-up and his philosophy. It was an element which Chesterton placed at the centre of his apologetic. He was keen to show that Orthodoxy alone could secure this kind of adventure. The desirability of adventure he takes to be axiomatic:

If we desire European civilisation to be a raid and a rescue, we shall insist rather that souls are in real peril than their peril is ultimately unreal.[9]

His frame of reference is one in which the idea of damnation does not represent primarily a fearful warning as in certain kinds of Christianity, or is underplayed and toned down, as in other kinds. It conveys a 'healthy idea of danger'.[10]

If Chesterton's lack of sympathy with Hobson suggests an element in his attitudes and tastes, his warm admiration for George

Wyndham strongly confirms this. It was much more than an interest in Wyndham's Irish land policy:

> I felt almost immediately that Wyndham's opinions were at least of the same general colour as my own. And if ever there was a man of whom the word 'colour' in his opinions and everything else, recurs naturally to the mind, it was he.[11]

The whole question of Chesterton and adventure is raised in its sharpest form by his repeatedly expressed interest in the ambience of a man idolised by the staff of the high Tory *National Observer*, by Charles Whibley, Henley and George Saintsbury, and a man whose own special interests in literature were 'adventure, chivalry, a dream of feudal honour and Renaissance courtliness';[12] a passionate Imperialist. History has not been kind to Wyndham in the political causes for which he stood, which would no doubt have gratified Chesterton the anti-Imperialist. It has also passed stern judgement on his whole atmosphere, his emotional climate, tastes and approach to life. A recent critic quotes Walter Raleigh's dedication of a book

> 'To George Wyndham, soldier, courtier, scholar in a year of high emotion, and the accomplishment of unimaginable destinies...'. The year was 1900 and for 'high emotion' read 'Mafeking'.[13]

The point is that Chesterton could, unlike many modern readers, distinguish high emotion from Mafeking. He was able whole-heartedly to oppose Wyndham's Imperialism and simultaneously to warm to that quality, 'generosity', 'gusto', 'natural mysticism' of the lover of adventure.

In seeking to understand Chesterton's view of the subject it is obviously necessary to grant adventure of this kind some initial imaginative sympathy, to lay aside social or political prejudices about the 'tragic deception of heroic attitudes so soon to be buried in the mud of Flanders' or psychological prejudices about 'romantic immaturity'. Such clichés prevent the necessary discrimination between different types of thought and response within an alien body of feeling; the recognition that some are more valuable and intelligent than others. Chesterton, starting from the premiss that 'adventure', a life of colour, heightened emotion and startling incident was desirable, thought the subject through, exposing what he felt were prevalent contemporary fallacies about romantic adventure, and seeking to reveal its true springs and nature.

While much of his criticism of Imperialism is social and political, it may also be considered as an attack on false adventure, a kind of life which purports to be interesting, to offer more intense, significant kinds of experience, while doing nothing of the kind. His distaste for Cecil Rhodes has a suggestion of a man who has detected a cheat, adventure which is no adventure. Interestingly, his picture of Rhodes ('The Sultan' in *A Miscellany of Men*) is a portrait of a bore. It is noticeable that Chesterton's descriptions of bores, those who diminish the possibilities of life, are generally scathing; few more so than that of Rhodes. Remarking that, paradoxically, the urge to spread one's ideas by force seems particularly strong among those whose ideas are wearing thin, he argues that the whole dream of 'Cape to Cairo' or a 'white South Africa' was not an adventure or an entry into a new world. In fact, Rhodes:

> had only a hasty but elaborate machinery for spreading the principles he hadn't got. What he called his ideals were only the dregs of a Darwinism which had already grown not only stagnant but poisonous.[14]

Rhodes offered not a fresh view or a life more abundant but tired clichés. He was not an explorer of uncharted regions but 'an honest and humble recipient of the plodding popular science of his time.'[15] Clearly as a phenomenon he was not radically divorced from the deadness and tedium of debating societies in which nothing was debated, the cultural ossification of the previous generation against which Chesterton was reacting. 'Like many another agnostic old bachelor of the Victorian era', Rhodes was intellectually tenth-rate. True adventure, Chesterton seems to feel, cannot coexist with intellectual poverty. It was, he stressed, an intellectual poverty of a peculiar kind:

> That very governing class which urges Occidental Imperialism has been deeply discoloured with Oriental mysticism and cosmology.[16]

Cultural and intellectual criticism of this kind exposes the inner weakness of a false adventure. Excitement and tension are found in risk which is moral and not merely physical, in the sense of struggling against the odds for an endangered ideal, one which is new, difficult of achievement, which, in some sense, goes against the grain of things, which challenges and disturbs. It may exist in riddles and contradictions, but never in the trite and threadbare; in, for example, Rhodes' 'one small genuine idea' that he was the agent of an inevitable fate.

In this piece on Rhodes, Chesterton seems incidentally to have laid his finger on a fault in the texture of much of the writing produced in pre-1914 flowering of the romantic adventure story: the curious combination of a yearning for a larger life with the inability to achieve a moral and religious, and therefore a true transcendence of circumstance. Chesterton was as convinced as many of the providers and consumers of the adventure dream, of the dull and constricted nature of much of the urban life offered. He would probably not have attacked the escapist impulse if only the escape had been a genuine one. In retrospect the intellectual weakness was a literary as well as a moral fault in the adventure writers. Frank Swinnerton draws attention to the disparity between the immensely popular Seton Merriman's creation of 'suspense' and the fatuity of his philosophic comments on life and character. These:

> were much influenced by Fitzgerald's version of Omar Khayyam which came out of copyright at the end of the nineteenth century and was printed in various delightful forms – 'The Moving Finger writes' etc. . . . And the moral is always that men should be brave, that women should be enduring, that the worldly hopes of human beings bring no satisfaction, and that the British are the salt of the earth.[17]

This is a very suggestive comment. Critics, on the whole, agree on a tone of deep sadness in Conrad and Kipling, a generalised note of melancholy wisdom, of stoicism and courage in the face of futility. Heroism and adventure, in both writers, are enacted against a bleak and meaningless background. Explanations for this, often highly plausible, are offered in terms of their private lives, or childhood experiences. Possibly these purely personal accounts omit to note the prevalence of this element in the writers of high adventure from 1890 to 1914. It is almost the dominant note which perhaps explains Chesterton's liking for even humbler writers, thrillers and detective fiction.

What is striking is the way in which second-rate writing, of some literary pretension, echoes or foretells passages in the major authors. Alan Quartermain before the battle in *King Solomon's Mines* has an 'overwhelming sense of the sadness of human life', of an unending and unmeaning permutation.

> Truly the universe is full of ghosts, not sheeted churchyard spectres, but the inextinguishable elements of individual life which having once been, can never *die*, though they blend and change and change again forever.[18]

In a sense, Haggard is typical of a whole late Victorian and Edwardian sensibility, a vague but powerful displaced religious urge, seeking answers and finding them in *outré*, exotic, often fatalistic and pessimistic cults. Morton Cohen's description of this element in Haggard's adventure stories strikes a familiar chord in the secondary literature of the period:

> His groping into Egyptian and Nordic archaeology, his scrapings in prehistoric temples and tombs, his toying with spiritualism and psychical phenomena, his strong belief in reincarnation – all are part of his quest for the answers. He felt within him deep spiritual soundings he could not understand.[19]

In *She* or *Ayesha*, there is a suggestion of some kind of portentous 'answer' involving reincarnation and the everlasting recurrence of the same love-triangle throughout eternity. Seton Merriman's speciality, unlike Rider Haggard's or Conan Doyle's was not re-incarnation but Fate. In *Barlasch of the Guard*, published two years before Chesterton's *The Napoleon of Notting Hill*, and a best-seller like Haggard's novels, he remarks that

> battles and revolutions and historical events are but the jagged instruments with which Fate rough hews our lives, leaving us to

shape them as we will. In other days, no doubt, man rough hewed while Fate shaped. But as civilisation advances men will wax so tender, so careful of the individual that they will never cut and slash, but move softly, very tolerant, very easy-going seeking the compromise that brings peace and breeds a small timid race of men.[20]

This passage is worth quoting since it suggests, in part, the mood of the opening *The Napoleon of Notting Hill*, the sense that heroism is departing or has already gone. It also hints, perhaps, at the nature of Chesterton's success in his first and best novel of adventure, a characteristically bold reversal of the formula used by his contemporaries.

This formula involved a combination of an exotic setting with a feeling of a hopeless, unaccommodating kind based on the knowledge that heroism, perhaps that all activity, is meaningless. With Kipling, one takes up the White Man's Burden in spite of the utter ingratitude of the natives and the fact that one's work will inevitably come to nothing. Like the Roman soldiers defending Hadrian's Wall or the officers in India, one struggles to preserve the state which disregards, despises and thwarts its preservers. In Kipling's greatest work *Kim* there is, surely, a sense that the Great Game and the pageant of the Grand Trunk Road are illusory compared with the Lama's pilgrimage to the River of the Arrow; his quest to free himself from the sorrowful Wheel of Eternal Change. If Kim returns to fight the good fight of Imperialism it is out of self-sacrifice and with his eyes open to its final emptiness.

Conrad's use of the formula, like Kipling's, is, of course, much more subtle than Seton Merriman's or Haggard's. But it is, nevertheless, in important ways, the same formula, the combination of colourful setting or exciting circumstances with an underlying sense of hopelessness. It is very hard to object to Jocelyn Baines' description of the magnificent *Nostromo*, with *Kim* the twin peak of the Edwardian adventure novel:

> Thus idealism and scepticism, faith and want of faith, both seem to lead to disaster. *Nostromo* is an intensely pessimistic book; it is the most impressive monument to futility ever created.[21]

Most significant of all, heroism itself is without meaning or value. It does not have, as in Kipling, a stoical grandeur. Nostromo himself dies as 'the victim of the disenchanted vanity which is the reward of all audacious action.'[22] Published in the same year as *The Napoleon of Notting Hill*, *Nostromo* helps to establish a context for Chesterton's work in the field of adventure, to make clearer the nature and value of his contribution to the novel of romantic incident. It is probably unnecessary to labour a point so well established in the critical study of individual writers, of the rooted pessimism of many of those authors who found their inspiration in individual heroism. Nor is it necessary, or perhaps even possible to speculate on the reasons for this prevalent feeling except perhaps to note a repeated suggestion that the growth of civilisation left no room for courage, nobility and adventure and that the greater one's knowledge of life, the greater one's disillusionment.

Chesterton's achievement was to marry two seeming incompatibles, to bring together an intellectual energy and hopefulness as great as his rival popularisers Shaw and Wells with heroic values and high romance which the author of *Arms and the Man* and the apostle of the Millennium through science presumably considered outdated; to combine the verve of the contemporary 'war of ideas' and intellectual adventure with the thrill of an older nobility which it might have been assumed to have rendered obsolete.

The Napoleon of Notting Hill, which we have already examined in connection with the Quixote myth, launches an attack on the sense of an inescapable process by which the heroic stage of man's life is left behind. In the first chapter 'Introductory Remarks on the Art of Prophecy', the whole notion of historical inevitability is gently but effectively mocked. There is no certain march to a more civilised, less virile society. In fact there is no certainty whatever in human affairs, except perhaps a delightful cross-grainedness, a refusal to conform to sensible predictions in terms of what is already known. Instead of sense and certainty there is a permanently reappearing frivolity, a spirit of play:

For human beings, being children, have the childish wilfulness and the childish secrecy. And they have never from the beginning

135

of the world done what wise men have seen to be inevitable. . . . Individually, men may present a more or less rational appearance, eating, sleeping and scheming. But humanity as a whole is changeful, mystical, fickle, delightful. Men are men, but Man is a woman.[23]

It is in this spirit, which Chesterton saw as in some sense feminine, that the first impulse and root cause of heroic or romantic adventure is found. The reality of free-will involves the right to be wilful, not itself always a perjorative term, the impulse to be perverse, extravagant, to take no account of common sense, self-interest or 'existing compromises', and for no other reason than that it pleases one so to do. Such behaviour is, of course, 'immature', but it is nevertheless a demonstration and affirmation of human freedom. Like Dostoevsky's 'underground man', Auberon Quin would rather be unhappy in his own way than happy in somebody else's. Dostoevsky's description of this awkward impulse seems pertinent to Chesterton's view of this origins of adventure. Man:

would deliberately desire to introduce into all this positive good sense his fatal fantastic element. It is just his fantastic dreams, his vulgar folly that he will desire to retain, simply in order to prove to himself that men still are men and not the keys of a piano.[24]

Chesterton differs from Dostoevsky in seeing this evidence of human free-will or wilfulness not as spite but as play. More significantly, he differs from Dostoevsky in seeing another element, essential to freedom, another element, the 'Father' as opposed to the 'Mother' of adventure. To the spirit of play, the child's preference for its own game over the adults' sound arrangements on its behalf, must, as has been seen in another connection, be conjoined the readiness to abide by the consequences of one's choice, the sense of honour which Chesterton had noticed in *A Defence of Rash Vows*. If perversity is an affirmation of the freedom of the personality, then the vow kept is an affirmation of its authenticity:

The man who makes a vow makes an appointment with himself at some distant time or place. The danger of it is that himself should not keep the appointment. And in modern times this terror of oneself, of the weakness and mutability of one's self has perilously increased.[25]

The Napoleon of Notting Hill may be and has been very profitably discussed from the social and political point of view as an attack on Imperialism or a contemporary tendency to feel that the future lay with larger and larger aggregations; on the contrary, a place must be limited before it can be loved. It may also be viewed as a study of the origin of adventure, a picture of a necessary tension or perhaps even a 'dialectic' between the humorist and the fanatic. This element is, I would suggest, illuminated by a remark of Chesterton's in a *Daily News* article of the previous year:

> We awake at our birth staring at a very funny place. After serious examination of it we receive two fairly definite impressions; the first, delight and the second, fear.[26]

The impulse to play, to produce art, to create festivals, to 'dance and kick about in the sunlight' and the impulse to institute rules and so create morality, to will and to restraint of will, were once both united in a coherent religious view of life. The loss of that view has damaged both impulses and caused the disintegration of that 'organic general view of life itself' which brings the human being to his full stature. What *The Napoleon of Notting Hill* shows is first the recovery of both these principles in their primal energy and then their interaction.

The initial moment of perception by Auberon Quin of the coat-tails of the two government officials he is following, not as coat-tails but as 'two black dragons looking at him with evil eyes',[27] is the recovery of the first of the primary motives for adventure, the sense of incongruity. Things in themselves are odd. They are arbitrary. Habit and daily expectation deaden this feeling. It may even, as in the bureaucratic despotism in which *The Napoleon of Notting Hill* opens, lay it to sleep for years:

> That vague and somewhat depressed reliance upon things happening as they have always happened which is with all Londoners a mood, had become an assumed condition.[28]

Habit, although very powerful, may be suddenly disrupted by an illumination, the sight of the thing in itself:

> If you look at a thing nine-hundred and ninety times, you are perfectly safe; if you look at it the thousandth time you are in frightful danger of seeing it for the first time.[29]

This is an important point. What is seen is not initially a fanciful vision but the thing itself seen for the first time. Also, more seems to be involved here than a sense of wonder. Before any moral connotation in the act of perception, there is the act of perception itself, a renewed sense of the physical reality of an object. In *Autobiography* Chesterton carefully distinguishes this child-like perception, 'a sort of white light on everything, cutting things out very clearly, and rather emphasising their solidity',[30] from a whimsical play with the unreal or the kind of heightened vision associated with first love or adolescence. To the child the fire itself is more interesting than the face in the fire. The beginning of adventure is not a fancy or a wild dream but this realisation of 'isness', of the thing in itself. What Auberon Quin has is a fresh sight of the buttons, cutting through traditional or habitual associations and attributions which surround them. They do not cease, of course, to be 'only two buttons at the back of a frock-coat' but they are discovered to be more solid, richer in imaginative potentialities, not constrained to be what men have made of them already. Speaking of imagination in *Autobiography*, Chesterton stresses that it is not an illusion, a dream or a deception from which the child awakens. On the contrary, 'pretending is not deceiving'. In order that imagination can work it must have physical objects, definite, solid and relished for their physicality:

> in the true sense images. The very word images means things necessary to imagination. But not things contrary to reason, no, not even in a child. For imagination is almost the opposite of illusion.[31]

Chesterton's view of the process of imagination as something dependent on the concrete reality and particularly of external objects is highly significant. Things are *there* and they are strange. They have an existing and a significance beyond anything that can be said about them. Pointing to a tree, Quin remarks that all frames of reference, the scientific, the political, even the ostensibly mystical, are less than the sheer arbitrary oddity, 'the humour of that tree'. 'The sublime victory of the joke that people do not see',[32] the last sanctity remains, as an inexhaustible source of wonder. As a later poem suggests, this sense precedes and outlasts emotional states which necessarily belong to particular times of human life:

> Romance and pride and passion pass
> And these are what remain
> Strange crawling carpets of the grass
> Wide windows of the sky...[33]

Outlasting the decline of strength and energy, this sense can in no way be destroyed by experience or disillusionment. It is only when we move from the thing itself into abstractions about it that such a consciousness is lost. As Chesterton remarked in an article two years before *The Napoleon of Notting Hill*:

> We see a green tree. It is the green tree that we fear; it is the green tree which we worship. Then because there are so many green trees, so many men, so many elephants, so many butterflies, so many daisies, so many animalculae, we coin the general term 'Life'. And then the mystic comes along and says that a green tree symbolises life. It is not so. Life symbolises a green tree. Just in so far as we get into the abstract we get away from the reality, we get away from the mystery.[34]

Seen with an awareness of its intrinsic mystery, no object or place lacks strangeness and it is not necessary to go to an exotic world to find wonder. The dichotomy between a 'dull mundane reality' and 'the romantic extraordinary' is seen to have no meaning.

Curiously, one way in which this sense of reality is likely to emerge is out of acute boredom:

> When the chord of monotony is stretched most tight it breaks with a sound like a song.[35]

Perhaps in what is called 'boredom' the mind is recalled to *things* themselves and away from what Chesterton had called in his article 'the faint, jaded symbols of the reality'[36] :Truth, Beauty, and Destiny of the Soul and so forth. In a later essay 'On the Thrills of Boredom,' he offers a somewhat different emphasis. Over-excitement may be a narcotic. Unfashionable hotels, empty waiting-rooms, watering places out of season give time 'to let certain nameless suggestions soak into us and make a richer soil of the subconscious.'[37] In 'The Glory of Grey' nearer the date of *The Napoleon of Notting Hill*, there is a similar suggestion of the value of the quiet, the subdued and the relatively unstimulating in somehow awakening hope and expectation:

> Grey is a colour that always seems to be on the eve of changing into some other colour; of brightening into blue or blanching into white or bursting into green and gold. So we may be perpetually reminded of the indefinite hope that is in doubt itself.[38]

Auberon Quin is more than a prankster. His initial perception is rooted in Chesterton's philosophical and aesthetic views. First acute boredom, then concentration on the thing itself, with an escape from habit and abstraction, then play, make-believe, fantasy. If, as was suggested at the time, Quin was modelled on Max Beerbohm whom Chesterton had just met and greatly liked, it is probable that it was not Beerbohm's superficial quality of artifice Chesterton drew on, so much as those traits which John Felstiner's *The Lies of Art* (1975) a study of Beerbohm, has noticed: childlikeness and freedom from abstract thought.

To the spirit of play rooted in the sense of the integrity of objects must be added honour, the sense of the integrity of self. Adam Wayne is the second essential ingredient of adventure. It is, of course, entirely correct to see Quin and Wayne as the humorist and the fanatic: the two halves of man's brain. But Chesterton is much more specific, detailed and more subtle than this. Quin expresses the liberation of man to be wilful, the rebuttal of rational self-interest as a motive for action, of a dreary consensus of 'all thinking people':

> Did Herbert Spencer ever convince you – did he ever convince anybody – did he ever for one mad moment convince himself that it must be to the interest of the individual to feel a public spirit?[39]

Freed from the constraints of imaginary general rules, it is possible to have a new relationship with the physical world, every object in which is itself freed from visual and emotional accretions. What Wayne provides is specifically related to this mysterious, well defined, solid otherness of material objects:

> Why should it be grotesque to say that a pillar-box is poetic when for a year I could not see a red pillar-box against the yellow evening in a certain street without being wracked with something of which God keeps the secret but which is stronger than sorrow or joy.[40]

What is involved here is a *loyalty* to the game, to the results of one's own choice, one's own 'humour', sensibility or way of looking at things. Wayne mentions specifically that Quin's words confirmed his own childhood fantasies, 'dreaming of great wars'. He loves Notting Hill 'because I had played boys' games there, fallen in love there and talked with my friends through nights that were nights of the gods.' The personality is an organic entity, abiding by, and being prepared to suffer for, its freely-chosen allegiances. Its perceptions are not a succession of unconnected instants or moments of pleasure without antecedents or consequences. There is no sense of a retreat, a back-door which is the 'sterilizing spirit of modern pleasure'.[41] Ultimately one is prepared to die for one's 'humour', to assert the integrity of the self and its own particular relationship with the external world, irreplaceable, unique, rooted in its own past, *sui generis*, like the Nicaraguan way of lassooing horses. Chesterton insists on the fact that Wayne's vision is rooted in his own past:

> The process began almost in babyhood and became habitual like a literal madness.[42]

It is, as the novel shows, a mode of perception, an angle on experience growing up gradually until it is 'the back and base of his brain'. Lacking artistic ability Wayne has, by himself, no power to express his vision, to make others share it. What he does possess is loyalty to it, without the least hint of insistence or aggression. Chesterton remarks on the psychological truth that the nearer defeat, the more endangered the vision is, the more it is loved. Like

Quin, Wayne is essentially a child. One has the child's freshness of perception and spirit of play; the other the child's intense loyalty to and absorption in his own game. It is out of a conjunction of the two that adventure is born. Offered his own dream-world through Quin's overthrow of the conventional world-view, Wayne transfigures the fantasy:

While the author and the victims alike treated the whole matter as a silly public charade, this one man by treating it seriously, sprang suddenly into the throne of artistic omnipotence.[43]

Play becomes that heightened life 'for which *The Iliad* is only a cheap substitute'. It is only through loyalty of this kind that choice can be significant at all. More than this, however, it has the power to give the whole freely-chosen course dignity through finality. After the 'Empire of Notting Hill' crashes to final ruin, Wayne sums up the whole matter of the integrity of the self:

'As the tree falleth so shall it lie', he said. Men have called that a gloomy text. It is the essence of all exultation. I am doing now what I have done all my life, what is the only happiness, what is the only universality. I am clinging to something.[44]

Powered by childhood fantasy, the recognition of the solid significance of the external world, and the coherence and continuity of the personality, adventure need never wilt. There need never be a process of disillusion since the imagination is continually creative and the reality of moral choice ensures that it is always possible to make one's existence approximate in some way to one's deepest and most persistent dreams. Chesterton devotes a much later and lighter book, *Tales of the Long Bow*, to the thesis that the most fantastic happenings are possible simply if one keep one's word and makes them happen:

In all our little adventures...we have all taken up some definite position and stuck to it, however difficult it might be; that was the whole fun of it.[45]

The point is found more movingly expressed in the 'Harp of Alfred' section of *The Ballad of the White Horse,* a distinction between true and false adventure, as well as true and false philosophy. Alfred's belief in the freedom of the will, and moral responsibility sets him apart from the Danes whose exploits take place in a hopeless void. He has an appetite for fresh experience and a hopefulness which may have not:

> We have more lust again to lose
> Than you to win again.[46]

Adventure, in Chesterton, touches on his view of imagination, of 'images', of personality, of the nature of choice and responsibility. All the facets of his attitude develop out of and express the religious origin of his thought. In a sense, however, the instinct as opposed to the philosophy of adventure was, in him, a religious instinct. His insistence on the value of the dramatic, the romantic, and the highly coloured, stems from his feeling that this was the ultimate nature of human life in time and in eternity.

In a late essay, 'Reading the Riddle'[47] he hazily recalled the odd fact that, years before, hundreds of people had bought a book with some such title as 'The Great Problem solved' under the illusion that it was a detective story and been grievously disappointed when they found it was a work of modernist optimistic theology; a pity, because fundamental questions and answers ought to be 'dark and drastic', gripping as a police romance, paradox rather than truism. Bernard Shaw, who thought the story of the Crucifixion too dramatic to be true has not recognised that not only religion, but heroic politics are 'terribly theatrical'. Even in the quietest life, however, there is that infinitely refreshing sense of mystery, resting on the sense of a Creator beyond all human rationalisations and abstractions from experience:

> We stare at a tree in an infinite leisure; but we know all the time that the real difference is between a stillness of mystery and an explosion of explanation. We know all the time that the question is whether it will continue to be a tree or turn into something else.[48]

VII

A RIGHT VIEW OF MYTH

The mythic as an element in literature and moral experience is, by any showing, of enormous importance in Chesterton's work. He was absorbed by legends and fairy-stories, both for themselves, and for what they suggest about the mind and life of man. His references to these related subjects in religious contexts are very numerous and, more significantly, discussion of them lies at the core of his two most important apologetics, in 'The Ethics of Elfland' chapter of *Orthodoxy* and in two chapters of *The Everlasting Man*, 'God and Comparative Religion' and 'Man and Mythologies'. In his literary criticism its role is equally central. It is, for example, the underlying theme in his early, deliberately combative study of Dickens and is an overt or implicit factor in all his literary judgements. For him, myth or fable are the vital ingredients omitted from the modern novel and the sophisticated literary culture of his own day, to their great loss. It was not so much, perhaps, that they were compelled thereby to lack popular appeal, although this as a proof of cultural fragmentation, was in itself regrettable. Chesterton insisted rather that without a dimension of myth or fable literature was incomplete. A fundamental need in the reader was disappointed because a fundamental way in which truth might be apprehended had been abandoned. In fact, it had even been despised and rejected.

Chesterton's view of fable may be examined in a philosophical context, partly as an answer or a corrective to earlier and contemporary theorising on myth and comparative religion. Or it may be seen in a literary setting, as a defence of popular culture in certain of its instinctive preferences and expectations about life and writing. Within both frames of reference his intentions were quite clearly controversial, and the second complements and completes the first. Myth was not a matter of archaic reconstruction, though it might be used to understand the past. It was a living issue, an appetite, a need and a faculty, which had not died out, although it had been partially suppressed. It hardly needs saying that at the very heart of Chesterton's apologetic writing lies the conception of the story intuited through man's myth-making faculty and finally fulfilled. Behind both the literary and religious judgements lies the second and related assumption of life having the configuration, the proportions or structure of a story, being *like* a story in its texture, rather than like a theory or a logical sequence.

In the case of fable or story, as in that of his interest in the grotesque, a full understanding of Chesterton's position requires an examination of its intellectual context. It is quite natural, though I believe incorrect, to regard Chesterton's views as personal intuitions and to ignore their background in controversy. One gains greatly by knowing what he was reacting against or attempting to answer.

Beneath many complex details, there are two substantial features in this intellectual context: first, the change of direction in the study of myth, connected in England with the work of Max Müller, and second, in literature, the developments typified, among much else, by George Eliot's novels and Henry James's criticism. These pointed towards an enhanced status for the novel, towards increasingly 'adult', sophisticated, 'mature' fictional concerns and to self-consciousness about form. These two broad areas of change, although, of course, they found expression in very many disparate phenomena, might be said to have a common impulse behind them, a movement of the cultivated away from primitive or popular conceptions or expectations.

The change of direction in the study of mythology is the more easily dated and formulated of the two. Ernst Cassirer, looking back in 1923, cogently summarised its nature:

The romantics followed in the way indicated by Herder; Schelling, too, sees in language a 'faded mythology', which preserves in formal, abstract distinctions what mythology still treats as living concrete differences.... Exactly the opposite course was taken by the 'comparative mythology' that was attempted in the second half of the nineteenth century especially by Adalbert Kuhn and Max Müller. Since this school adopted the *methodological* principle of basing mythological comparisons on linguistic comparisons, the factual primacy of verbal concepts over mythic seemed to them to be implied in their procedure. Thus mythology appeared as the result of language.[1]

Cassirer here seems to suggest that they mistook the convenience of a methodology for its objective truth. Whatever may be the case, parts of that methodology are still in use in the study of myth. Lévi-Strauss, as much as Max Müller, though in a far more sophisticated fashion, interprets myth through analogies drawn from language, admittedly from linguistic structures, rather than philology.

Chesterton's studies of myth, lacking as they do a scientific terminology, may perhaps seem amateurish and subjective. Here, too, the modern reader inherits attitudes and expectations which were coalescing in the period around Chesterton's birth. It was another effect of Max Müller's writings with their intimidating multiplicity of detail to introduce this 'scientific' frame of reference in the latter half of the nineteenth century, to make it appropriate or even obligatory. The success of Müller might be regarded as the success of methodology. It was also, probably, a reaction to those over-emotional obscurantist elements in the German romantics' view of folklore and myth, their inflated claims for primitive wisdom and the primal sensibility. Isaiah Berlin[2] has touched on certain irrationalist elements in the approach to myth of writers such as J.G. Hamann or even Herder. He summarises their approach in a way which implies its imbalance and possible dangers, a constant exaltation of the sensuous imaginative and irrational, of images rather than logic, proverbs rather than rational conclusions, a corresponding denigration of reason, denying its proper function, a cult of the primitive and instinctual, Berlin strongly suggests that romantic

146

mythography was anti-rational and anti-scientific. Its overt hostility to the intellectual investigation of the mind of primitive man and its exaltation of instinct as in all circumstances the surest guide must have served to arouse suspicion. One has besides only to note the vague poetic afflatus, almost rhapsody, of the translation (1827) of Herder's *Treatise on the Origin of Language*,[3] to realise how such writing on myth would seem lacking both in facts and method, compared with Müller.

Perhaps these excesses both of matter and manner explain the vulnerability of the German romantic view of myth, hitherto the most developed and enthusiastic, to rational and scientific attack. Müller, as the editor of the 1909 edition of *Comparative Mythology* pointed out, was pre-eminently a clear and temperate writer, his involved terminology and vast information 'set off with the graces of a beautifully picturesque and lucid style of which he was master. His English for a foreigner was marvellous.'[4] What this clarity reveals is a very definite set of attitudes both cultural and religious. Max Müller is remarkably honest and direct in expressing his revulsion from the grotesque element in early myths. In the seminal and highly influential essay *Comparative Mythology* (1856), for example, he remarks on the seemingly unbridgable gulf between the beginnings of religion, laws or political societies in early communities of which it is possible to form some picture, and the preceding stage of myth-making. What possible link can there be between the high civilis-ation of the world shown in the Homeric poems, far advanced in the fine arts, with public meetings and elaborate judicial pleadings, and characters such as Nestor or Odysseus with their mature wisdom or cunning, and the mere mental darkness of the myth-makers? How is it possible to believe that the rich culture of the Greeks at the dawn of history could have been antedated by 'a race of men whose chief amusement consisted in inventing absurd tales about gods and other nondescript beings?'[5] Later poets may have lent some of these fables a degree of charm but most of them, taken literally, are absurd, and irrational. So great is the difference between the mind which created and delighted in them and the later achievements of Greek moral and religious thought that one might almost believe that there was 'a period of temporary insanity through which the human mind had to

147

pass.'[6] His own argument for a derivation of myth from language seems to offer an alternative to the 'violent and repugnant theory' of repeated catastrophes due to upheavals from the depths of human consciousness, a notion which must clearly render a reasoned account of man's intellectual development impossible.

Müller's explanations of myth, widely challenged in their own day and rapidly superseded, are less interesting and significant than the religious or philosophical premiss which underlies them. Expressed with an unguarded ingenuousness by the founding father of comparative mythology in English, it appears in a more cautious form in his more sophisticated successors such as Frazer or Gilbert Murray. It is essentially the distaste of a civilised man for the primitive and for fable, an inability to see how the latter could possibly have any kind of religious significance. Müller's language is that of repugnance bordering on disgust. How, he asks, can one believe that a few generations before Solon and Lykurgos:

> the highest notions of the Godhead among the Greeks were adequately expressed by the story of Uranos maimed by Kronos – of Kronos eating his children...? Among the lowest tribes of Africa and America we hardly find anything more hideous and revolting.[7]

Traced to its source, his reaction stems from his judgement of the nature of religious experience. It is evident that he took a reverent interest in spirituality but felt that it transcended 'those regions within which language has its natural origin.'[8] Metaphor and myth are inevitable if regrettable incrustations around a real, although ineffable, sense of the holy or the Godhead. One may, however, take consolation from the thought that just as a diseased body presupposes a healthy body, so a mythological religion presupposes a 'healthy' religion. It is always possible to detect glimpses of the original stem through the 'rank and poisonous growth of mythic phraseology.'[9] The tendency to embody spiritual truths in concrete forms, along with the demand for a visible God, is an understandable inclination of man's primitive intellect, gradually lost as the race develops. In the course of that growth it is certain that much of the language of the New Testament will have to be surrendered. Müller is sometimes prepared to be indulgent to myth considered in this way as an outgrown, puerile phenomenon:

> Those who spoke of God as walking about in Paradise spoke as children, did the best they could, gave all they had, and who shall say that their two mites were in the sight of God less precious than all our creeds and philosophies.[10]

At the heart of Müller's thinking lies a radical divorce between the other-worldly realm of religious meaning and that of tangible physical phenomena and our 'ordinary' experience. Spirituality *is* real but it cannot, of its nature, be manifested in the world we know, or in our language. Certainly, for modern man, perhaps for all men, myth obscures and corrupts, rather than clarifies, the intimation of God we gain through a direct awareness of the numinous and through the moral sense. Müller resists the whole idea of story or myth in a religious context, as part of a wider distaste for any giving of spiritual experience a local habitation and a name. It is quite simply, as far as he is concerned, a degradation. What is possibly most disconcerting is that these attitudes affect Müller's approach to the subject in which he achieved greatest distinction. It is surely, as his recent biographer Nirad Chaudhuri[11] points out in a highly sympathetic study, on his pioneer work in the field of Hindu myth and religion that Müller's reputation now rests. Through his energy in personal contacts in Oxford and through his indefatigable efforts as an editor, he might be said to have been the founder of this whole field of study. For him, however, Hindu myth was certainly a revelation of human weakness rather than a fascinating kingdom of the imagination:

> If we want to know whither the human mind, though endowed with a natural consciousness of a divine power, is driven neces-sarily and inevitably by the irresistible force of language as applied to supernatural and abstract idea, we must read the Veda; and if we want to tell the Hindus what they are worshipping – mere names of natural phenomena, gradually obscured, per-sonified and deified, we must make them read the Veda.[12]

Müller's whole career and his work in bringing Indian religion to the notice of the educated world of his time suggests that his view of Vedic myth was not simply a Eurocentric prejudice but was coloured by his attitude to myth in general and rooted in his distaste for or incomprehension of the primitive and the fabulous. It would be reasonable to infer that this distaste persisted in the major writers on myth who succeeded him. Müller's frame of reference in other ways was, of course, soon superseded. Obsolescent at his death in 1900, when Chesterton's career was beginning, it had been utterly outmoded by the mid-1920s, the time of Chesterton's ripest consideration of myth in *The Everlasting Man*. However, he remains, without doubt the largest single factor in the context of Chesterton's view of fable ancient and modern. Müller, as Chaudhuri points out, was much more than a specialised scholar. He coloured 'the mental history of his times. . . . His fame spread out from the scholarly field like that of Darwin or Einstein.[13] Müller's deep and repeated distrust of the mythic embodiment of religion, of the myths as stories, of the very urge towards mythic expression, becomes an important element in the culture of his and later times.

Although turning, as is well known, more and more to anthropology in the years immediately before and after the First World War, the study of myth retained the imprint of his initial distrust of primitive story-telling. It is striking that there appeared to be no questioning of that division, which was Müller's psychological and moral starting point, the gulf between an exalted and spiritual religion on the one hand and stories as concrete embodiments of religious insights and experience on the other. Nor is there any hint that myth is not somehow *inferior* to the pure and direct intimation of the holy. Frazer devotes several pages to establishing such a hierarchy of value as the point of departure for *The Golden Bough*. He draws a sharp distinction, throughout an entire chapter, between 'magic', the attempt of men to 'force the great powers of nature to do their pleasure',[14] and which is the origin of the dying and resurrected God, scapegoat and sacrifice, and its periphery of attendant figures and related stories and, far removed from this, 'religion' which is a subsequent and ethically much higher development, 'a perfect submission to the divine will in all things'[15] and an imitation, so far as human imperfection allows, of God's moral nature. He speaks of religion, as he defines it, with great respect; of magic, and the myths which he believes embody it, in a tone either patronising or openly contemptuous. It and they retain their hold among 'the dull, the weak, the ignorant, the superstitious, who constitute, unfortunately, the vast majority of mankind.'[16] The mythopoeic temper, connected with a belief in the efficacy of magic, is a standing menace to civilisation, a solid layer of savagery among the subterranean masses throughout the world, barely held in check by the cultured and intelligent few who maintain civilised standards, reason and morals. Frazer's sense of his own superiority to the mind of the primitive savage and that of the contemporary populace, which are indeed fundamentally the same, is expressed with an innocent directness:

One of the great achievements of the nineteenth century was to run shafts down into this low mental stratum in many parts of the world and thus discover its substantial identity everywhere. It is beneath our feet...[17]

Behind any particular doubts or difficulties in the contemporary views of myth, or any specific points in them Chesterton might have wished to take up, lies the great dilemma of a cultural split to which they bear witness. They express with peculiar militancy the views of a self-consciously intellectual minority. Müller and Frazer adopt very different explanations of myth but in both writers the opening terms of their arguments are dictated by a distrust of story, of the *concrete* embodiment of the supernatural. It must, their readers are made to feel, be irrational, the impulse behind it, with Frazer, or its incidental features, with Müller, exciting distaste.

In the leading figures of the anthropological school which dominated Edwardian, as opposed to Victorian views of myth, Gilbert Murray and Jane Harrison, there is no such overt expression of distaste for the primitive imagination, for fable and for the concrete realisation and personification of the supernatural. The devaluation of the appetite for fable is more subtle, and more effective. For Murray, 'religion' is the inevitable relationship a man must have to the uncharted tracts of life, involving his whole being rather than simply the conscious reason. What is gained from it is a precious possession, hard to define, but lying at the 'heart not only of religion, but of art and poetry and all the higher strivings of human emotion',[18] namely practical guidance in some questions where experience and argument fail. Where Jane Harrison was sympathetic to the primitive mind and its 'religion of fear',[19] Murray, who popularised her work, was not. His tone was harder and more categorical, and his influence much greater. Within the religious impulse, which he, though an agnostic, accepts as a noble one, the solid particularity and concreteness of the way in which the Greeks saw their gods is a very lowly element:

The process of making winds and rivers into anthropomorphic gods is, for the most part, not the result of using the imagination with special vigour. It is the result of not doing so.[20]

Of course, this effect of 'normal human laziness' was fortified and adorned by literary art of a high order in Homer. If, however, we penetrate behind 'these gods of the artist's workshop and the romance-maker's imagination'[21] we find entirely different conceptions. In the age of the highest civilisation, 'the religious thinkers of the great period' have conceptions of God which are subtle and rarified, not easy for primitive man to grasp. In the mind of primitive man is found not the God of the philosophers, nor the anthropomorphic gods and heroes of the myths embellished by artists in a literary culture but 'collective desire' and 'collective dread' concentrated 'on two things, the food-supply and the tribe-supply, the desire not to die of famine and not to be harried or conquered by a neighbouring tribe.'[22] Murray's account suggests that these straightforward physical needs and the placatory rites to which they give birth are the roots of the religious impulse. The advent of the Olympian Gods, the second of the 'five stages' of Greek religion represents a moral expurgation and a bringing of intellectual order, reducing to a minimal remnant the rites connected with Food-supply and Tribe-supply. Finally, Murray remarks, in a passage which explicitly and interestingly reveals his sympathies:

the Olympian movement swept away also for two splendid centuries, the worship of the man-god, with its diseased atmosphere
of megalomania and blood lust. These things return after the fall
of Hellenism.[23]

Philosophy and the moulding of beautiful anthropomorphic creations in art and myth are the result of a temporary victory of human
reason and dignity. The appeal of myth is not that it is a fundamental
human impulse or need. Its attractiveness is a quality imparted by
gifted artists in a minority culture. The fears of the masses wait to
return and swamp this higher civilisation of the élite and the rise of
Christianity and its rival oriental cults are, in Murray's well-known
phrase, simply 'the failure of nerve'.

A glance at the point of departure for some of the most important
studies of myth before and during Chesterton's career is interesting
in several ways. It reveals, for one thing, the arbitrariness and
fragility of the assumptions on which professional careers and
academic frames of reference have been founded. For another, it
suggests that the faults within a discipline may well lie in assumptions, especially cultural attitudes, rather than in a failure of scholarly procedures or factual accuracy. Precision over dates and
references was not Chesterton's, as it undoubtedly was Müller's,
strongest point. However, his apparent instinct to turn away from
minute scholarship to look rather at structures of feeling, premises
to arguments, the unspoken or unspecified backgrounds or contexts
of the views he combatted, may often have been adequately justified.
This is rarely more strikingly the case than in his work on myth.

In important respects, the assumptions behind Müller's, Frazer's
and Murray's writings are similar. Historically, they are of course,
curiously dated, very much linked to the temporary dominance of
Western Europe over Africa and Asia. In Frazer's case, Edmund
Leach has explicitly pointed to *The Golden Bough* as an apology for
colonialism:

The overall effect is to represent 'savages' as stupid. . . . Frazer was
writing at precisely the point when European colonial expansion
had reached its peak: It must have been consoling for many

153

liberal-minded imperialists to find that the 'White Man's Burden' could be justified by such detached scholarly procedures.[24]

However, while this may have been applicable to Frazer, it hardly seems fair to the radical anti-imperialist Gilbert Murray. Perhaps it is sounder to place these writers within a cultural rather than a simple political context. They illustrate a fear and suspicion of the beauties and satisfactions of fable and unite in denying that myth-making is a joyful act of creation, valuable at a 'primitive level'. They refuse to accept or discuss it as a primal human urge. Related to this, in each of them, there appears to be a distaste for popular, that is to say concrete, embodiments of religious experience. Underlying all their responses to the question of myth, is detectable the reaction of an embattled intellectual minority against the mass.

If one notes the literary, as opposed to the religious or anthropological climate in which Chesterton undertook his work on myth, the case is strengthened for believing that his greatest problem in that work was bridging a contemporary cultural division. Indeed it is reasonable to infer this from the time he gives in *The Defendant* essays, which launched him before the public, to the defence of popular culture and specifically to those elements of the art of fiction which had been rejected by the educated. They are, in a word, its mythic elements. The most clearly influential, the seminal statements on literary art in the later nineteenth century, standing as they do at the beginning of the novel-form's rise to dominance, are notable, among much else, for this rejection. George Eliot's declaration of the nature and scope of her art in *Adam Bede*[25] and Henry James's essay on 'The Art of Fiction', to name the most obvious examples, announce a change of direction, intended to make the novel fully adult, suitable for an intelligent mature reader, for a serious criticism of life. Involved in the new claims, for Eliot, are sacrifices, of the effort to transcend experience, to render it as more beautiful or mysterious than it is, of that 'glamour' which Chesterton in *The Victorian Age in Literature* criticised her for lacking.[26] It is easy, she says, to draw a griffin, much harder and more worthwhile to render things as they are in the light of common day. For James what must be sacrificed are the thrilling qualities of fiction, the long, involved, exciting plots which stir curiosity rather than the faculty of moral and psychological discrimination and which overturn the design necessary in finished art. Both of these programmes for the novel's future involve surrendering what Chesterton later singled out as those very traits which make for a sense of *timelessness* in prose narrative, rather than a sense of bondage to time and circumstance. They are the qualities of epic and of myth; absorption, exaltation, celebration, satisfactions basic to story-telling from its earliest history. Now, as Chesterton tried to show from the time of his first defences of popular culture, it was in 'Penny-Dreadfuls' and detective stories, despised and banished by the educated, that the remnants of these vital fictive concerns still lingered on. Chesterton was conscious from the outset of that division between the story-tellers and the philosophers on which he laid emphasis in *The Everlasting Man*. He seems, in fact, to have viewed it as the leading cultural feature of his time.

(It is, perhaps, hardly necessary to argue that Chesterton's philosophical defence of popular culture and the mythopoeic imagination was altogether more different, much more serious, than the self-conscious 'intellectual slumming' of his near contemporary Andrew Lang, discussed by John Gross.[27] Lang's scholarly work on myth was of considerable stature but as Gross makes clear his defences of adventure stories did not represent an interest in their mythic qualities. Rather it was deliberately aimed at a middle-brow public and was partly, also, the result of his own intellectual laziness and moral timidity in the face of disturbing issues in fiction).

Chesterton encountered the distaste for myth as a mode of discourse in specific tasks he set himself. Obviously his first work on Dickens (1906) can scarcely be fully understood unless it is seen, in very considerable part, as a reaction to the study (1898) George Gissing had published a little before. It is not an attack on Gissing personally but a controversial book taking issue with a spokesman of the advanced literary culture of the time. The most significant matter of debate is the function and value of myth and fable in writing. Gissing, mentioned by name at important points in *Charles Dickens*, is the implied adversary throughout Chesterton's effort to establish the opening terms of his debate, his frame of reference.

Gissing may be seen as the counterpart, in the purely literary field, of the cultural limitations embodied by Müller, Frazer and Murray in comparative mythology. He provides a representative example of the other half of the context necessary to a fuller understanding of Chesterton's view of myth and fable.

Charles Dickens: a critical study offers a reasoned and weighty defence of its subject, a plea for considering him seriously as an artist. Gissing assumes himself, and takes it that his readers will feel, that exaggeration, fantasy, fable, the mythic, are inadmissible. His tactic is to prove that everything that resembles them in Dickens' writing is really something else. Dickens' characters are not like 'figures in the Old Moralities', a kind of art Gissing takes to be indefensible. They are:

> not abstractions, but men and women of such loud peculiarities, so aggressively individual in mind and form that they forever proclaim themselves the children of a certain country, of a certain time, of a certain rank. Clothed abstractions do not take upon the memory as the people of Dickens did from the day of their coming to life.[28]

The secret of their power lies in the 'actuality'. True they may at times seem strange but eccentrics and grotesques were more common sixty years before in that repellent period every aspect of which, in Gissing's view, was ugly, although this had been alleviated by the growth of culture between Dickens' early years and his own. Dickens was the 'later school of English fiction'. By 'taking hold upon the life nearest to him, making use of it for literature and proving that it *was* of interest',[29] he initiated that kind of social realism of which Gissing himself was a practitioner. Indeed had the word then been in use, Dickens would certainly have called himself a Realist. Admittedly there were fairy-story, popular or non-realistic elements in his novels:

> Everybody (or all but everybody) is to be made happy for ever after; knavish hearts are softened by gratitude and those of the good beat high in satisfied benevolence. This is the kind of thing that delights the public.[30]

Gissing, as the tone of this comment suggests, regards such facets of Dickens' art as weaknesses, concessions to popular taste which he implies are bad in themselves. He roundly condemns Dickens at the point where he was most rooted in the popular art and sensibility of the times, in those plays of sentiment and melodrama which dominated the theatres and commanded huge audiences until the 'reforms' and realism associated with Tom Robertson, the Bancrofts and Pinero. The exaggeration, histrionics, rhetoric and feeling inseparable from this kind of art are, in Gissing's view simply bad:

> Dickens's love for the stage was assuredly a misfortune to him as an author and man.[31]

Such a view leads naturally enough to a determination to see individual characters where they succeed as successes of the realistic method, exact pieces of social observation: (Bagstock and Toots represent quite as truthfully figures possible in a certain class, as do Thackeray's characters in another).[32] Gissing avoids the problems of his frame of reference by deft manoeuvres in specific instances. Realism is the highest kind of art, perhaps the only admissible kind. Dickens is clearly of the highest quality. Therefore Dickens must be a realist. Exaggeration and the fabulous are bad. Dickens cannot then really exaggerate. Instead, he must report. How, then, can one explain Mrs Gamp? She is, he insists, realistic, 'a sick nurse, living in Kingsgate Street, Holborn, in a filthy room, somewhere upstairs ... a very loathsome creature; a sluttish, drunken, avaricious, dishonest woman.'[33] So repulsive is she, that Dickens in order to render her acceptable to persons of good taste, makes her funny:

> In Mrs Gamp, Dickens has done his own Bowdlerizing but with a dexterity, which serves only to heighten his figure's effectiveness.... Vileness on the other hand becomes grotesquerie, wonderfully converted into the subject of laughter.[34]

This tortuous reasoning is worth quoting not only because Gissing's book is one of the immediate occasions of Chesterton's Dickensian studies, but also as an instance of the lengths to which an able writer may be driven to reconcile intransigent facts he cannot avoid seeing

with artistic premisses he will not abandon. Curiously and reveal-
ingly, Gissing does, at least once, touch the frontiers of the mythic
but he does so in a fashion which shows he finds the subject jejune.
He remarks of *Pickwick* that 'one may discourse about it in good set
terms, pointing out that it belongs to a very old school of narrative
and indicating resemblances with no less a work than Don
Quixote,'[35] if, presumably, one finds such an approach worth
pursuing, or such an 'old school of narrative' worth talking about,
both of which seem doubtful.

Not surprisingly, Gissing greatly prefers the later Dickens, especially *Little Dorrit*, which may be more easily accommodated to his
literary criteria. This novel he views as the adult, as opposed to the
childish, Dickens, critical terms which are themselves symptomatic:

> The reason is plain, in this book, Dickens has comparatively little
> of his wonted buoyancy.... Whereas a competent judge, taking
> up the book as he would any other will find in it some of the best
> work of Dickens, especially in this matter of characteristic pic-
> tures, so wholly admirable, so marvellously observed.[36]

The impression Gissing's study gives is an odd one. The points he
makes are not indefensible in themselves but he is unwilling or
unable wholeheartedly to *enjoy* Dickens. He must defend or extenu-
ate by strained arguments and in an inappropriate idiom, what is
most vital and attractive in the Dickens world, its mythic quality.

The critic's problem is his own artistic ideology. Perhaps one's
misgivings about the words missing from his vocabulary, or the
conceptions absent from his mental landscape arise particularly in
relation to Gissing's description of Mr Sapsea's epitaph on his wife in
Edwin Drood. His remark that in this case Dickens has been 'guilty of
a piece of exaggeration altogether exceeding the limits of art',[37]
epitomises the prevailing tendency of his analysis. He is plainly
embarrassed by the exuberant, the larger than life, the escape of the
human personality from the limits of 'real' time, 'real' circumstance,
verisimilitude. Beneath the critical vocabulary Gissing employs, as
beneath the scholarly apparatus of Müller, Frazer and Murray,
lurks a 'religious' or philosophical attitude. With him, as with them,
it is neither demonstrated nor argued. It is simply assumed.

Chesterton was not unique in grasping the importance of the cultural split which had developed in the later nineteenth century. It could be plausibly argued that much of Kipling's inspiration and popularity stemmed from understanding it and from exploiting some of the literary potential of popular sensibility and artistic forms.

In pointed defiance of the preciosity of the 'l'art pour l'art' school he chose to model himself on the ballad maker who functioned as the mere vehicle of folk memory and whose aim was to convey to ordinary men the truths implicit in their own experience.[38]

The comparison with Chesterton is an illuminating one. Kipling, unlike Chesterton, approached the field as a series of questions about technique, of what he as an artist could get out of the deliberate cultivation of vulgarity, the metre or spirit of music-hall, the linguistic resources of slang. He is not concerned to explore the philosophical or religious implication of the gulf he is bridging in his, often extremely fruitful, raids into another consciousness. The spoils are enough, for him and his readers. At the limits of his mind there does exist, somewhat poignantly, an intimation of the 'mythic' or 'fabulous' quality of the material he utilised:

Some day a man will rise up from Bermondsey, Battersea or Bow and he will be coarse but clear-sighted, hard, but infinitely and tenderly humorous, speaking the people's tongue, steeped in their lines, and telling them in swinging, urging ringing verse what it is their inarticulate lips would express. He will make them songs. Such songs! And all the little poets who pretend to sing to the people will scuttle away like rabbits, for the Girl, (who, as you have seen, is, of course Wisdom) will tell that Soldier (who is Hercules bowed under his labours) all that she knows of Life and Death and Love. And the same they say is vulgarity.[39]

As far as Kipling has a terminology to express this intimation about his material, it is that of astrology. It does not really fit the case. In the above quotation something beyond the external facts of experience is certainly announced but it cannot be particularised. The Soldier and the Girl remain as portentous, rigid classification.

Kipling's few attempts to explore the mythic are undeveloped, largely perhaps because of his inadequate terminology and his lack of a grasp of general ideas.

Comparison with Kipling reveals the nature of the contribution Chesterton was peculiarly equipped to make. He was strong in the area where Kipling was weakest, the ability to take an argument back fruitfully to first principles, to expose the opening terms of his contemporaries' account of, or failure to account for, myth, in thought and in literature. It may be urged that in following this concern in Chesterton's work there is a danger of blurring too many edges, in thought, (historical, political, cultural) and in genre; that in seeking to gain a synthetic view, too much material is being compared over too long a period. However, with regard to the first point, one leading aspect of Chesterton's critique was that the age of myth and fable had not ceased. The appetite and the faculty continued to exist in humble, unsuspected places. A seemingly light essay on 'Penny-Dreadfuls' might, then, offer an insight as necessary to the full understanding of his position as a considered account of primitive religious myths. The length of time covered by the writing suggests a running battle between Chesterton and his time, a constant returning to points he felt necessary but that his contemporaries seemed unable to see.

'A Defence of Penny Dreadfuls' like the other defences of popular culture in Chesterton's first important book, is concerned to expose buried, but living traditions, slighted by the educated élite, neglect of which upsets the balance of their view of life. Chesterton connects the 'invisible dramatis personae' of the child's first imaginary world, the professional story-teller of the East, the ballads of Robin Hood and the boys' comics of his own time, as manifestations of a fictive urge more significant and universal than the aesthetic ideals and concerns of the few:

> The simple need for some kind of ideal world in which fictitious persons play an ideal part is infinitely deeper and older than the rules of good art, and much more important.[40]

The comics are not some new manifestation of cultural degeneration or declining standards. The story-telling impulse has always existed and has no necessary connection with form, construction or technique, the hall-marks of high art.

Literature and fiction are two entirely different things. Literature is a luxury; fiction is a necessity.[41]

Literature is written to show the author's wit or skill, as a *tour-de-force*, or for the satisfaction of making an object as perfect as possible. Fiction, on the other hand, celebrates the sense of timelessness and freedom. The impulses behind them are too different for fruitful comparison:

A work of art can hardly be too short for its climax is its merit. A story can never be too long, for its conclusion is merely to be deplored.[42]

The 'increase in the artistic conscience' tends more and more to brevity and impressionism. The popular myths, whether of Robin Hood or Dick Deadshot, have no end since 'these two heroes are deliberately conceived as immortal.'[43]

This last remark is not a casual verbal flourish. Chesterton quite clearly connects fiction, in his meaning of the term, with a sense of, or hunger for, the supernatural, for immortality in fact. The distinction, drawn in 'A Defence of Penny Dreadfuls' is developed and deepened five years later, in the chapter on *The Pickwick Papers* in *Charles Dickens*, one of the most cogent and attractive of Chesterton's early discussions of myth.

This important account opens by pinpointing the mythic element underlying Dickens's creation, the fact that the surface movement and machinery of the novels are intended to display *static* character:

Things in the Dickens story shift and change only in order to give us glimpses of great characters who do not change at all.[44]

Colonel Newcome, in Thackeray's realistic novel, lives in the medium of time. Pickwick does not. To most modern readers this will seem praise of Thackeray, criticism of Dickens:

161

But this only shows how few modern people understand Dickens. It also shows how few people understand the faiths and fables of mankind.[45]

Myth and fable are, in one of their essential aspects, a celebration of timelessness, a quality retained in the 'fading supernaturalism' of much popular literature:

> The popular preference for a story with a happy ending is not, or at least was not, a mere sweet-stuff optimism; it is the remains of the old idea of the triumph of the dragon-slayer, the ultimate apotheosis of the man beloved of heaven.[46]

Where old myth and its contemporary traces, (the latter 'stormed at by silly magistrates, sneered at by silly schoolmasters') escape mortality, the literature of the educated minority is in thrall to it. This new 'literature' is really a very recent and somewhat curious phenomenon, a fancy for writing down our own or similar lives in order to look at them.

> It imitates not only life, but the limitations of life; it not only reproduces life, it reproduces death.[47]

The preference for the short story in modern writing is not 'an accident of form' but has its roots in religious or philosophical attitudes:

> It is the sign of a real sense of fleetingness and fragility.[48]

Realistic 'mature' literature is concerned with limits. Myth, fable, or folklore extend 'quite normal desires' beyond such limitations. The first mode of narrative is endorsed as adult and intellectually respectable by those who form educated opinion. The second is condemned. But both endorsement and condemnation are the result of metaphysical assumptions about the nature of reality.

They are also, Chesterton feels, partly caused by inhibitions, by an inability to enjoy or to accept a common experience of heightened reality, by a failure, in some at least, to appreciate the meaning of those occasions when the 'god-like' shows itself. The often-quoted passage in which this point is made is not, perhaps, what it looks out

A Right View of Myth

of context, a praise of conviviality or alcoholic expansiveness. Rather it is a hint of what Mircea Eliade has called 'Great Time' or the 'Paradisiac state':

To every man alive, one must hope, it has in some manner happened that he has talked with his more fascinating friends round a table some one night when all the numerous personalities unfolded themselves like great tropical flowers. All fell into their parts as in some delightful impromptu play. Every man was more himself than he had ever been in this vale of tears.[49]

These normal and natural visitations of ecstasy, or a reality behind what daily routine or material circumstances allow to appear are a hint of the appetite which makes myths and ensures that 'the whole moral world is a factory of immortals'. The important point is not that personality is unreal or an illusion. It is more real, more stable and strongly defined, more joyfully itself than habits or mundane events and worries allow it to appear. A problem in understanding this part of the mythic impulse is the fading in the modern educated mind of the desire for endless or timeless joy, of the life that lasts forever:

Both popular religion with its endless joys and the old comic story with its endless jokes, have in our time faded together. We are too weak to desire that undying vigour. We believe you can have too much of a good thing.[50]

Chesterton sees the process which brings mythologising to an end not in the manner of his contemporaries as a loss of superstitious awe, or of the sense of mystery under the onset of reason or science, a regrettable or admirable process but, in any case an inevitable one; rather it is the difficult psychological problem of the loss of a love of life in many educated men of his own time: 'We have come to be afraid of an eternity of joy.'[51] Clearly one does not wish for more, and more abundant, life if one does not greatly care for life in the first place.

It is easy, therefore, to see why Chesterton in attempting to answer Gissing's misinterpretation of Dickens, his undervaluing of myth, should concentrate, initially on the matter of joy. Incidentally, of course, as Chesterton points out Gissing sees the early Dickens period as hard and cruel because he omits the note of hope born of a new post-1789 value of the common man and popular culture and aspiration:

> Its education, its public habits, its rhetoric were all addressed towards encouraging the greatness in everybody.[52]

It is, to some extent, the waning of this liberal tide after 1870 which cuts a despondent intelligentsia from a sense of the value of ordinary life, of the generality of men and their creative possibilities, and of the popular roots of myth. Chesterton remarks in a political context that:

> the note of the last few decades in art and ethics has been that man is stamped with an irrevocable psychology and is cramped for perpetuity in the prison of his own skull.[53]

Beyond the political and social lie the moral, emotional and psychological aspects of the problem of the loss of a capacity in many of Chesterton's generation for creating myths and appreciating a mythic art like that of Dickens. There has been a withering of the urge to endless celebratory stories, to the heightening and extension of experience in heroic cycles, or towards imagining characters outside time. Here, the difficulty, at heart, is a habit of sadness. Chesterton exhorts his educated readers, if they are to understand a mythic art, at least in imagination, to 'surrender the very flower of your culture; give up the very jewel of your pride; abandon hopelessness all ye who enter here.'[54] It is surely not accidental that in considering this art where plot is an 'invocation for calling down a god' Chesterton should single out as expressing the essential Dickens, Mr Sapsea's epitaph on his wife which Gissing had used to illustrate Dickens' excess or failure. This suggests a deliberate rebuttal of the Gissing conception of reality, stressing that important element of myth, the escape from time:

> You could scarcely have such immortal folly as that in a world where there is also death. Mr Sapsea is one of the golden things stored up for us in a better world.[55]

(It is worth noting, incidentally, the boldness and novelty of Chesterton's valuation of the mythic in art. Writing on children's literature where, in a sense, the mythic held its own in the later nineteenth century, such as that of Ruskin, of Andrew Lang or such a well-reasoned pedagogical defence as that of J. Newby Hetherington, confine themselves to asserting that fairy-stories *are* suitable for children and that the older versions should be left alone, and not moralised or sentimentalised. They make no such claims as those of Chesterton).

The groundwork of Chesterton's working out of his philosophy of myth both embodies, and displays the value of the dichotomy in his nature. Clearly Chesterton had two sides to his head. Both were brought into play in his consideration of myth, to achieve a peculiarly comprehensive and balanced view of the subject. When one remembers the deficiencies and dangers of the intellectual context against which he worked, these qualities of inclusiveness and sanity are specially notable. One side of Chesterton has received ample notice. This is the rational Chesterton with his stress on the concreteness of things, on reason, logic, form and definition, on order and the 'Roman heritage'. The other side, though a little less well known, is no less important; the Chesterton of the grotesque, of myth, fable, folklore and story, of the non-verbal language of *Manalive*, convinced that life and reality are mysteriously themselves, not explicable by reason or categorising, being, in essence, more like a fable than a logical sequence. Chesterton needed both of the chief weapons of his intellectual armoury, since he was fighting a war on two fronts. On the first of these he had to insist on the validity of myth against scholars such as Müller who saw the *Rig Veda* as the first stage in the development of the Aryan mind towards its fulfilment in Kant's *Critique of Pure Reason*, myth, that is, as only a feeble anticipation of philosophy and against literary critics like Gissing who viewed myth only as childish intrusions or lapses in the presentation of 'reality'. In his fight against these tendencies Chesterton emphasised the rights of fable to a place of honour in the minds and culture of men:

The only two things that can satisfy the soul are a person and a story; and even a story must be about a person. There are indeed very voluptuous appetites and enjoyments in mere abstractions – like mathematics, logic or chess. But these mere pleasures of the mind are like mere pleasures of the body. That is, they are mere pleasures...; they can never by mere increase of themselves amount to happiness.[56]

Myth is not an outmoded first glimmering of philosophy or of a more 'spiritual' religion. It does not stand for or symbolise the ultimate reality which is the external world. Rather external objects symbolise the ultimate reality which is spiritual.

In his first sustained examination of the nature of the moral institutions fable and popular folk tales offer, 'The Ethics of Elfland', he claims that the mythic view presents a truer picture of the world because unlike a materialist science it has no simple belief in the 'law' of cause and effect. The sense of wonder, from which myth springs and to which it ministers, might be called a 'higher agnosticism' since it does not try to impose on an essentially mysterious universe as a law what is merely an association of two events, a notion that 'because one incomprehensible thing constantly follows another incomprehensible thing the two somehow make up a comprehensible thing.'[57] The sharp feeling of amazement the fables evoke is part of a mythic art which tries to touch a nerve gone dead, a primal sense of wonder which is the first and truest reaction to experience. This wonder, like the feeling of timelessness, is forgotten in the delusive sense of life as normal, ordinary, or routine:

All that we call common sense and practicality and positivism only means that for certain dead levels of our life we forget that we have forgotten. All that we call spirit and art and ecstasy only means that for one awful moment we remember that we forget.[58]

I have confined myself in this chapter to *part* of the controversial context of Chesterton's early view of myth, that governed by the literary and philosophical hostility to mythic apprehension. Obviously, however, it is necessary to appreciate the other front on which he was fighting to realise the phenomenon of displaced or perverted myth as a dominant factor in shaping his views towards their mature expression in *The Everlasting Man*. The second half of the context would require an essay to itself. It is also, perhaps, more familiar to the reader of Chesterton.

Paradoxically, though hostile to myth and fable as the spontaneous creations and expressions of popular feelings, apprehensions and moral intuitions, the climate of the whole of Chesterton's career was exceedingly indulgent to myths fostered by intellectuals themselves. It is a truism that history, and scientific and social thought in his time were dominated by myths which were not recognised as such. Chesterton, the advocate of myth in its true role and right place, was the implacable opponent of the displaced or perverted mythopoeic faculty in action, which increasingly produced much of what passed for thought in his time. One need only recall his attacks on the Superman, the eugenics, on doctrines of racial superiority and inferiority, on the abuses of evolutionary theory, on the historicism which proved the 'inevitable' rise or decline of civilisations, all of which coloured the minds of very many of his contemporaries. His position in challenging these obsessions relied on logic and reason. He questioned the premises and connecting links in the arguments which supported these myths and pointed out fallacies and *non-sequiturs*. He defended philosophy against mythopoeic insult as he had buttressed myth against intellectual contempt.

The unfolding of Chesterton's thought on this subject is towards a balance of reason and imagination, fable and philosophy. *The Everlasting Man* is, of course, the point where this is fully treated, becoming, in fact, the focus for a sketch of human thought and history. It offers, among much else, a sympathetic but not uncritical picture of the mind of the 'philosophers', an 'intellectual aristocracy' with a delight in theorising and a prevailing temptation to insane simplifications; the cast of mind in effect, of Chesterton's early adversaries in his defence of myth. But it also represents the conclusion of that other defence, of objective fact and of logic against perverted myth, a degenerate hybrid of imagination and impulses of fatalism, boredom and the hunger for power and quick results. Chesterton examines the limits of both the mythic and the reasoning faculty, their need to be joined in a synthesis, their need, above all, for an objective conclusion, fulfilling both the stories and the theories, satisfying and bringing into harness two impulses which otherwise could never meet and which wrongly denied each other's validity. At first, his final view of myth may seem cautious, compared with the first defences of 'Penny-Dreadfuls' and of the art of Dickens, but it is conditioned partly by a different polemical need, partly by a wish to strike a balance between two divergent impulses. There is a sense in which his description of the last stages of the pagan world seems appropriate to the cultural split to which he was opposed in his own time:

Mythology is a *search*; it is something that combines a recurrent desire with a recurrent doubt, mixing a most hungry sincerity in the idea of seeking for a place with a most dark and deep and mysterious levity about all the places found. So far could the lonely imagination lead, and we must turn later to the lonely reason. Nowhere along this road did the two ever travel together.[59]

VIII

A TRUE SENSE OF THE GROTESQUE

Borges' important short piece on Chesterton singles out, probably rightly, the two critical studies with which he made his literary début as in some way typical of his essential nature:

> His personality leaned towards the nightmarish, something secret, blind and central. Not in vain did he dedicate his first works to the justification of two great Gothic craftsmen, Browning and Dickens.[1]

Most readers interested in Chesterton, while grateful for this contribution to the recent increase of serious attention he has been getting, are likely to feel that Borges' reading of his innermost spirit is wrong. Yet, they might accept that while the conclusion is false, the area of emphasis is correct. Much of vital significance about Chesterton is displayed in those combative, deliberately controversial rehabilitations, a concern, above all, with the grotesque, in experience and in art. This chapter will explore Chesterton's view of the grotesque in its intellectual context, especially his return to the first formulations and spirit of Victor Hugo, which had been either forgotten or misinterpreted by his contemporaries and immediate predecessors.

In his two early critical forays, on Browning and on Dickens, Chesterton engaged in a number of tasks. Both books were obviously and successfully rescues: of Dickens, from critics or defenders who attacked or condoned his superficiality; of Browning from those

reverent admirers who insisted on his 'profundity'. Characteristically good tempered, they are outstanding examples of literary
polemic, the overwhelmingly convincing demolition of a false and
time-wasting view of a subject. Chesterton rendered it impossible to
view Dickens or Browning as George Gissing or Professor Forman
viewed them. Fruitful and important as this work of demolition was,
it is, perhaps, less significant than Chesterton's deeper controversial
intention. Beyond the removal of misconceptions about individual
authors, the underlying direction of the two books is towards a
wholesale examination and defence of the 'larger than life' element
in art. The studies of Browning and Dickens are seminal statements
of Chesterton's aesthetic views.

Conveniently they break the 'larger than life' into two separate
elements: the nature of fable, the basis of consideration in the work
on Dickens, and the 'grotesque', the primary subject of study in
Robert Browning. The grotesque Chesterton sees as the proof of
Nature's energy, or rather the energy of God in nature, 'energy that
takes its own forms and goes its own way'.[2] The grotesque is the
refusal of the living force of Nature to conform to narrow aesthetic
views, the conventionally 'beautiful' harmony of proportion and
form, the diluted heritage of Greek classicism. It is, too, evidence of
an artistic energy which escapes jejune or limited notions of what is
beautiful, those which concentrate on the supposed needs of civilised
man, or defer to the received opinions of art critics.

Readers will at once recall instances of Chesterton's excursions
into this field in his very early work: 'A Defence of Skeletons', or 'A
Defence of Ugly Things', (both 1900), first traces of a tendency
which was to undergo some alteration before it culminated in *The
Man who was Thursday* as a fictional concern, and in essay form in 'On
the Book of Job' (1929). It is in 'A Defence of Ugly Things' that
Chesterton, leaning, as will be shown, on Hugo's *Preface to Cromwell*,
makes his most trenchant and direct attack on the Greek classical
ideal of harmony and proportion. This short manifesto on behalf of
the grotesque, among the very first of his articles published in the
Speaker, is interesting because it stands at the very start of his literary
career, antedating even the book on Browning. He roundly attacks
the classical ideal as 'a worship of one aesthetic type alone.'[3] The

170

Greeks 'carried their police regulations into elfland'[4] out of a timid avoidance of the wild ideas, the violent combinations of the imagination which mankind naturally love. Consequently their fantasy is anaemic compared with fairy-tale or 'Scandinavian story'. Chesterton adds, borrowing from Hugo:

Who ever feels that the giants in Greek art and poetry were really big – big as some folk-lore giants have been.[5]

What applies in the realm of imagination affects also our way of seeing the world. Greek restraint 'this disgraceful *via media*, this pitiful sense of dignity' makes us, against our instinct, view powerful and endearing faces as ugly, silly and repulsive faces as beautiful. Left to itself, mankind spontaneously prefers 'size, vitality, variety, energy, ugliness',[6] which ultimately are qualities of Nature. 'Ugliness' in aesthetics is a recognition of the primal quality of Nature or life. It is not at this stage, as it became, significantly, later in Chesterton's view, a question of humour. Rather Nature is considered as an artist breaking fresh ground by 'her bold experiments, her definite departures, her fearlessness and her savage pride in her children.'[7]

It would be hard to deny that, in themselves, these early statements possess little more than a passing interest, one derived mainly from such light as they presumptively throw on Chesterton's mature use of the grotesque and as little seeds or faint anticipations of *The Man who was Thursday*. It would, however, be a mistake to view them only looking forward to Chesterton's later career. To understand their true significance it is necessary to look backwards, to see them within their intellectual context. Chesterton's liking for the grotesque and his writing on it, have, besides, been discussed very much within a framework of his personality and psychology, where of necessity much must be guesswork and assumption. Their background in terms of debate and the history of ideas, vitally important in a career built so much and so consciously on intellectual controversy has, perhaps, not been given sufficient attention. The tone and manner of Chesterton's utterances on the grotesque seem more likely to stem from what others had said or failed to say than from some conjectural subconscious motive.

It is probable that Chesterton wrote against the current of a view of the grotesque originating in Walter Pater, specifically in Pater's misinterpretation of Hugo. However, the full understanding of the debate requires a still wider context. It is useful to see what directions Hugo's original view of the grotesque had, and how Pater changed its tone and emphasis. But also how, because of the tendency among other critics writing in English on the grotesque, to underrate it and fail either to explore or do it justice, Pater's powerful and subtle views held the field at the time when Chesterton began to formulate his theories, largely in opposition to them; theories which were, in essence, a return to Hugo's first pronouncements.

Victor Hugo's name is clearly central to the assumed background of the debate in which Chesterton was involved, since the *Preface to Cromwell* (1827) must be taken as the seminal document on the grotesque, at least in England. Hugo's *Preface*, rather than Hegel's *Essay on the Grotesque* was the probable point of departure for English readers because it is written in an accessible style where Hegel is peculiarly dense and technical and likely to appeal only to a minority among professional philosophers, even in a period when Hegelianism was highly influential. It is, of course, true, as Clayborough has pointed out,[8] that the *Preface to Cromwell* uses a basically Hegelian framework, one which stresses the antithetical elements of man working towards resolution, and a tripartite division of human history into primitive or the age of the ode, classical or the age of the epic, and romantic or the age of the drama, in the last of which a synthesis of the material and spiritual is reached. The *Preface*, however, is a bright succession of striking generalisations rather than a laborious treatise. It is a lively sketch of human history offered with a polemical purpose in the context of Hugo's war against 'Classical' canons in the French theatre leading up to the scandal and triumph of *Hernani*, and in the current of liberalism moving towards the 1830 Revolution. Its appeal is instantaneous.

Perhaps the most significant point about Hugo's view of the grotesque, taken up, after a long interval, by Chesterton, is his placing of it firmly as an aspect of necessary and desirable moral and social development, and extension of human sympathy connected explicitly with growing political freedom. First, in his sketch, comes the innocence of primitive times, 'when man is just awakened', when the earth imposes no fetters on the individual man and 'he is still so near God that all his meditations are ecstatic, all his dreams are visions.'[9] It is time when his 'Lyre has but three strings God; the soul; creation; but this three-fold mystery enwraps everything; this three-fold thought includes everything.'[10] In this first age the poetic temperament is one of prayer and finds expression in the ode. The classical age which follows, Hugo, for polemical purposes, portrays as a falling off from this first freedom and innocence. Dogma lays its hold on worship. Theocracy succeeds patriarchal community. An impressive gravity prevails in public and private morals and an epic spirit dominates, even in the plays. The Greek drama, Hugo states, was essentially a vast civic and religious ritual:

Its characters are still heroes, demigods, gods; its motives, dreams, oracles, fatality; its tableaux, funeral rites and combats.[11]

Everything was remorselessly sacrificed to one ideal standard of beauty, a perfection of physical form and a concentration on the socially exalted. The advent of Christianity Hugo sees as an attack upon a civilisation which had hardened and degenerated. The new religion preached a division of flesh and spirit in man, foreign to a purely materialistic paganism. With the new more complex human model appeared a hitherto unknown sense of contradiction which Hugo calls 'melancholy', the disparity between man's immortal and temporal concerns. The simplicity and harmony of pagan classicism were no longer possible.

This moral change was connected with a social change:

Up to that time catastrophes which befell empires rarely reached to the heart of the people. Kings fell, majestic personages vanished, but that was all.[12]

But now, the violence which brought the Roman Empire to an end affected the great mass of the population. Influenced by it and by Christianity, a religion of 'equality, liberty and charity', there was a much greater sense of social equality:

173

Man, taking thought to himself in the presence of the vicissitudes among the great, began to take pity on his kind and to reflect on the bitter ironies of life.[13]

The logical and fullest development of this spirit, Hugo states, is just emerging in the romantic art, especially drama, of his own time. The new spirit of this art:

will feel that everything in creation is not *beautiful* from the standpoint of mankind, that the ugly exists besides the beautiful, the misshapen besides the graceful, the grotesque beside the sublime.[14]

It will decline to 'set God to right' by rejecting so much of his creation to obtain an ideal beauty by mutilation, to cut man in two.

Hugo sees the Middle Ages, as might be expected of the future author of *Notre Dame de Paris*, as the first great flood of the grotesque, in heraldry, in 'that wonderful architecture', in manners, in laws and eventually in the Church and religion. He describes it, with exhilaration and delight, as a spirit of vigour and creative power.

In considering the treatment of the grotesque by English writers in the fifty years before Chesterton it is hard to dispute Kayser's generalisation that the discussion fell back from 'the high place of the definitions between 1770 and 1830.'[15] In general, apart from the special and very important exception of Pater, a straightforward 'loss of status' for the whole concept of the grotesque may be traced during the period from 1830 to 1900. Much the most significant feature of this process, however, was the refusal of writer after writer to accept the notion of the grotesque as part of a social development: the historical consciousness which was the essence of Hugo's analysis of the term and its moral meaning.

At first, in Ruskin's well-known account in *The Stones of Venice* (1851-3), the grotesque still occupied a relatively high rank. It is, of course, inferior, even in Dante, to the sublimity of the highest art since it results from a sportive instinct which a perfect nature does not partake of:

It is evident that the idea of any kind of play can only be associated with the idea of an imperfect, childish fatigable spirit.[16]

The grotesque impulse, for Ruskin, chiefly occupies a middle rank in the human temper between the perfect, and those either too morose, dull or exhausted to invent a jest. He divides grotesque art into the noble or terrible and the ignoble. The existence of the noble grotesque in art Ruskin takes as a kind of index of the quality of a civilisation. The phenomenon as a whole he sees, much as Hugo in this particular, as a result of the contradiction, consequent upon Christianity, between flesh and spirit:

the fallen human soul, at its best, must be as a diminishing glass, and that a broken one, to the mighty truths of the universe around it.[17]

Ruskin's thoughtful analysis lays weight on the description of spiritual states which seem to be given permanent facts of human nature rather than on any historical process. The temperaments which produce different kinds of art, it would seem, recur in age after age. Along with the loss of historical consciousness and sense of development found in Hugo, there is a tendency to blunt the edge of the grotesque, to soften any bizarre or uncouth quality it might have. The 'noble grotesque' sounds a humourless affair as well as a hardly conceivable hybrid. By importing the notion of 'nobility' Ruskin accommodates the grotesque to contemporary tastes by limiting its capacity to shock.

Later critics showed a disposition to retreat from Ruskin's carefully qualified but nonetheless important place for the grotesque. Clayborough remarks that:

in the later nineteenth century when the romantic view of grotesque art as possessing a 'numinous' transcendental quality loses ground, a ... view of the grotesque becomes current according to which the grotesque is neither a rejection of reality nor an actual part of it; the view that it is a fantasy with a practical aspect; parody burlesque, mockery, caricature.[18]

There seems, also, to lie behind their various dilutions or disintegrations of the concept of the grotesque a persistent sense that art should be dignified and that the grotesque must derogate from it; that its nobility and beauty are the supreme truth and that to admit other elements would overturn the proper and natural hierarchy of aesthetic value.

Walter Bagehot, although well aware of the grotesque on a personal level,[19] was unwilling, in his essay 'Wordsworth, Tennyson and Browning; or, Pure, Ornate and Grotesque Art in English Poetry' (1864), to grant it, except in theory, any significant stature. In spite of a technical admission that 'grotesque art' (a term which he uses to mean ugly or monstrous rather than fantastic) within its limits might be as valid as pure art, he makes it clear that since grotesque subjects require highly specialised treatment the artist had much better leave them alone. In any case and in practice, the grotesque of Browning is far inferior to the pure poetry of Wordsworth or even the ornate poetry of Tennyson.[20]

In Thomas Wright (1865), J.A. Symonds (1890) and George Santayana (1896), there is a perceptible movement further and further away from Hugo's view of the grotesque. The constituents of that view, namely the connection between the grotesque and the religious sense; the 'melancholy' awareness of human contradiction; the link insisted upon between the emergence of the grotesque and the growth of a wider social and human sympathy; the essential part Hugo assigned to it in a fuller view of man and the world, freed from the mutilation caused by a limited aesthetic ideal; the notion of the grotesque as, above all, a token of creative energy; all the rich and suggestive ideas broached in the *Preface to Cromwell* have been abandoned. Wright's simple *History of Caricature and the Grotesque in Literature and Art* states that 'the monstrous is closely allied to the grotesque and both come within the province of caricature when we take this in its widest sense.'[21] It is a definition so loose as to be almost valueless. Nevertheless the intention is plainly to rob the grotesque of deeper psychological or spiritual meaning or significance. For Symonds, in his essay 'Caricature, the Fantastic, the Grotesque':

the grotesque is a branch of the fantastic. Its specific difference lies in the fact of the element of caricature, whether deliberately intruded or imported by the craftsman's spontaneity of humour.[22]

It is, he feels, particularly found in the Teutonic races, and is lacking in Greeks and Orientals. It is, possibly, scarcely necessary to observe that the notion of 'caricature', like that of 'nobility', in the grotesque represents a demotion of the whole category. In Symonds' view it can have no originality and must be parasitic on the 'real' world. Santayana considers the grotesque simply as a name given to artistic novelty and aesthetic effect for a while striking and new in its 'divergence from the natural'. When, however, the effect is more fully understood 'the incongruity with the conventional type disappears and what was impossible and ridiculous at first, takes its place among the recognised ideals.[23] This disappearance of what is startling, Santayana seems to regard as highly desirable. (It is interesting to note that he, like Bagehot, depreciated the grotesque art of Browning which Chesterton was to rehabilitate). Perhaps the ultimate point in this gradual denial of meaning and significance to the grotesque is found in T. Tyndall Wildridge's *The Grotesque in Church Art* (1899) where it is suggested that it resulted from the copying of earlier work 'without a knowledge of its serious meaning',[24] that it was, in fact, a form of incompetence or ignorance.

The movement from Ruskin to Santayana was nothing less than a drying up of interest in a whole category of art and experience. There are some curious paradoxes about this dwindling away of a potentiality. One is the great and continuing popularity with educated Englishmen of Victor Hugo as a playwright, poet and dramatist and his role acknowledged by critics, such as Pater, in the general development of Romanticism, for which, of course, the *Preface to Cromwell* is a prime source. Yet in spite of this, there was a strange unwillingness to take up the ideas on the grotesque contained in the *Preface*. Another anomaly in this failure of intellectual response is suggested by the recollection that it coincided, in England, with the full flood of the Gothic Revival. Surely, one might feel, there ought to have been some connection between the grotesque and the Gothic.

The paradox that this element played little part in the interpretations of Pugin, Ruskin or William Morris is readily explained. They were serious moralists, in their various ways convinced that Gothic art was connected with the simple moral goodness, religious purity or superior social organisation of the medieval world which produced it. It was this which absorbed them rather than the bizarre or fantastic vision as such.

In short, the full range of insights offered by Hugo were too disturbing and wide ranging, raising too many questions both moral and aesthetic. It was preferable to see the grotesque as 'caricature' or as an artist's desire for an original effect because this blunted any challenge it might have to accepted taste or moral standards. Perhaps the whole process of attenuating the sphere and meaning of the grotesque is best viewed as a rear-guard action of intellectual conservatism.

There is, however, one striking exception to the process briefly sketched; Pater's exploration of the connection of the grotesque with the romantic spirit and its animating and vivifying role in art. This sophisticated treatment of the subject, with its obvious influence on the aesthetes of the 1880s and 1890s, is to be found in the 'Postscript' to *Appreciations* (1889), an essay which, however, first appeared as 'Romanticism' in 1876. Because, as has been suggested, other critics abdicated from serious discussion of the grotesque, Pater's view was the most weighty and considered one available, and the one Chesterton felt called upon to encounter.

It has been suggested that Pater's essay, so sharp a contrast to Arnold's 'The Study of Poetry', was itself written as an implicit reply to Arnold, setting energy and sharp contrasts against the moralistic Arnoldian criteria of seriousness and restraint.[25] Certainly the placing of the 'Postscript' in *Appreciations*, analogous to the 'Conclusion' in *The Renaissance*, suggests that it was meant as some kind of credo or definitive summation of the individual studies in the volume.

Pater, recalling Hugo, describes classical restraint and romantic love of the grotesque as two 'tendencies really at work at all times in art, moulding it with the balance sometimes a little on one side, sometimes a little on the other.'[26] Significantly, however, Hugo's scheme of a moral and social *development* is dropped, since the two tendencies have always been present. Pater's notion of a delicate and necessary balance between two conflicting ideals as being the pre-condition of the highest art has some affinity with the 'synthesis' of romantic art in the *Preface to Cromwell* but seems much more an affair of deliberate, and calculating design on the artist's part than a cultural and social phenomenon.

The romantic spirit, according to Pater refuses, though it loves beauty, to have it 'unless the condition of strangeness be first fulfilled.'[27] It must be a beauty born out of the conjunction of unlikely elements, by experiment and a bold alchemy 'a charm which wrings it even out of terrible things.'[28] Recognising the piquancy of the grotesque, Pater sees it as a difficult but essential undertaste in a work of art, a subtle ingredient in the whole effect. The 'eager, excited' romantic spirit 'will have strength, the grotesque first of all'. If enough sweetness and beauty is incorporated the result will be a 'genuine classic', 'and a trace of distortion, of the genuine grotesque, may perhaps linger, as an additional element of expression, about its ultimate grace.'[29] This is like, yet crucially unlike, Hugo's balancing of the sublime and the grotesque. Hugo suggests a broader human sympathy, Pater a more sophisticated artistic effect. Having subtly altered Hugo's views, Pater illustrates the effect he means by drawing several examples from Hugo's own novels. 'The Postscript' is altogether a very deft performance.

Chesterton's relationship to the Aesthetic Movement of the 1880s and 1890s was a more complex one than is often allowed. By selective and familiar quotation it might be made to seem as if he simply combatted their pessimism with cheerfulness, their morbidity with healthy-mindedness, their ideals of art with a jolly popularism. This matter of the grotesque shows the relationship in a different light. He evidently shared Pater's taste for unlikely combinations, deliberate discords or at least was unwilling to surrender the possibilities of vitality and freshness in art which the grotesque might supply.

The persuasiveness of the views Chesterton encountered, ema-nating from Pater's 'Postscript' must be admitted, especially set against the obvious deficiency of the Arnoldian ideal on which they themselves were a covert attack. Even in his controversy on transla-tion with F.W. Newman there is, for most readers, a sense that Arnold is limited, that he is ignoring the value, as artistic resources,

of the rough, the bizarre, the uncouth or the grotesque. Too much
has been sacrificed to dignity and restraint. He is vulnerable to
Pater's quiet but deeply subversive response. Yet, restrained as
Pater characteristically is, his position is open to abuse by coarser
minds, such as that of Oscar Wilde.

The 'Postscript's' emphasis throughout is on the highly self-
conscious artist exploiting the grotesque. The artist seizes on it with
delight, drawn to it for the energy it brings his work. But then he
elaborates upon it, combining it with 'sweetness', achieving an
'alchemy' as Hugo, Pater suggests, does in the figures of Marius and
Cosette. Pater's analysis gives the process an unspontaneous, recondite flavour. Significantly, he describes those periods when this
'temperament' has dominated as those when:

> curiosity may be noticed to take the lead, when men come to art
> and poetry with a deep thirst for intellectual excitement, after a
> long ennui in reaction against the strain of outward practical
> things.[30]

'Curiosity', 'ennui', 'thirst for intellectual excitement' a movement,
above all, away from outward practical things, every characteristic
Pater associates with the grotesque, reverses Hugo's view with its
stress on wider social sympathy and involvement. In more vulgar or
less restrained minds than Pater's his teachings lend themselves to
mere titillation, a cold exploitation of horrible or distasteful elements
for effect. In this sense, Pater's are the views behind that 1890s
dabbling with the bizarre against which Chesterton reacted.

Chesterton's response is subtle. He senses the inadequacy of
balance alone, of a purely negative kind of restraint. (His description
of Arnold's ideal figure Goethe is a striking example of damning with
faint praise).[31] He is as alert as Pater to the value of the grotesque
and its connection with energy in art. Without surrendering these
undoubted advantages, the benefits, established by Hugo of dis-
owning a stereotype, such as that of Greek or Renaissance
classicism, he effects a fundamental shift in the basis of Pater's
analysis of the grotesque. This may be seen partly in his account of
Victor Hugo, Pater's chief exemplar.

Chesterton's essay on 'Victor Hugo' (1902), belongs to the same

period as 'A Defence of Ugly Things' and *Robert Browning*. Its full
effect, as with the book on Browning and other of Chesterton's
examinations of the grotesque is best understood if his approach is
contrasted with Pater's. With Hugo, as with Browning, (and, incidentally, when he examines the related concept of the fabulous in
Dickens), Chesterton's first and most important effort goes to establishing a context in the recent past in which the figure and his
'grotesque art' may be understood. In 'Victor Hugo', the techniques
employed a year later in *Robert Browning* may be seen in miniature.
Chesterton emphasises the point that with Hugo, as with
Browning:

> we are divided from the generations that immediately precede us
> by a gulf far more unfathomable than that which divides us from
> the darkest ages and the most distant lands.[32]

This represents a familiar preoccupation of Chesterton. Repeatedly
he developed the thesis that the period from 1789 to 1871, from the
French Revolution to the defeat of France by Prussia, was one
cultural unit, that of the high-tide of reformist liberalism. After this
hopeful and expansive period, which produced the writers he
rehabilitated, Dickens, Browning, and in a sense, Hugo, the age just
before his own, 1871 to 1900, represented a failure of nerve, a decline
into pessimism and fatalism in philosophy and literature, into loss of
hope and capacity for action in politics.[33]
The twin revolutions of Romanticism and Democracy which
produced Hugo, Browning and Dickens are incomprehensible
because they 'have conquered and become commonplace'.[34]
Chesterton's position is destructive of the historical detachment of
the Paterian cultural arbiter moving with scholarly ease from age to
age. The 'languid and aesthetic collector' lavishes praise on Byz-
antine painting, Persian carpets and Fijiean idols, but has no real
sympathy or understanding for, no involvement in, the age in which
he lives, the movements and ideas which, even though he chooses to
ignore them, provide the background of his own mind. Without such
sympathy he cannot understand the eruption of the grotesque into
the work of the great nineteenth-century writers.
This is very far from being, as Pater describes it, a love of the

strange stemming from an ennui of practical things, but a rescue of the seemingly mundane from insignificance, a rescue intimately connected with a new sense of human value, produced by the rise of democracy. For Hugo:

there is neither a large thing nor a small one; he has abolished the meanest and most absurd of all human words, the word 'insignificant'; he knows that it is impossible for anything to signify nothing.[35]

The essence of Chesterton's view of the grotesque lies in his giving it a context in the recent past.

In his essay 'On Gargoyles' (1910) Chesterton returns to the division of human history in the *Preface to Cromwell* with one significant difference. For Hugo there had been an age of primitive innocence; then classicism; then romanticism. Chesterton sketches first the childlike innocence:

They worshipped the sun, not idolatrously but as the golden crown of the god whom all such infants see almost as plainly as the sun.[36]

The priest then orders the people to build a temple in a style suggestive of Hugo's age of classicism:

He would have nothing grotesque or obscure. . . . He would have all the arches as light as laughter and as candid as logic.[37]

As in the *Preface to Cromwell*, barbarian invasion, 'years of horror and humiliation' break up this simplicity and serenity. There comes the realisation that:

the temple is of the noon; it is made of white marble cloud and sapphire sky. But the sun is not always of the noon. The sun dies daily; every night he is crucified in blood and fire. . . . The sun, the symbol of our father, gives life to all those earthly things that are full of ugliness and energy. . . . The ugly animals praise God as much as the beautiful.[38]

Under this 'new inspiration', they plan a Gothic cathedral, 'all the possible ugly things making one common beauty.'[39] But the plan was never completed. Although (almost in Hugo's very words) 'this was romantic, this was Christian art; this was the whole advance of Shakespeare on Sophocles',[40] it was never carried through. The 'rich' obstructed it. The design which unified the ugly details into a scheme of grotesque beauty was lost and the result was that chaos of meaningless absurdity, Realism. (Realism is simply Romanticism that has lost its reason).[41] The political liberalism and movement towards democracy of 1789 to 1871, which might again be renewed, was presumably an attempt to redress this, restoring, incidentally, the grotesque in literature, in restoring the social and moral condition on which it must depend. Chesterton is, in effect, returning to Hugo's position of 1830, after the retreat of the years 1871 to 1900.

Chesterton's critique of the assumptions of aestheticism seems more often concerned with its provinciality than with its unhealthiness. Its notions of what are strange or exaggerated situations or reactions are often the result of a timid and sheltered English gentility, cut off, in spite of its claim to range countries and centuries, from European culture and common humanity. The last words of Danton, for example, were very much in the spirit of Hugo and 'the extravagant appropriateness of Hugo's conversations are thoroughly in harmony with the extravagant appropriateness of the actual incidents of French History.'[42]

Chesterton's attitude to the grotesque involves, among much else, an attempt to recapture from the aesthetes and decadents their most defensible insight into the nature of art, the real value of unexpected combinations and their connection with energy.

Perhaps a close comparison will show the manner in which Chesterton changed the emphasis and the tone of speaking of the grotesque adopted by the aesthetes. The change is a delicate and subtle one; far from a rude breeze of heartiness dispelling preciosity. Pater describes the pity for odd neglected characters and situations, inseparable from Romanticism in these terms:

Penetrating so finely into all situations which appeal to pity, into all special or exceptional phases of such feeling, the romantic

humour is not afraid of the quaintness or singularity of its circumstances or expression, pity indeed being the essence of humour, so
that Victor Hugo does but turn his romanticism into practice, in
his hunger and thirst after practical *Justice*! – a justice which shall
no longer wrong children, or animals, for instance by ignoring in a
stupid mere breadth of view, minute facts about them. Yet the
romantics are antinomian too, because of the love of energy and
beauty, of distinction in passion, tended naturally to become a
little *bizarre*, plunging into the Middle Age, into the secrets of old
Italian story . . . [43]

Pater admits the impulse and mentions certain of its leading features.
Yet the effect is odd, because of the curious placing of emphasis in the
passage. The instinct of pity is made to seem a recondite elaboration
of feeling, highly sophisticated, tending to operate most effectively in
contexts chosen for their strangeness, their 'special or exceptional
phases'. There is something distant about this 'pity', and the way in
which Pater italicises *Justice* gives it an air of a bold, uncouth concept.
'And whatever next'! he seems to be saying. The mention of sympathy for children in the context of quaint and singular emotions
speaks for itself. The ideal of the detached scholar-artist could hardly
be carried further. It is almost with a sigh of relief that Pater then
returns to the thought that the impulse was really antinomian. The
romantics were more concerned with the *bizarre* than with moral
qualities of any kind. The whole passage is an act of delicate subver-
sion, having the effect of taking Hugo's most important insight about
the grotesque and draining it of value. It is all the more effective
because Pater admits the impulse to wider human sympathy while he
is, at the same time, gently robbing it of significance.

Contrast this with Chesterton's account of the odd prosaic details
in Browning's love poems, part, as he says, of the material for that
'general accusation against Browning in connection with his use of
the grotesque.'[44] Chesterton tackles head on and completely breaks
up the false detachment of the aesthete or scholar-artist. Browning's
oddities touch a common human feeling, rooted in one's sense of
things, not some outré or far-fetched artistic instinct, reacting against
boredom or conventionality:

So great a power have these dead things, taking hold on the living spirit, that I question whether any one could read through the catalogue of a miscellaneous auction sale, without coming upon things which, if realised for a moment would be near to the elemental tears. And if any of us or all of us are truly optimists and believe as Browning did, that existence has a value wholly inexpressible, we are most truly compelled to that sentiment not by any argument or triumphant justification of the cosmos, but by a few of these momentary sights and sounds, a gesture, an old song, a portrait, a piano, an old door.[45]

The grotesque, here, is connected with the concrete and the particular, the 'little details' which affect a man 'who has really lived'. The 'suburban streets, garden rakes, medicine bottles, pianos, window-blinds, burnt cork, fashionable fur hats' of Browning's love poetry are connected with 'insatiable realism' of sentiment and emotion. Thought and intellect, Chesterton remarks, can accept abstractions but sentiment must have concrete particularities and Chesterton characteristically appeals to common experience here:

It awakens in every man the memories of that immortal instant when common and dead things had a meaning beyond the power of any dictionary to utter ... [46]

It is, in other words, the 'melancholy' of Hugo, the sense of disparity and yet connection between material objects or mundane sights and spiritual or emotional realities. The most telling difference between the early views of Chesterton and those of Pater on the grotesque lie in Chesterton's assumption of a humanity shared by intellectual and non-intellectual, an involvement in the business of living common to himself and his readers, of experiences more fundamental than cultivation or the lack of it; and secondly, in his assertion that the grotesque is *natural*, a basic part of the condition of our lives, not a rare element for which one goes in search.

Whether he considers the grotesque in scenery, in domestic details, or in startling emotional juxtapositions, Chesterton is concerned to point out that it forms the texture of existence. We cannot avoid it and it cuts through the pretence of intellectual detachment

185

or indeed any of the moods and postures with which we deceive ourselves. As he points out in 'A Defence of Skeletons':

However much my face clouds with sombre vanity, or vulgar vengeance, or contemptible contempt, the bones of my skull are laughing forever.[47]

His manner of treating the grotesque is human, relaxed and less entrenched in the fallacious certainties of high culture than that of the aesthetes. Being aware that one cannot escape it makes for humility, based eventually and most importantly, on a sense of mystery. Chesterton points out that all that was profound or even tolerable in the aesthetes of the 1880s or the decadents of the 1890s was anticipated by Browning's grand conception that every point of view was interesting, however jaundiced or bloodshot. The vital difference between Browning and the decadents was his confidence that the grotesque quality of experience was a mystery too great for human comprehension, a meaning too large for human reason to fathom. Speaking of different interpretations of the ancient fable of the blind men and the elephant, Chesterton declares:

There is a vital distinction between the mystical view of Browning that the blind men were misled because there is so much for them to learn and the purely impressionistic and agnostic view of the modern poet, that the blind men were misled because there is nothing for them to learn.[48]

One has the sense in Chesterton's early efforts to expound his view of the grotesque, of having moved out of a closed circle of assumptions. We are made to feel, in a salutary way, how little we know. There are things larger than intellect, or hard as this may be to accept, than good taste.

The first appearance of a concern with the grotesque in Chesterton's writing, itself contemporary with his first essays, appears to be polemical. Its drift is better understood by contrast with the aesthetes' view of the subject than in relation to Chesterton's notional secret fears. To connect it, as Chesterton does with democratic and liberal movements and universal human experience returns to first principles in Hugo. It changes it from a private, exclusive element, the concern of a self-conscious artistic and cultural élite, which rather than any inherent 'unhealthiness' was its undesirable element. Chesterton undertakes a campaign of demystification, a dispelling of the secretive and portentous element which, even in Pater, and much more in his cruder imitators, tended to hang about the grotesque. (It is an aim of letting in the light, found, in brief, in an early essay such as 'A Defence of Publicity' republished in *The Defendant* and at length, of course, in *The Man who was Thursday*). In terms of the history of ideas, he effectively is the link with Hugo's first formulations, the restorer and begetter of the fuller meaning of the concept 'grotesque' in English.

What, perhaps, suggests that Chesterton's view of what Borges calls the 'nightmarish', related more to public literary debate than to private phobias, is the marked change of tone between his earlier and later views of the subject. Passages suggesting that the universe and the creatures in it are wild and fantastic may be found in all periods of his writing and to a cursory view they may seem to contain much the same meaning. If, however, the earliest and some of the latest pronouncements are placed together then it appears that some important alteration has taken place. In 'A Defence of Skeletons' (1901) we find this passage:

> This is the deepest, the oldest, the most wholesome and religious sense of the value of nature – the value which comes from her immense babyishness. She is as top-heavy, as grotesque, as solemn, and as happy as a child. The mood does come when we see all her shapes like shapes that a baby scrawls on a slate – simple, rudimentary, a million years older and stronger than the whole disease that is called art.[49]

The emphasis, here, is on the innocence and goodness of the primal energy, its innate happiness. It has no enigmas. Our relation to it in such moods is one of 'lucidity' and 'levity' as 'simple as a dancing lunatic'. Taken from its contemporary context of a debate on the nature of the grotesque this might seem to lend itself to the charge of emotional special pleading; Chesterton is talking too loudly, he is trying to argue down some inner terror or uncertainty. And the tone of this passage, it might be remarked, may be found several times elsewhere in his early work.

However, if this extract is compared with a quotation from the essay on 'The Book of Job' (1929), a shift may be detected in the inner meaning Chesterton attaches to the grotesque. The playful element found in 'In Defence of Skeletons', as in early references to the Book of Job itself, is much less marked. The comic and ludicrous quality of strangeness is insisted on much less than its 'positive and palpable unreason'.

> God will make man see things if only it is against the black background of nonentity. God will make men see a startling universe if He can only do it by making Job see an idiotic universe.[50]

What seems to have happened in Chesterton's continuing consideration of the grotesque has been a movement from the celebration of the 'intrinsically miraculous character of the object itself', the wonder and delight of 'the sense of the uproarious force in things' towards a feeling of the mysterious and enigmatic. Of course, this later element had been innate or implied in the earlier work but it had been submerged in the sense of joy, of energy, of the naturalness and freedom from aesthetic or cultural constraints contained in the sense of the grotesque. The characteristic images of the essay on 'The Book of Job', of joy breaking 'through agnosticism like fiery gold round the edge of a black cloud',[51] or of 'light seen for an instant through the cracks of a closed door',[52] involve a somewhat different attitude to the grotesque element in Nature. The strangeness of the physical world is rather an arresting oddity, destructive of facile explanations and mechanical optimism and making us suspect some great secret. In 'A Defence of Ugly Things', the gaining of a sense of joy, of a feeling of being at home in the world appears easy:

> The moment we have snapped the spell of conventional beauty, there are a million beautiful faces waiting for us everywhere, just as there are a million beautiful spirits.[53]

More notably, as here, the problem is seen in aesthetic terms, the need to reject a false or constricted way of apprehending the world.

In the explorations of the grotesque in the late phase, there is a moral rather than an aesthetic emphasis, an accent on 'impenetrable enigma' in the grotesque vision. There is an explicit denial of any simple solution or liberation into enjoyment but 'the refusal of God to explain His design is itself a burning hint of His design. The riddles of God are more satisfying than the solutions of men.'[54] (Comments involving similar attitudes may be seen elsewhere in Chesterton's later writings).

What the change involves it is, perhaps, impossible to answer with a dogmatic certainty. One might suggest, however, that in the early work in particular, polemical necessity may have lead him to dwell especially on the naturalness and universality of the grotesque, and its connection with a creative energy. An attempt to explain the change in psychological terms involves multiplying hypotheses. Such an explanation requires not merely a suppositious emotional state or a neurosis for Chesterton, but a whole theory of its development into something else quite different; an elaboration of guesswork for which there is no hard evidence. If, however, one sets Chesterton's early views against contemporary and previous accounts of the grotesque, especially Pater's, then the need for just the particular accent he gave his views becomes clear. He wanted the grotesque, but he wanted it without misconceptions. By the later writings this polemical need had disappeared and much wider and more fruitful conceptions of the term 'grotesque' had formed.

It is, perhaps, even possible to detect in *The Man who was Thursday*, a crucial instance of the movement from joyful celebration of the grotesque towards an exploration of its deeper ambiguities. The dark inscrutable Sunday represents the manifestation of God's energies in Nature, rather than God himself. His strange notes fill Syme with a joy connected with a recognition of Nature's incongruities:

> He remembered a hornbill which was simply a huge yellow beak with a small bird tied on behind it. The whole gave him a sensation, the vividness of which he could not explain, that Nature was always making quite mysterious jokes.[55]

What is important, as it is also very moving in the novel, is the acknowledgement, stated with great tenderness and pity, that there are those who do not see the jokes. Minds like the Secretary's or

Gregory's, sensitive, scrupulous and literal-minded, who, in spite of Syme's plea, refuse to joy in the abundant energy of a grotesque creation. This point in Chesterton's development (1908) might well be taken as dividing the earlier and later phases of his involvement with the grotesque.

IX

THE REACTION AGAINST IMPRESSIONISM

The use of the term 'Impressionism' is almost inevitable in any even moderately lengthy discussion of Chesterton. His philosophical and moral objections to a loss of definition, a melting of one object or entity into another one, are, by any showing, central to his view of life and of the times through which he lived, and, naturally enough, are noted and discussed by most critical writers on him. These considerations enter, in a moral sense, as we have seen, into his attacks on the myths of the Superman, evolutionary transcendence, or of blending into the Absolute. They obviously affected his view of art, of that great artistic revolution, a major cultural event of the last century and of his lifetime, by which a broadly representational drawing and painting governed largely by the canons of the Italian Renaissance, gave way to the waves of experiment, of which Impressionism was one of the earliest, and which attempted to discover a visual truth beyond the conventionally realistic or representational; the reproduction of which, for those who wanted it, was often said by the artistic innovators, to have been relegated to the new technique of photography.

Chesterton's comments on the phases of this artistic revolution, largely negative and often crusty, have, perhaps, seemed one of the least interesting aspects of his response to the cultural crisis. He objected to the loss of visual definition and to the divorce of a 'minority art' from mass taste and expectations and there is little more to be said. In fact his view of the whole matter was more subtle and defensible than is often credited.

Chesterton and the Edwardian Cultural Crisis

The visual in Chesterton's work has an importance which is readily and generally granted. The implications of shapes, tints of sky, or landscape are, however, much less frequently examined than other outstanding features of his work. Paradox, philosophical allegory, or the defence of sanity, as well as being almost inexhaustible fields of discussion for the literary critic are more easily apprehended than a subject bordering on art appreciation or aesthetics. The result of this comparative neglect has been to confirm Bernard Bergonzi's view that Chesterton was exclusively concerned with the rational mind and conscious will. Ignoring his original intuitions in the field of perception, leads to the view that he had no interest in sensation or the instinctual where they could not serve an argument.

A convenient starting point is his description of childhood perception in *Autobiography*. He singles out sharpness, clearness of definition, as its primary quality. The object is seen in itself, as it is, with a clarity of which subsequent 'memories', however interesting in themselves, are modifications or dilutions:

> Really, the things we remember are the things we forget. I mean that when a memory comes back sharply and suddenly, piercing the protection of oblivion, it appears for an instant exactly as it was. If we think of it often, while its essentials doubtless remain true, it becomes more and more our memory of the thing rather than the thing remembered.[1]

We remember too often, in the sense that accretions of associations form around the original impression, literary reminiscence perhaps or the experience of romantic love. The perception of first love may have the sharp-edged definition in the object seen, characteristic of the child's perception. It may also have that quality of being set within a frame like the images of the children's toy theatre Chesterton declared had coloured his mind from infancy. In other ways it is crucially different. The vision of first love, tinged with the sense that what is loved be lost, is to that extent, 'the wreck of something divine'. More significantly:

> it did not, and does not, make me think the other windows and

192

houses were all almost equally interesting; and that is just what the glimpse of the babies' wonderland does.[2]

Perhaps this point may be missed in a concentration on one much more fully emphasised, the strange and solid otherness of objects.

Stephen Medcalf has drawn a distinction between Chesterton's own interest in the quiddity of objects and Aquinas's theories of perception with which he certainly sympathised. Chesterton was concerned not so much as Aquinas was with the 'essential singularities' of the concrete thing as with

'its overall weight and impact, especially its unexpectedness.'[3]

One might go beyond Medcalf's suggestions to note another vital element. In a passage in *Autobiography*, Chesterton draws together some of his leading preoccupations, the solidity of objects and the frame which limits the vision but he then stresses another factor; the sense of what is *not* in the picture:

> My point here is that we can test the childish mood by thinking, not only of what was there, but of what must have been there. I think of the backs of the houses of which I saw only the fronts; the streets that stretched away behind the streets I knew; the things that remained round the corner and they still give me a thrill.[4]

The limiting of the vision to what is seen within the frame does indeed enforce a concentration on the objects which can be seen, emphasising their concreteness. The solid reality of what is disclosed represents a mysterious quiddity outside the self. Beyond this, however, the visible entity is a pointer to, almost a guarantee of, many more, equally substantial, equally mysterious things, not possible to see, but possible to imagine. Chesterton glancingly suggests that the limits have two functions: to preserve the integrity of objects and to stimulate the sense of wonder, the appetite for fresh visual and imaginative experience.[5]

Chesterton's childhood perceptions have great intensity. The image of the white horse's head is retained from the nursery and recalled throughout life at all its most important and deeply felt moments. The scene from the toy theatre 'glows in my memory like a glimpse of some incredible paradise; and, for all I know, I shall still remember it when all other memory is gone out of my mind.'[6] Statements like these seem to have a kinship with a common thread in the romantic sensibility, beginning with Wordsworth's 'spots of time' and culminating in Walter Pater's privileged moments of vision. However, Chesterton's kinship with this tradition is less significant than his divergence from it. He perceived intensely enough at given moments to found, like Pater, a cult of momentary perception, yet he did not do so.

Pater's sense of the moment of transfiguring vision with no before or after, finds many expressions in his writings, as for example, in the essay on Du Bellay in *Studies in the History of the Renaissance*.[7] Here perceptions are offered as details, almost 'framed' as Chesterton prefers his should be, for great concentration. Yet, though intense, they are not solid. Rather they are vehicles for some external force which 'transfigures' them, for an instantaneous accidental vision of which there is no certain repetition.

'The Child in the House' (1878), Pater's semi-autobiographical fragment, provides a useful comparison with Chesterton's own childhood memories of visual impression. Pater, unlike Chesterton, sees impressions as haphazard, important as agents for the discovery of larger realities, principally those of our own nature;[8] of a higher quality because isolated from the normal flow of experience and as hints of some more significant kind of life. What they are in themselves or how they relate spatially or in a moral or emotional sense to other things are of no significance.

These early 'epiphanies', as Stephen Dedalus calls them in Joyce's Paterian *Portrait of the Artist as a Young Man*, are mainly interesting as foretastes of more refined aesthetic sensations. The child delights in the gold of dandelions 'in the lack of better ministeries to its desire for beauty'.[9] When the individual's nature has reached the culminating point in a process of self-conscious refinement, he may have a 'peculiar and privileged hour'. Marius, in Pater's novel has, by an unexpected chance, a reverie in an inn garden, 'the scene and the hour still conspiring', in which the objects he sees, fall, in some seemingly fortuitous way, into an alignment with his inner thoughts and feelings.[10] For Pater, in *Marius the Epicurean*, if not in *Studies in the*

History of the Renaissance, the aesthetic intensity hints at an 'Ideal' comprehensible in terms of religious experience. The perceptions are stray gleams which transfigure this lower realm.

Pater, in fact, seems to draw two distinct inferences from such moments of vision. The epilogue to *Studies in the History of the Renaissance* carries the famous exhortation to clutch at every exquisite passion 'while the ground melts beneath our feet'. The golden moments are the only reality in a meaningless flux. In *Marius*, a few years later, they point to a certain kind of spirituality quietly contemptuous of the ordinary material world. In neither case are they rooted in other material things. The picture or scene is defined by its own perfection, not framed to produce an artistic effect in conjunction with a real or assumed background. It is likely that Chesterton would find the religiously tinged revision of Pater's view of perception as unpalatable as the frank hedonism of the original version.

The relevance of this brief resumé of Pater's teaching is based on more than his general importance in the 'Aesthetic Movement' against which Chesterton revolted. Pater's teaching had a role in Chesterton's own period of art education at the Slade, (1892–5), a period of emotional crisis the importance of which is generally admitted. While Chesterton is remarkably frank about his own mental state during the period, he is much less informative about the curriculum and official atmosphere of the Slade. Maisie Ward represents him as untouched by its teaching. He was, however, clearly affected, after a somewhat sheltered childhood, by contact with other students, as both *Autobiography* and a grave essay 'The Diabolist'[11] make clear. His reticence about the intellectual origin of the influences he encountered may have been due to a feeling that those among his teachers who endorsed 'Impressionism' had not foreseen its consequences.

It might be possible to suggest an hypothesis which would illuminate Chesterton's Slade years: what exactly he meant by 'Impressionism' and the precise nature of his hostility towards it. The subject has, hitherto, been coloured by a pseudo-psychological explanation; Chesterton's defence of well-defined outlines, of frames, limits, order and structure in perception express, in the language of art criticism, a fear of the breakdown of his own mind. Superficially plausible, although reductionist, such an account distorts a much more complex process. Chesterton's hostility to what he called 'Impressionism' was not that it opened the floodgates but that it destroyed imagination by fixing it to one aspect of one object seen at one time unrelated to anything else.

It is worth noting a number of points which clarify Chesterton's early relationship to 'Impressionism'; the importance of George Moore who in *Confessions of a Young Man* (1888) and *Modern Painting* (1893) is acknowledged to have introduced the French Impressionists to the English public, the fact of Moore's friendship with and intellectual influence on Henry Tonks, the drawing master of the Slade and Moore's deep admiration for and vulgarisation of, Walter Pater. What Chesterton encountered was not Impressionism, a certain technique, or a school of French painting, but 'Impressionism' as seen by Moore, a set of attitudes, or a way of perceiving, hostile to Chesterton's childhood vision, his sense of the relationship of object to object in the material world.

Moore was dedicated to the great French painters whom he met in Paris, after his conversion to their work in the later 1870s, to making them understood by the insular English art world. His brilliant propaganda succeeded. Art historians have accepted his subsequent (1916) claim for *Confessions of a Young Man* that it contained the first eulogies written of Monet, Degas, Whistler, Manet or Pissaro in English or almost in any language.[12] Moore, writing before Roger Fry (1910) established the division between Impressionism and Post-Impressionism, of course adopts categories different from the modern ones. More significantly, what he presented as 'Impressionism' reflected his own temperamental and intellectual bias.

Confessions of a Young Man reveals that Moore's enthusiasm for the French Impressionists was more than equalled by his devotion to his own very partial, indeed perversely misinterpreted, view of Pater's *Marius the Epicurean*. Moore jettisoned Pater's spiritual velleities, his ambiguities of tone, his reticence, and equated the meaning of *Marius* with Gautier's *Mademoiselle de Maupin*. Both, he stated, taught that the beauty of the material world sufficed for all the needs of life.[13] Pater's letter to Moore thanking him for *Confessions* reveals, along with great politeness, reservations of tone somewhat reminiscent of his review of Wilde's *The Picture of Dorian Gray*. In each case, Pater appeared to feel he was being distorted.

Moore went beyond Wilde even, in dissociating the visionary moment of aesthetic delight from any kind of moral or emotional framework. It had no relationship to anything else and if it cost others pain or hardship, then so much the better. Speaking of Ingres' *La Source* for which the 'price' was the seduction and death of the model through drink, he remarks that 'the knowledge that a wrong was done... that a girl or a thousand girls, died in the hospital for that one virginal thing, is an added pleasure which I could not afford to spare.'[14] While dissociating the visionary moment from any kind of moral or emotional framework and from Pater's kind of spirituality, Moore continued to retain, from Pater, the glowing afflatus with which the 'epiphanies' were described.

The literary rodomontades of *Confessions of a Young Man* represent the flavour of Moore's conversations or rather monologues, which several witnesses have described as brilliant performances. They suggest what he is likely to have declaimed in Tonk's hearing, while carrying out his mission to popularise the Impressionists. One of Moore's later biographers quotes from two letters of 1893 confirming his generous and energetic role as a self-conscious propagandist at this time.[15] The fighting qualities Chesterton readily granted in *Heretics* are the other essential element in Moore's personal influence on English art in the 1890s.

Moore's single-handed crusade on behalf of Impressionism (*c.* 1887–95) overlaps Chesterton's years at the Slade. The acclaimed best seller *Modern Painting* appeared almost in the middle of his time at the school. Moore's friendship with the newly appointed drawing-master Henry Tonks dates from the autumn of 1894. However, he was already closely associated with Steer and Brown, the head of the Slade, and had been acting 'for some years as the critic of the New English Art Club', the literary mouthpiece of Steer's and Brown's attacks on the Academy and its values. Throughout Chesterton's time at the Slade, the school was associated with a new combatively expressed view of painting of which Moore was the fugleman. With Tonks' arrival, the effect of Moore's influence, particularly of his picture of Impressionism, probably became even more pronounced. At least this is a reasonable inference from the portrait of his friend Moore presented many years later in *Conversations in Ebury Street*. A surgeon before he aspired, relatively late, to be a painter, Tonks suffered severely from having to leave his profession and 'face the world naked and ashamed'. Several accounts confirm Moore's picture of an intense ascetic, anxious to a perhaps excessive degree, to improve his technical skill, leaning on others for intellectual support, 'praying that the secret might be vouchsafed to him, for art had become Tonks's religion.[16] The personal problem of a highly-strung conscientious man trying to acquire a new self affected Tonks's approach to the techniques of painting and further coloured the 'Impressionism' mediated through Moore's urgent hedonism and Pater's cult of the 'golden moment' of perception.

The influences on Chesterton during his time at the Slade were of a complex character, produced by the interaction of several factors at a particular time and requiring careful delineation, a more precise context than a generalised 'decadence'. One curious point may be noted. Deliquescence may have been a philosophic meaning of 'Impressionism'. In actual execution or composition it meant not a loosening of technique but an increased stringency. Gaunt points out that the aesthetic doctrines of the New English Art Club and the Slade:

> produced 'this anxious feeling', a continuous anxiety about 'tones' and 'values' . . . a keen consciousness of mistakes and the possibility of making them, a fretful recourse to the plumbline.[17]

It is perhaps scarcely surprising that Sickert, Steer, Tonks and their disciples failed to produce an art comparable to the French Impressionists they admired.

Undoubtedly admirable and conscientious, Tonks must have reinforced what was already a strained and constricted attitude to painting. The perfectionism inherent in the doctrine of the 'golden moment' drawn out of Pater through Moore was confirmed by an obsession with exactitude in the techniques by which a momentary aspect of a scene or a figure might be rendered. Moore had already emphasised the magnificent execution, the sheer professional skill of Whistler and Manet. In practical terms Tonks's temperament and teaching, his 'awe-inspiring manner and exterior' which 'had the effect of keying his pupils up to a pitch of effort which was the result both of fear and affection',[18] may have produced a worried concern with the particular nuance; an anxiety which lends substance to Chesterton's casual remark in *Autobiography* about the atmosphere of the Slade:

> The very latest thing was to keep abreast of Whistler; to take him by the white forlock, as if he were time himself.[19]

The subject of Chesterton's relationship with 'Impressionism' may be approached in two ways: first, and more obviously, through its seeming connection with moral and philosophical positions against which he fought throughout his career, and secondly, through his view of the visual. Impressionism, he also remarks in *Autobiography*:

> naturally lends itself to the metaphysical suggestion that things only exist as we perceive them, or that things do not exist at all.[20]

This is familiar ground in Chesterton, the solipsist bugbear, which he feared in his own early manhood and detected as an insidious current in contemporary thought. Discussing the intellectual fore-runners of the aesthetic he encountered at the Slade, he made this the centre of his criticism. Pater's desire to stay at the point where the keenest emotions meet, he declared, involves the certainty of feeling none of them.[21] Emotion must be rooted in choice, paid for. 'Golden moments' whether of emotion or sensuous feeling do not come out of nothing and relate to nothing. Chesterton's well-known and very amusing characterisation of Moore restates the point with slightly different emphasis. Moore's taking up of unrelated, inconsistent positions, a kind of 'moral Impressionism' means that although self-display is his object, all his tones and shades and aspects coalesce into nothing definite, no clear-cut personality.[22]

Familiar features of the Chesterton landscape, central to his philosophical position, the arguments by which Pater and Moore are challenged represent a transference into moral and intellectual terms of intuitions which had in their original form an *aesthetic* dimension. The 'Diabolist' embraces the aesthetic as well as the moral, the spectacle of an 'Impressionist painting' of the fire lit before the steps of the Slade by a gardener and the argument about 'real things' between Chesterton and the sinister young man. One gives rise to the other and they are bound up together.

Rather than rehearse the well-known, though fruitful, case against solipsism, it might be as well to return to that meeting on a winter's evening in 1893, and to note that Chesterton's view involved a sense of visual as well as moral contingency. His sense of wonder could never be confined to what was actually seen. It depended for its full effect on a sense of 'the backs of the houses'. Aesthetically it was opposed to the kind of concentration and isolation taught at the Slade as Impressionism. Objects could never be confined to a vivid aspect. To deny an object visual relationship to an unseen background was hostile to imagination. The 'Impressionism' of Brown and Tonks, an overdisciplining of the perceptual faculty, tried to focus on an isolated vision at the expense of flow, movement, connection and mystery. The over-anxious quality Gaunt mentions was certainly inimical to Chesterton's artistic temper, to that vigorous, bold, unembarrassed way of drawing remembered by Nicholas Bentley.[23] Much more important was his revulsion against the 'closed-in' picture, the picture which is a final statement. (Chesterton in his study of Blake remarked that the clarity with which Blake saw objects was, as in fourteenth-century illumination, an affirmation of their meaning as a spiritual *design*, a misunderstood story or an uncomprehended hieroglyphic perhaps, but not a meaningless flux. In the affirmation of the concrete reality and relatedness lies the highest affirmation of the spiritual.[24] Chesterton's conception of the relation of physical and spiritual is clearly totally alien to Pater's).

George Santayana's criticism of Impressionism in *The Sense of Beauty* which appeared in the year after Chesterton left the Slade makes an interesting comparison because he said what Chesterton is wrongly accused of saying. Their objections to Impressionism are really fundamentally different. Santayana reproaches it with offering 'vague stimuli' to the sense of perception which it is unable to shape into recognisable form.[25] Chesterton sees it as flat and literal minded, a truncating of the process of imagination and of the kinetic relationship of one object with another, of the seen to the unseen.

Chesterton's intuitions on the subject of perception mark a sharp break with the 'Impressionism' of the Slade and the aesthetic of Pater upon which it was founded. But also, they are a break with Santayana's criticism of Impressionism. (In fact the Slade teachers and Santayana share a common frame of reference. In the modern terminology of perception, they would both be seen to endorse analytic *gestalt* vision, a way of seeing which advanced writers on art such as Anton Ehrenzweig have recently exposed to searching criticism).[26]

Chesterton, in his art criticism, is, above all, concerned to discover a visual language, a way of rendering objects which allows for their mystery, which opens out the ways in which they can be seen and widens the range of possible relationships they can have with each other and above all does justice to their complex effect on the human mind. In his study of *G.F. Watts* (1904) Chesterton offers, incidentally, a picture of his own aesthetic frame of reference, the expectations about painting he had formed. (The choice of Watts may perhaps have been intended to mark a reaction from the ethos of the Slade. However, Watts has not benefited from the recent revival of interest in the Pre-Raphaelites and it is likely that in linking the expression of his views with the work of an admittedly somewhat inferior painter Chesterton did not do them justice). It is clear however that Chesterton felt an artist should not be concerned with an 'impression', a perfect moment, an aspect, but should rather attempt to engage the deepest levels of man's consciousness, providing a form for the vast unknown pattern of perception or knowledge which exist there. Speaking of Watts' painting *Hope* he declares:

the philosophical meaning of the word in the conscious mind of man, is merely a part of something immensely larger in the unconscious mind, that the gusty light of language only falls for a moment on a fragment, and that only a semi-detached unfinished fragment of a certain definite pattern on the dark tapestries of reality.[27]

The existence of a vast unknown relatedness between colour, line and moral sensations, themselves quite definite, but not definable given the crude nature of language, is the subject of a large part of this early book. Clearly, this hidden order interested Chesterton. The view of perception suggested in *G.F. Watts* does not exalt unrelated epiphanies, celebrated either for their own sake or as glimpses of an other-worldly kind. It does not seek satisfaction in a picture complete in itself. Perception for Chesterton is the discovery of unknown modes of relatedness. He praises Watts for providing in his painting a new, precise, coherent, visual expression of a certain nuance about hope. Stephen Medcalf suggests a contrast between the early view which Chesterton expresses in *G.F. Watts* and that given much later in *St Thomas Aquinas*. In the first, he feels, Chesterton is saying that 'both language and painting [are] parallel attempts to symbolise something beyond adequate expression.'[28] In the second Chesterton has decided that it is possible to make 'a certain contact with the essences of things'. There is some doubt as to the strong distinction Mr Medcalf proposes. The general tenor of the passage on *Hope* in *G.F. Watts* and its effect on the perceiver, is that something really *has* been discovered, relations between visual forms and subconscious elements in the mind have been recognised. The emphasis is on a finding of what is already there, although complex and hard to grasp. Chesterton describes a dawning sense of understanding in the mind of an imaginary viewer of *Hope*, when he had overcome an initial resistance.

> But if we imagine that he overcame these preliminary feelings and that he stared at the twilight picture, a dim and powerful sense of meaning began to grow upon him – what would he see? He would see something for which there is neither speech nor language, which has been too vast for an eye to see, and too secret for any religion to utter, even as an esoteric doctrine. Standing before that picture he finds himself in the presence of a great truth.[29]

The exact nature of the 'dim and powerful sense of meaning' is partly moral and emotional, but has also, most importantly, a definable relationship with visual form. It is possible to move from one way of speaking to another. They are not so much, perhaps, parallel attempts to express the inexpressible, as parts of some vast contingency or relationship which the adult mind is continually putting together, if it is hard-working and fortunate. In childish perception, as Chesterton described it, the sense of relationship existed without effort or strain, intimately connected with the sense of wonder. Watts' *Hope* represents a drawing together of dispersed areas of apprehension, fragments of knowledge. Lines, shapes and colours are not chosen to *symbolise* some truth abstracted from past experience. The relationship between the visual and the moral and emotional is more intimate and organic.

If we find ourselves gazing at some monument of the fragile and eternal faith of man, at some ruined chapel, at some nameless altar, at some fragment of Jacobin eloquence, we might eventually find our own minds moving in certain curves that centre in the curved back of Watts' 'Hope'.[30]

Chesterton shows little interest in the conventional symbols; icons, military, civic, commercial or moral which are exact equivalents of some sentiment or truism. Art of that kind is scarcely worth the trouble. Neither, however, although he uses the word 'allegory' to describe the aspect of Watts' art which he admires, does the expression fully encompass what he seems to be aiming at. It is not so much an affair of 'allegory', 'symbol', 'objective correlative' or 'analogy' as simply that of activating another level of the mind, of perceiving in another way with a wider extension of understanding. 'Our minds move in certain curves'. They do not discover, intellectually, a symbol or analogy for a truth, intellectually arrived at.

Perhaps Chesterton's conception of the nature and potentiality of perception is best seen in the practical use to which he put it in his own descriptions of landscape. The visual effects in some of the Father Brown stories are unforgettable. It is often, and perhaps with justice, said that the visual descriptions in these stories remain with the reader much longer than the not always entirely satisfactory plots. Mostly, however, they are praised as if they were set pieces, elaborate, highly wrought and fantastic exercises in scene setting at the start of the story, images of a place which, admittedly, bears some analogy to 'the inner weather which (rather than the crime itself) is the real subject of each story.[31] Certainly they can be examined in this way but it is important to recognise that the scenes are dynamic. They are not fixed impressions. The visual effects move and change within the stories, approximating to the effects of film. Nor, except in the simplest instances, are they symbolic equivalents of some fairly simple change in atmosphere. Rather they are a perception of another kind; suggestions of new meanings discovered on the subconscious level. They point, invariably, to a restoration of health and balance, a 'seeing round the backs of the houses', a limiting or localising of some evil or horrifying vision.

'The Sign of the Broken Sword,' for example, opens with the 'grey' and 'silver forest' and 'dark-green-blue sky', stars bleak like 'splintered ice'. The 'dark spaces between the trees' suggest that what cannot be seen is even colder than what can. In fact, the cold horror has no limit. It is 'bottomless', 'incalculable'. A mention of how the scene looks on 'glowing summer afternoons' with their wagonettes of American tourists seems only to intensify the opening effect. Even they find it oddly dumb and neglected. The monument of the recumbent soldier, marked by a 'small silver pencil of starlight', is massive and strangely contrasting with the featureless graves all around. Intellectually, as has been suggested, the cold isolation of the opening tale is appropriate to its solution. The buried hero is, as it were, in a Dantean hell of cold, the place of the traitors.

The image, however, does not remain fixed. 'The Sign of the Broken Sword' ends in the warmth of the tavern with its 'strong scarlet light' and its red curtain. On the table stands a silver model of the tomb. The image is offered again, its colour drowned in another light, not bottomless or incalculable but somehow petty, diminished.

Chesterton delights in setting up powerful initial visions and then subverting them or at least showing their relativity. 'The Wrong Shape', for example, begins by an evocative journey along one of the great roads out of London. Moving along, the imaginary eye focuses on a long low house. Carefully and fairly slowly, from a sense of slight oddity, Chesterton begins to move to an effect of greater and greater strangeness. The plan of the house is precisely given. When the hall door is open, it is possible to see into the conservatory, 'a perspective of rich apartments to something like a transformation scene in a fairy

play; purple clouds and golden suns and crimson stars that were at
once scorchingly vivid and yet transparent and far away.'[32] The
visual climax of the opening is not the conservatory, however, but
the fantasy world of the drug-addicted poet Leonard Quinton,
'tropical heavens of burning gold and blood-red copper'. Having
orchestrated an effect of greater and greater oppressiveness,
Chesterton proceeds to clear the air, or wash the landscape clean by
a storm of rain in the darkness. The earlier vision seems to resist:

> The terrible tropic flowers still seemed to keep a crimson memory
> of the sunset.[33]

By the end of the story the first colour impression has been extin-
guished, 'and the wet waterproofs of several policemen gleamed in
the road outside.'[34] What interests Chesterton is a flow of visual
effect, a rhythm of perception, corresponding to a rhythm in the
subconscious mind; not simply objective correlative to an intellectual solution but a pattern of response expressed in a movement of
tones, shades and forms. 'The Sins of Prince Saradine' opens with a
river journey into regions of greater and greater strangeness and
beauty. It is unearthly, a lemon yellow moon, a sky of vivid violet
blue. It seems also to be a journey into childhood or fairyland.

> Standing up thus against the large low moon the daisies really
> seemed to be giant daisies, the dandelions to be giant dandelions.
> Somehow it reminded him of the dado of a nursery wall-paper.[35]

The first impression then dissolves 'into working daylight'. The
houses are long and low 'like huge red cattle'. The vision has been
deliberately modulated into something mundane. 'Long and low' is
repeated three times and then the magical quality fades.

> The sloping rods that made the roof were of darker red or brown
> and the otherwise long low house was a thing of repetition and
> monotony.[36]

The vision halts for a while in the interior of the house, with its
repeated mirrors and its 'dead sunlight'. The light and the unsub-
stantialness of the place, its nondescript quality is broken by a
second movement of the colour composition. Among the 'pictures of

a quiet kind', the 'grey photographs' is an arrestingly different red chalk sketch of two brothers. The colour red is repeated in references to the sketch and culminates in a mention of the red waistcoat of the would-be avenger Antonelli. Simultaneously the outlines grow sharper until every detail of the two duellists is visible in the distance. The effect of the brightly-coloured tiny figures is bizarre:

> They looked like two butterflies trying to pin each other to a cork.[37]

The red motif reaches its climax in the breaking of a big rose tree and a cloud of red earth thrown up by one of the men. 'The Sicilian had made a blood offering to the ghost of his father.' Once more the light dies. The last visual effect in the story is the melting away of Prince Saradine's treacherous note in green ink, torn and thrown into the water by Flambeau:

> The last gleam of the white card and the green ink was drowned and darkened; a faint and vibrant colour as of morning changed the sky and the moon behind the grasses grew paler.[38]

In each of these three instances pictorial rhythm in the story is used in an exceedingly sophisticated fashion which relates to changing moods in the perceiver. There is a movement towards the establishment of a visual configuration which is then dissolved or localised.

The patterns do not appear to act as symbolic counters for some simple truth. They have moral meanings, or at least moral parallels may, without too much straining, be found for them. But often these extend, rather than confirm, the meaning of the story. In the last example it may appear that first Flambeau is the observer. His are the bright tints, the vision of entry into fairyland about which Father Brown cautions him. Brown detects the dreary grey and blood red, the hatred of brothers and murder. The final melting is like the dispelling of illusion in Flambeau's mind. The false letter was based on a trick he himself had once played. He comes, perhaps, to see the true nature of crime, without romantic or adventurous disguise. (There are parallels both visual and moral to the process in two other stories concerned with Flambeau's moral education, 'The Blue Cross' and 'The Flying Stars').

At their best Chesterton's dynamic images, his method of taking a picture and developing it visually, function in ways which enrich, by adding a different dimension, to the line of his logical argument. One interesting example of this is his use of a panoramic vision of the landscape of Palestine, an actual journey down the steep road from Jerusalem to the Dead Sea in the chapter entitled 'The Battle with the Dragon' from *The New Jerusalem*. He remarks that most scenes from the Holy Land are impressions of particular things:

> This gigantic gesture of geography or geology, this sweep as of a universal landslide, is the sort of thing that is never conveyed by any maps or books or even pictures. All the pictures of Palestine I have ever seen are descriptive details, groups of costume or corners of architecture, at most views of famous places; they cannot give the bottomless vision of this long descent.[39]

The way in which the visual element is made to work throughout the chapter amounts to a complex strategy to enable the reader's mind to open out to fresh perceptions, to become sensitive to nuances of sensation which the bare bones of the argument cannot convey. Chesterton is, it may seem, very aware of structure and development in these images. He seems to wish to emulate a stylistic effect which he detects in the New Testament parable of the 'Lilies of the Field', brilliantly analysed in the same chapter.[40]

Such a 'power of thinking on three levels' is, he goes on to remark, much needed in modern discussion. The visual element in his writings may often be seen as a reaction against the single visions of Impressionism and of discursive reason, an attempt to regain perceptual mobility, to return to 'thinking on three levels'.

The chapter opens with a discussion of St George and the dragon as symbolic of the casting out of evil. Chesterton plays lightly with the notion that we may wish to believe in St George as an actual historical figure embodying certain desirable ethical ideals. He imagines the dismay of researchers who found no direct testimony to such a figure but abundant evidence of the dragon they had dismissed as a legendary accretion. At this point he introduces his first visual effect, a sweeping picture of a rapid journey from Jerusalem, 'down steep and jagged roads among ribbed and columned cliffs.'[41]

He recalls the descent of the Gadarene swine down a steep place
into the sea and ends his first visual excursion with a bizarre effect:

I even had a fancy one might fish for them and find them in
such a sea turned into monsters, sea-swine or four-legged fishes,
swollen and with evil eyes, grown over with sea-grass; the ghosts
of Gadara.[42]

Returning to his logical line, he next sketches a brief history of
modern thought from the ethical humanism of T.H. Huxley,
which consisted of Christian ethics divorced from religious sanc-
tions, to the contemporary spirit which repudiates the morality
Huxley thought unanswerable but dabbles continually in various
forms of the supernatural he thought exploded. At first it may
appear the Gadarene swine are being introduced as a well-worn,
although serviceable, symbol of this intellectual descent. Chesterton has other ends in view than merely to reinforce a censorious
verdict on the tendencies of the time from which he and his
readers are, by implication, divorced. Returning to his image, he
takes us over the journey again, pointing up its visual effects to the
full; the divisions of hills and crags with the sense of 'silent catas-
trophe and fundamental cleavage'; the cold wan blue of the level
skies; the fact that the sky seems to be still while the ground is
moving. Carefully, the effect of visual horror is made to mount
until we arrive at the sight of Sodom and Gomorrah, 'wasting
white and silver and grey with mere dots of decadent vegetation.'
These things are hateful, he suggests, because in the darkness of
our brains are buried things as bad 'as any buried in that bitter
sea'. It is to destroy these, rather than to enunciate ethical senti-
ments, that Christ came. The road down seems now rather to
suggest a journey into the self.

From this abyss the eye travels back across the stages of the
way, through the rocks and gorges to the distant spire of the
Russian Church in Jerusalem. The images of cleavage, the suggestions of violent energy in the landscape take on a different
meaning 'not so much a scene as an act', the triumph of good over
evil:

Sodom lay like Satan flat on the floor of the world. And far away and aloft, faint with height and distance, small but still visible, stood up the spire of the Ascension like the sword of the Archangel lifted in salute after a stroke.[43]

The way into the journey from Jerusalem to the Dead Sea is used, illustrates Chesterton's rejection of a pictorial effect which stays in one place or 'means' one thing. Rather, he seeks a visual quality which flows, in counterpoint with his argument, suggesting, not some single moment of illumination but a continuous perceptual quest, linking more and more into a mysterious coherence.

X

IDEOLOGY AND THE INDIVIDUAL MIND

Some of Chesterton's most abiding concerns were with the mental effects on the individual of the wider cultural malaise, with the emotional damage, possibly not recognised as such, which the simplifications and ideologies caused. He was concerned too, with the way in which it might be diagnosed and cured.

Although Chesterton would probably not have cared to be called a psychologist, even the most cursory knowledge of his work suggests a continued interest in the health and afflictions of the mind, in the cause and cure of mental and emotional illness, in the nature of sanity. As might be expected from his active intelligence and from such a long-lasting preoccupation with a complex absorbing matter, Chesterton's views did not remain static. Without giving up any of his basic ideas, his original set of perceptions, he did modify them appreciably. He turned the subject about under many lights, examining and re-examining it. Shifts of emphasis may be observed, a bringing forward of some aspects of the matter, a lessening stress on others.

There is, however, another reason for Chesterton's changing view. Madness and sanity are social phenomena, and were seen as such by him. He was aware of living in a society changing in ways he deplored. The scene was, in some senses, a darkening one in which the pursuit of sanity was to grow more difficult. But there was a gain in this process. His mind sharpened by new tensions, Chesterton responded with new insights.

210

An examination of the phases of this intellectual involvement has several uses. It offers a good picture of Chesterton's mind at work, of his essentially dynamic intellect, in which a wish for firm definitions and established first principles was allied to a readiness to take a fresh look again and again at a subject; a mental characteristic which was the most heartening of his many paradoxes. The 'pursuit of sanity' suggests also another feature of Chesterton's personality, the way in which, with him, emotion was transcended. Rooted, obviously, in his own readily admitted and fairly-faced experience of adolescent morbidity, Chesterton's preoccupation issues out into intellectual discussion. In spite of the interest the subject had for him there is nothing self-indulgent in his treatment of it. The predominant elements are rather pity for the victims and that sheer pleasure in thinking through a matter which he rated one of the highest of human functions. Chesterton sensed how many, especially young, people are mentally self-tormenting. Barbara Traill in the first of the stories in *Four Faultless Felons* (1930) strikes a familiar chord:

> She told herself again and again she was being morbid, and she told herself again and again that she was only morbid because she was mad. But she was not in the least mad, she was only young, and thousands of young people go through such a phase of nightmare, and nobody knows or helps.[1]

She reminds the reader of many other instances. It was a country Chesterton knew well. His arguably most persuasive apologetic work, *Orthodoxy* and his undoubtedly most impressive novel, *The Man who was Thursday*, had both dealt in their different ways, with escape from a world of private nightmare. They both suggested, furthermore, that as early as 1908, he had well-defined ideas on the subject of madness, its cause and cure. His analysis of the unbalanced mind, in Chapter II of *Orthodoxy*, 'The Maniac' is noteworthy for several reasons. The strategy of starting his apologetic with the fact of mental illness rather than the traditional point of departure 'the conviction of sin' implies a feeling that a new approach is needed. The facts remain but the language which describes them has become jejune; part of a structure of thinking and feeling no longer commonly shared. But although men deny sin, 'we all still agree that there is a collapse of the intellect as unmistakable as a falling house.'[2] More important for the present purpose than Chesterton's sense of the need for a new idiom for the Christian argument, is the frame of reference he uses in discussing mental illness. It is necessary, he seems to feel, to define the 'collapse of the intellect' accurately since he is living at a time when such a collapse is widespread.

In part, Chesterton's view of madness in *Orthodoxy* shows the influence of the Augustan moralists in whose writings he was steeped. He was later to connect himself with the Tory tradition of the late seventeenth and eighteenth centuries,[3] very different, of course, from modern Toryism. His admiration for Dr Johnson is well known. But, when little more than a boy, Chesterton had been complimented by W.P. Ker for taking pleasure in the then unfashionable Pope.[4] The quotation from Dryden in 'The Maniac' is highly functional and germane to Chesterton's argument.

It may be very reasonably objected that Chesterton's pictures of madness are not medically realistic, that they are not recognisable pictures of the distressing symptoms of nervous breakdown, depression, paranoia or other common forms of such illness. Chesterton's 'Madmen' seem altogether too bright, cheerful and argumentative. Chesterton knew of emotional and nervous distress directly. His wife appears to have suffered from prolonged and acute depression. His brother-in-law committed suicide under its effects. He does not, however, choose in his novels to show this kind of emotional distress. He concentrates rather on the theme of *ideological* madness, devising, I would suggest, a range of characters who, not intended to be realistic, symbolise types of cultural and intellectual lunacy. To say that Chesterton's individual madmen are metaphors of the collective ideological insanities of the twentieth century, is not, of course, to suggest that such mental illness does not exist on a personal level. Chesterton's position is that much mental abnormality and emotional damage has to do with cultural currents, with ideas and above all, specifically, with two strands of dominant contemporary thought: first, materialist determinism and the denial of free-will and moral responsibility; secondly, the widespread tendency to deny the reality of the physical world. If these do not cause mental illness, they certainly exacerbate it. The essential truth about such illness, given the force of habit by which terminologies are maintained, would not be reached by case-histories of symptoms, but by exposing the mental pressures which through false logic or ideological bombardment bring about breakdown or depression. This can only be done through the non-realistic mode of making the mad argue, defend, justify and extrapolate their illness, when, in reality they might be more likely to retreat into silence.

Madness or neurosis Chesterton sees not as the result of excessive repression of the instinctual life in the Freudian manner, nor as until quite recently fashionable psychologists have done, as the consequence of stresses within the family. His basic emphasis is, like that of Johnson in the *Adventurer* No.85[5] or Swift in 'A Digression on Madness',[6] on the danger of trusting the reasoning faculty divorced from the commonsense and common feeling of the community. This is the weight behind Chesterton's quotation from 'Absolom and Achitophel', Dryden's accusation that Shaftsbury/Achitophel sets mere fluent cleverness against common sense and common quiet. Johnson's astronomer in *Rasselas* is cured not by reasoning but by linking himself to the general life. Imlac advises him:

> When scruples importune you which in your lucid moments you know to be vain, do not stand at parley but fly to business or to Pekuah, and keep this thought always prevalent, that you are only one atom in the mass of humanity.[7]

Chesterton stresses that man cannot think himself out of mental evil since the most unmistakable mark of madness is logical completeness. The only answer is like Johnson's, to admit no parley, 'decision is the whole business here'. 'A door must be shut forever' and one must connect oneself resolutely with a life which will correct the follies of solitary reasoning:

> I admit that your explanation explains a good deal; but what a great deal it leaves out! Are there no stories in the world but yours?[8]

A second aspect of the cure is a readiness to accept mystery, to cease to attempt to explain everything. Chesterton's criticism of materialist philosophers like Haeckel is essentially that of Johnson's rebuke of Soame Jenyns, that of trivialising life and death, beautiful, deeply painful and inscrutable by utterly inadequate rationalisations. Present in both writers is a protest against philosophies in which the explanation of the whole seems less than its separate aspects. Chesterton's often expressed admiration for 'The Book of Job' is part of a feeling that only acknowledged mystery can heal and console. Shallow rationality merely makes matters worse. While 'mysticism keeps men sane. As long as you have mystery you have health... . The ordinary man has always been sane because the ordinary man has always been a mystic. He has permitted the twilight.'[9] In Chesterton, as in Johnson, the key words in the cure of insanity are community and mystery. Both see mystery essentially in religious terms. The problem for Chesterton is in community. How is the delusion of the solitary reasoner to be corrected without a sane community to which to refer him? For him, of course, the family was of prime value. Unlike R.D. Laing he saw it, not as an engine of torment, but as a bracing challenge to the idiosyncrasies of the individual, his potential cliquishness.[10] His defence of the institution of the family against the attacks which were beginning to be made against it both by psychologists and, he felt, by legislators, underlines the problem Chesterton was increasingly to have with community. It was the radical difference between his situation and that of Johnson who could rest on acknowledged cultural, social and moral values. Chesterton is above all an author of cultural crisis. England, he recognised, had ceased to be Christian.[11] The pursuit of sanity is much more than a personal matter for individuals in his novels. It is the fever chart of the times in which he lived.

It is the most important, though not the only, theme of his greatest novel. *The Man who was Thursday* (1908) is a complex, and in some ways mystifying, book whose allegorical meaning escapes neat paraphrase. At one simple level, it is, as the dedicatory poem to E.C. Bentley makes clear, a metaphorical record of Chesterton's private crisis at the Slade, of his reaction against the solipsism and pessimism of the 1890s. It studies, from the standpoint of an assured sanity and intellectual certitude the 'old fears' and 'empty hells' of the youth who saw the universe as meaningless or worse, as governed by hostile, inexorable forces. The novel's subtitle 'A Nightmare' implies the lifting of this 1890s vision. It was only a nightmare after all.

On another level, *The Man who was Thursday*, from the very form of its plot, is a political novel, addressing itself to the public danger posed by intellectual nihilism. (The book, needless to say, had its topical side. Overt anarchism, culminating in a series of murders, including those of a President of the USA, a King of Italy, a Prime Minister of Spain and an Empress of Austria, was a political fact of the time. Chesterton's novel, as much as Conrad's very different *The Secret Agent* grew out of a recognition of this danger). The mass of anarchists are really, Chesterton feels, quite harmless, sincere and misguided romantic revolutionaries, but there does indeed exist an inner core of wealthy cynics and pessimists who manipulate the revolutionary movement as Dostoevsky's Stavrogin manipulates 'the Possessed'.

At first sight these two separate strands of the novel seem to be saying two different things. The private allegory seems to suggest that the universe is far friendlier than it appeared, that things are not what they seem but much better, as the conspiracy of anarchists melts away into the forces of law and each man who had looked an enemy is revealed as a friend. So optimistic is this side of the novel that it may even lend itself to the notion that evil is an illusion, a misreading Chesterton was at pains to dispel in a later essay:

> I was not then considering whether anything is really evil, but whether everything is really evil; and in relation to the latter nightmare it still does seem to be relevant to say that the night-mares are not true.[12]

The political strand of the novel seems, on the contrary, to assert the reality of a world-wide conspiracy of wealthy nihilists in which the rich men who are perverting the community join hands with these intellectual enemies of meaning and order whose revolutionary zeal is, in fact, a hunger for death. However, this divergence in the meaning of the book is only superficial. The nihilism to which the core of the anarchist movement has yielded, is, in essence, identical with those private fears, that feeling of inevitability and hopelessness which are the starting point of the private allegory. The victory in the

personal battle for sanity, which inaugurates a new vision of life and
of the universe is also a victory over those forces intellectual and
material which threaten the community.

The Man who was Thursday begins with a quarrel, set in Saffron
Park, an artists' colony, between a young poet Syme and Gregory,
another poet and the one real anarchist in the novel. Syme has
reacted against his unconventional, half-crazy family into sanity and
respectability and has become a police detective. Through the
quarrel, he comes to hear of a secret grand council of anarchists,
taking their names from the days of the week and acting under the
leadership of the strange, terrifying giant, Sunday. Syme takes
advantage of Gregory's introduction of him to this body to ask to
become the replacement for Thursday who has recently died. This is
granted and Syme seems to have entered an enclosed, evil, all-
powerful group. Once he conquers his fears, however, he finds he is
not alone. One by one, in a series of startling incidents, each member
of the anarchist council is revealed as a detective in the same
organisation as Syme, engaged, like him in the fight against anarchism. Sunday's bewildered followers pursue him as, leaving behind
a series of enigmatic messages, he flies off in a balloon to his estate. In
the novel's allegory this huge but in fact harmless, if mischievous
figure is, perhaps, life, Nature or, more accurately God's energies in
Nature. Each man sees in the estate the happiest scenes of his own
youth. When the unreconciled true anarchist Gregory confronts
Sunday with the accusation that he has never known the horror felt
by his lieutenants, Sunday answers in Christ's words 'Can you drink
of the cup I drink of'? The novel seems to be saying, in its religious
essence, that the mystery of life becomes bearable, capable of
meaning and joy, through acceptance of one's own suffering in
acknowledgement of the suffering of God.

The situation of the morbid, neurotic or mentally disturbed would
be hopeless but for the most important element in Chesterton's
analysis of their problem, his belief in the power of self-
determination through an act of will, in the fact of human responsibility. Syme's throwing aside of fear on hearing the music of the
barrel-organ in *The Man who was Thursday* is a two-fold process. It is a
splendid evocation of both community and mystery. Syme feels

linked to 'these common and kindly people in the street, who everyday marched into battle to the music of the barrel-organ.'[13] Equally important with this feeling of kinship with the common life is the readiness to embrace mystery, to submit to the fact of death:

This liberation of his spirit from the load of his weakness went with a clear decision to embrace death.[14]

In choosing to die for the sake of his integrity he is dying for something the anarchists could never understand. The music of the barrel-organ combines the two elements, 'all the trumpets of the pride of life, the drums of the pride of death.'[15] Much might be written about the design of *The Man who was Thursday* and critics have suggested how carefully every detail in the novel fits within the whole intellectual scheme; so different is the real Chesterton from the diffuse boulevardier of popular myth. Into this pattern the pursuit of sanity and Chesterton's analysis of the cause and cure of mental illness is central. Saffron Park, the starting point for the quest may be seen as an allegorical picture of the modern intellectual world. Drawn from the Bedford Park of his early courtship, it is made to display those features of modern thought which he was to describe in some of the most amusing passages in *Autobiography*.[16] Like the Ethical Society Chesterton recalled there, which altered its doctrines completely to accommodate each succeeding lecturer, the inhabitants of Saffron Park are lacking in intellectual seriousness. They are not actually committed to anything. It is a pleasant place, but a place of poseurs, of 'characters' striking attitudes, listened to by their 'emancipated' but curiously indulgent womenfolk.

Chesterton seems to wish to establish two points about this limbo: first, that the absence of firm and consistent principles lays men open to certain abiding dangers, which he examines throughout his later work, namely mad rationalism and superstition; secondly, that it is only by seeking to live through the consequences of a real moral choice that one succeeds in passing out of the half-world of the modern intellectual. Saffron Park is, significantly, described as 'written comedy', a kind of stage set. The images of dissolving skies and unreal sunsets with which the novel opens are functional, as a recent critic has shown. Chesterton, without being in the least censorious, notes that it is an artificial paradise 'as separate as a drifting cloud'[17] from the economic, social and emotional life of most men. It is in such a world that the dangers of madness, individual and collective, most threaten.

The anarchist threat proves, of course, to be a delusion which collapses when it is faced; a fundamentally hopeful attitude which Chesterton never retracted, but which he later noticeably modified. Although eventually unreal, the threat posed by the anarchists is palpable and terrifying and its symptoms are carefully described. They fall into two groups. Much of the anarchism of Syme's parents and of the conspirators he later meets is insane logic, arguments based on false or narrow premises and carried to absurdity. By the time Syme's mother has come to the point of advocating compulsory vegetarianism, his father is preaching cannibalism. The 'heroic worker' who occupied the post of Thursday, has died 'through his belief in a hygenic mixture of chalk and water as a substitute for milk,'[18] which he feels involves cruelty to cows. This abstract humanitarianism ends too in cruelty and Syme is made aware of the anarchist danger by an actual terrorist outrage. Here again Chesterton's relationship to the eighteenth century may be noted. His critique of pedantic humanitarian rationalism issuing in ideological barbarity rests ultimately on Burke,[19] one of the leading figures of the tradition he admired.

The other salient feature of the attack on sanity is fear. A feeling of fear permeates much of the book, essentially a superstitious fear based on the sense of inevitable fate. The fatality is something hostile to human life and feeling and expressed in grotesque images which recur in Chesterton's work, like the one of the crooked or wrongly-shaped coffin containing something non-natural. Much of Chesterton's writing is an attack on this fatalism, incarnated in the 'gods behind the gods' worshipped by the Danes in *The Ballad of the White Horse* or by Carthage in *The Everlasting Man*, and often associated by him with the East. It explains his attacks on such figures as Nietzsche, Spengler and Marinetti, prophets of fate and force.

He seems to have felt he was living in an increasingly superstitious age, which, lacking true beliefs, was given over more and more to morbid fearfulness. The description of Syme's first view of Sunday's

218

face is a careful piece of analysis. Syme is described as over-sensitive to 'nameless psychological influences':

Utterly devoid of fear in physical dangers, he was a great deal too sensitive to the smell of spiritual evil. Twice already that night little unmeaning things had peeped out at him almost pruriently and given him the sense of drawing near to the headquarters of hell.[20]

It recalls a childish fancy, the face of Memnon in the British Museum. Chesterton is pointing out, as Lamb did in 'Witches and Other Night Fears,' that there is in every human being, an innate fearfulness, which will find some object; a point he elaborated later with reference to the childhood of his brother Cecil in an essay 'The Fear of the Film' in *Fancies Versus Fads* (1923). Fear is born with us and always remains in the substratum of the mind. With the weakening of the religious sense of free-will, these childish terrors revive, attaching themselves to trivial chances and mere coincidence, 'little unmeaning things'. The result can be a mind or will paralysed or forced along a certain course by a feeling that it is inevitable, as when Syme begins to feel Sunday is a Superman. This perception was to form the basis of Chesterton's remarkably clear account of the predicament of Macbeth and it is interesting and significant that a whole volume of Father Brown stories *The Incredulity of Father Brown* is devoted to cases of superstitious fatalism.

Chesterton in *The Man who was Thursday* develops in careful stages the remedy for such a sapping of the mind. Clearly nothing can be done unless one leaves the world of Saffron Park behind and begins to make decisions and hold opinions to which one's whole personality is bound. The action of the novel really begins when Syme condemns the comic talking-shop of the modern intellectuals:

I should think very little of a man who didn't keep something more serious in the background of his life that was more serious than all this talking.[21]

As Chesterton pointed out later, the figures in 'The Book of Job' do not agree to differ, do not refer divergent opinions to questions of temperament.[22] Consequently urgent matters can be discussed. It might even be possible to reach the truth. This, of course, is the premiss of Chesterton's philosophical novels.

As the action of the story unfolds, the lonely individual finds he is a part of a community, joined to others who have made a similar decision to take sides, in a battle which involves life and death. A part of the individual's cure lies simply in breaking out of his isolation and learning to trust others, as Syme does when he overcomes his fear of treachery.[23] Community is found with the poor, in the symbol of the barrel-organ. It is found with the past, in the image of the lantern with the cross on it which Syme holds up before the surging crowd:

> There is not a street you walk on, there is not a thread you wear, that was not made as this lantern was, by denying your philosophy of dirt and rats.[24]

Above all, community is found still existing in France, a country of small farmers, where the poor have dignity. They are not down-trodden, 'clinging to the decencies and charities of Christendom', like the working people of London, but members of a society which allows them property and equality. Looking at the Norman peasant, Syme remarks that he will never be an anarchist and Colonel Ducroix replies:

> Mr Syme is right enough there, if only for the reason that he has plenty of property to defend. But I forgot that in your country you are not used to peasants being wealthy.[25]

This is the meaning of the French denouement of *The Man who was Thursday*. In a healthy society, which France approximately is, insanity based on fear and fatalism cannot take root. Chesterton is fully aware, then, of the social dimensions of the pursuit of sanity.

Mystery, inseparably linked with community as the remedy of the disease, is, of course, identified with the figure of Sunday. Critics have noted the similarities between the seemingly fearful enigmas of Sunday and some of the writings of Kafka. The similarities are certainly present, but Chesterton, towards the end of his life, guarded himself against the suggestion that the dark, terrifying and unknowable Sunday was a picture of the Divine Nature. The mystery he describes was not another version of the bleak inscrutable God outlined by Kierkegaard and Barth. Such a mystery could hardly be an answer to fatalism.

Chesterton's essay on 'The Book of Job' throws some light on his intention in the figure of Sunday, not in fact God, but the manifestation of God's energies in Nature. The mystery is not designed to intimidate but to sweep aside trains of false logic, narrow rationalisms, like the mechanical equalities of the anarchists or the mechanical rewards and punishments of Job's comforters:

> God will make Job see a startling universe if he can only do it by making Job see an idiotic universe.[26]

This comment on God's answer to Job out of the whirlwind 'a long panorama of created things'[27] full of hints of joy, strongly suggests the reason for Syme's reaction to Sunday's strange notes:

> He remembered a hornbill, which was simply a huge yellow beak with a small bird tied on behind it. The whole gave him a sensation, the vividness of which he could not explain, that Nature was always making quite mysterious jokes.[28]

Chesterton firmly insists on this great secret, too good to be told, which God is keeping back, but of which there are innumerable hints, an enigma very different in spirit and effect from Kafka's tormenting riddles.

If, however, the history of the pursuit of sanity in Chesterton's later work is sketched, it becomes clear that his position is very far from unqualified optimism. Even in *The Man who was Thursday* there are shadows. True community can only be found in France, since the social condition of England is desperate. Sadder even than this, there are minds like the Secretary's and Gregory's who resist the mystery, who do not accept that it solves anything. It is notable that they never retract their accusations:

> If you were from the first our father and our friend, why were you also our greatest enemy?[29]

There is a final revelation of a suffering God but, significantly, there is no comforting conclusion for Gregory, Gogol and the secretary, no

221

answer to Syme's plea 'Oh, most unhappy man try to be happy.'[30] Perhaps there are those who simply lack that capacity. At least they are free to choose and we never learn that they do, in fact, make the right choice. There is never the least pretence that the pursuit of sanity is easy even in *Orthodoxy* and *The Man who was Thursday*.

In *Manalive* (1912), however, there has been a significant change. The setting of this book is in interesting contrast to those of the earlier novels. Instead of wide-ranging incident, adventures and flights across country, the action is confined to a suburban boarding house. The inmates of Beacon House, unlike the characters of previous novels, are not rebels or colourful personalities. They are washed-out, despondent victims of fatalistic modern psychological and sociological teachings, who see their surroundings as drab, and the business of living as a jejune affair without purpose or interest, a dreary series of foregone conclusions. Innocent Smith bursts in upon this dismal backwater in a symbolic high wind, and, through a series of seemingly eccentric actions, brings the lodgers new zest and their little world a new colour and excitement. Persuading them to establish their own 'sovereign state', with its own laws, customs and rituals, he enhances their sense of the boarding house's potentialities. He disrupts the settled tedium of their lives, encouraging them to paint, sing, dance and picnic on the roof.

Ronald Knox and other commentators have noticed a resemblance between the plot of *Manalive* and Jerome K. Jerome's play *The Passing of the Third Floor Back*, then enjoying an undeserved popularity, in which a Christ-figure transforms the lives of a group of lodgers. The difference is more striking than the superficial similarity. In Jerome's piece, as Max Beerbohm pointed out in a justifiably scathing notice (*Saturday Review* 5 September 1908) the characters are cardboard types of various kinds of stock immorality, whom the mysterious stranger 'saves' by telling each one how good he or she really is. Innocent Smith, on the contrary operates through various sophisticated psychological strategies and he has to deal with aspects of a much more intractable psychological malaise.

One of the most interesting themes of *Manalive* is that of justice embodied in its central incident, the 'trial' of Smith by a family court composed of the lodgers of Beacon House, on the charge that his wild behaviour proves he is insane. The prosecution consists of Dr Pym, the American criminologist and Moses Gould, who represent respectively an intellectual nullity, concealed by elaborate and useless terminologies, and a reductionist materialism hostile to ideals and zest. The defence consists of two others, Arthur Inglewood and Michael Moon, the embodiments of English modesty and decency and Irish realism.

The 'court' hears as evidence letters written about Smith alternately by individuals he has offended and by friends who provide innocent explanations for their charges of murder, burglary, desertion and bigamy. It emerges that Smith renews the excitement of his life by such devices as breaking into his own house like a burglar to rediscover the joys of possession, eloping with his wife to experience afresh the joys of marriage and walking around the earth in order to see his home with fresh enthusiasm.

The curious narrative devices of the trial enable Chesterton to explore themes dear to him, the value of the home and the family unit, against the modern state and current ideologies. The letters, several of which narrate encounters Smith has on his travels with representatives of different cultures, French middle class, Russian liberal, Chinese Confucian and deracinated modern American, enable Chesterton to examine the value and limitations of those traditions and to show both what Smith learns from them and how he, in turn, affects them.

In *Manalive*, the enemy of sanity is not a conspiracy without substance. It is the 'real world', the habitual, mundane matter-of-fact life of Dr Warner and Moses Gould. There is a very real possibility that a truly sane man runs a risk of being certified as a lunatic in a world becoming increasingly crazy. Chesterton's political disillusionment (1906–14) has a bearing on the pursuit of sanity. In 'The Mad Official' published in the *Daily News* in 1912, he raised the connection between routine and madness in societies and individuals. There are peoples who have lost the power of astonishment at their own actions and 'one of these countries is modern England'. The essay is a piece of energetic journalism written to expose a specific injustice. Some hyperbole might be expected, as in the comparison of medical evidence with Chinese ceremonial torture. The opening of *Manalive*, however, sketches seemingly ordinary people who are, in fact, victims of a loss of mental balance. Warner is:

> the embodiment of silkiness and solidity. He was a big, bland, bored, and (as some said) boring man, with flat, fair hair and handsome, heavy features.[31]

Inglewood, who admires him, is a timid soul:

> unmarried, moral, decidedly intelligent, living on a little money of his own, and hiding himself in the two hobbies of photography and cycling.[32]

Michael Moon is one of the earliest versions of a recurring figure in Chesterton's fiction, the unhappy Irish rebel. Moon is at odds with his life, without apparently being able fully to define the reasons for his discontent. He is drawn to and yet repelled by Moses Gould, the fourth of the quartet of psychologically damaged men who are to be challenged by the great wind and by the advent of Innocent Smith. Taken together, the four are a microcosm of the emotional effect of materialism and determinism. Warner, bland and self-satisfied, has been dead for years[33] but his view of life provides a mental prison for his disciple Inglewood:

> Under the Warnerian scepticism and science of hopeless human types, Inglewood had long come to regard himself as a timid, insufficient and 'weak' type, who would never marry; to regard Diana Duke as a materialistic maid-servant.[34]

Ideas have consequences and Chesterton shows their effect on Inglewood. It is perfectly possible to be emotionally and mentally crippled even to the point when both will and perception cease to function. Inglewood simply does not see things as they are and is losing his sense of life's possibilities. He is becoming increasingly isolated and out of touch with others. Isolation and inability to see partly recalls Syme, but the tone is very different. There is nothing colourful or dramatic about Inglewood's ailment. It is simply a wasting disease.

Moon, 'intelligent without ambition', is a more obvious misfit.

Like Dalroy in *The Flying Inn*, he is a romantic, sad, flippant and ironic. He prefers 'low company' and to listen rather than talk. Chesterton pictures a man who cannot square his inner life and perceptions with the world around him. Moon's preference for the company of his intellectual inferiors is as depressing a symptom as Inglewood's isolation. Rather than cut himself off from others, he prefers to find those he can patronise and laugh at.

Inglewood and Moon are at least unhappy. Warner and Gould are all too thoroughly 'integrated' into their world. Unlike Warner, Gould is not unpleasant.

> Moses Gould was as good a fellow in his way as ever lived; far kinder to his family than more refined men of pleasure; simple and steadfast in his admirations; a thoroughly wholesome animal and a thoroughly genuine character.[35]

He simply has no sense of a spiritual dimension in life. The nerve is dead. He is the cynic triumphant. There is none of the agonised questioning of the accusers at the end of *The Man who was Thursday*. The suggestion conveyed by the figures of Warner and Gould is a sombre one. The human mind might be permanently reduced in scale. Its spiritual or emotional life permanently maimed. Offered the possibility of more abundant life, of transcendence, even of joy, such a mind cannot accept it. When Gould is asked whether he thinks being perfectly good in all respects would make a man merry, he simply denies it 'with an unusual and convincing gravity'.[36]

The task Chesterton proposes to himself in *Manalive* is less an enquiry into madness in its wider philosophical bearings, as in *The Man who was Thursday*, as an attempt to grapple with it in its specific day-to-day expression, to suggest 'therapies' for those whose condition is desperate, though, like Inglewood, their symptoms are undramatic. As in the 'hole in heaven' sequence of *The Flying Inn*, or the dressing-up at the end of *The Man who was Thursday*, there is a stress on the importance of recovering the element of play, the fantasy and games of children.

Innocent Smith succeeds in making the lodgers at Beacon House feel that they are a family. He encourages each one to define and heighten his own personality:

Each person with a hobby found it turning into an institution.[37]

His use of the old trick of reproducing the same figure twice on a photographic plate becomes 'moral photography', a turning of the individual's sense of himself into something playful. Smith seems to be trying to make Inglewood like himself more and paradoxically take himself less seriously:

> One highly successful trilogy – representing Inglewood recognizing Inglewood, Inglewood prostrating himself before Inglewood, and Inglewood severely beating Inglewood with an umbrella – Innocent Smith wanted to have enlarged and put up in the hall, with the inscription –
> Self-reverence, self-knowledge, self-control –
> These three alone will make a man a prig.[38]

Smith's use of dance and painting, like his use of photography, is as Moon sees and analyses, deliberate means of expression which sidestep conversational clichés, the prisons of structured language and ideas, to give new weight of meaning to communication, and to reach and awaken areas of the mind not being brought into play.

The whole framework of *Manalive* in which Smith, instead of being certified at once as Warner wishes, is 'tried' by a 'family court', is a deliberate challenge by him, and by Chesterton, to conventional ideas of sanity and insanity. Smith seems to wish his judges to examine their own emotional lives. More than this, the trial is a sustained attack on psychological classification of individuals into types, with certain innate characteristics, who do not act out of choice but out of pathological necessity. (Chesterton sees little difference between this new fashion in psychology and the decaying 'science' of phrenology he mocked in 'The Criminal Head' in *Alarms and Discursions* (1910). Under the pretence of a more humane view, the expert Cyrus Pym reduces men to automata. The question has been:

> thoroughly elucidated by ... our great secret-guessing Sonnenschein, in his great work, *The Destructive Type*. We do not denounce Smith as a murderer, but rather as a murderous man. The type is such that its very life – I may say its very health – is in killing.[39]

Michael Moon, arguing for the defence, counters this by quoting a non-existent Dr Moonenschein's monograph to the effect that Warner belongs to a type naturally prone to be murdered. Sadly what Chesterton intended as a *reductio ad absurdum* is now a widely canvassed psychological theory.

In *Manalive*, Chesterton's view of mental illness and its treatment has developed from the premises suggested in *Orthodoxy*. Community can only be restored by strengthening the family to the point where it is independent of the state. Mystery can only be restored by the drastic tactics of Innocent Smith, the sane man turned outlaw. The pervading force of fatalistic psychologists and philosophers, entrenched in the medical profession and in education, exploiting the official powers of the modern state can only be locally shaken by wild practical jokes. In possibly the finest section of the book, already touched on, Smith routs the arguments of his College Tutor, a follower of Shopenhauer, that life is a worthless illusion, by attempting to murder him to put him out of his misery. The point, however, is that Smith must break the mental hold of this philosophy or himself succumb to it. It is the implied desperation in *Manalive* about the threats to sanity in modern life which gives the book a somewhat hectic quality. An underlying element in *Manalive's* frenetic energy is the notion that only such antics could penetrate the cloud of routine obtuseness, such as that of Canon Hawkins.

Smith's mischievousness, his liking for the roofs of houses, his almost non-human energy, his sudden entry into the private lives of total strangers suggests, incidentally, another eighteenth-century moralist Le Sage. Belloc regarded *Le Diable Boiteaux* in its English version *The Devil on Two Sticks* as 'one of the best books in the language not only as an English book but as a translation',[40] and it is possible that he may have communicated his enthusiasm to Chesterton.

However where in *The Devil on Two Sticks* reality in Paul Hazard's words 'spells ugliness, unloveliness of soul, unloveliness of body',[41] what Innocent Smith sees from his rooftops is unexplored potentiality. Smith who, curiously, bears a strong physical resemblance to Chesterton himself, gets below conventional appearance to reveal not emptiness but wasted power. The vision of Cambridge Dr

Eames sees from the flying buttress awakens him to the unexpected and arresting beauty in what he had thought banal.

Just round the corner of the College, and visible from his crazy perch, were the brightest specks on that bright landscape, the villa with the spotted blinds which he had made his text that night. He wondered for the first time what people lived in them.[42]

The rooftops are a place where the dulled perceptions and habitual ways of seeing are challenged. The strange vision of the coloured smoke of London awakens the curate Mr Percy to the *unnatural* quality of modern civilisation; something as fantastic as an illustration to *The Arabian Nights* and essentially wrong:

And yet, though the tints were all varied, they all seemed unnatural, like fumes from a witch's pot.[43]

Percy's journey over the roofs, however, is a progressive revelation. Its second stage is a sense of the triviality of property and social laws and regulations:

I had reached, as it were, a higher level of that mountain of vaporous visions, the heaven of a higher levity.[44]

The culminating perception, as Smith recalling Santa Claus, makes his way down his own chimney, is that stealing is as cruel as taking a child's toys. The curate's rooftop journey has taken him from the stultified respectability of his colleague Hawkins, through an understandable but destructive view that property is theft, to a right sense of its value.

Innocent Smith, an eccentric in danger of being certified, is the adversary of a deadened and repetitive attitude to life which in the end produces madness. Yet, powerful as the tyranny of habit is, there is still the sense in *Manalive* that the trivialising of life, the loss of joy which causes mental illness might have a simple answer, to see things from another angle. A new language or form of expression, a rooftop journey or going round the world in order to return home are all devices intended to produce such a change of vision.

In Chesterton's later explorations of the theme of insanity, the picture is darker and more complex. The doctors who try to certify

Gabriel Gale in *The Poet and the Lunatics* (1929) are not merely imper-
cipient. They are evil and perverse. They attempt to persuade Gale
that he is suffering from 'a mode of modified monomania' because
'you never see a cat without thinking of a tiger or a lizard without
thinking of a dragon.'[45] In other words, his strong sense of the essence
of an object, of its distinctive qualities, his perception of sharply
defined independent entities is in itself a proof of madness. Gale
retorts that Wolf's mind is incapable of grasping 'the thing called a
thing', that it is 'a chaos of exceptions and no rule'.[46] Since Wolf has
no sense of what constitutes normality he could present a plausible
case for anyone being mad. Both Wolf's lack of a sense of definition
and of a moral conscience are both explicitly connected with his
atheism. In his colleague Starkey the condition is more pronounced
and the result more sinister. Gale points out that unlike Wolf, Starkey
does not have a sceptical philosophy. He has been a persistent liar
'and from so early an age that you could never see anything as it is,
but only as it could be made to look.'[47] To a lack of a sense of definition is added, in his case, an instinct for the 'deceptive potentialities'
of an object the way in which 'anything could be used as anything
else'. His instinct for the misuse of things is part of a general capacity
to snatch up ideas 'as swiftly as a pickpocket'.

With Gould and Warner there is merely, though sadly, something
lacking. In *The Poet and the Lunatics* evil is actively embodied in fluent
cleverness without a moral centre or sense of definition, exploiting
ideas and terminology and prostituting science. (In a much lighter
vein, Chesterton was to show, in the almost contemporary *Four
Faultless Felons*, the ease with which a wholly imaginary mental illness
might be invented. Believing the father of the woman he loves is a
murderer, John Judson coins the 'disease of duodiapsychosis',
tricked out with an elaborate terminology and spurious list of symptoms to help him escape a charge. The whole bluff is made to depend
on the authority of the 'great Dr Doone', now a vain and irritable
pedant, mulling over past feuds. The anecdote suggests that much of
what passes for science is trickery, jargon and a superstitious rever-
ence for established reputations).

The evil doctors of *The Poet and the Lunatics* knowingly use the terminology of psychology against the social or political nonconformist.

Unlike the attempt to certify Innocent Smith in *Manalive* their scheme to have Gabriel Gale put away is not a mistake made in good faith by men of limited perceptions or invincible ignorance. It is not a matter of their having lost, through a sincerely held materialistic determinism, a sense of the joy of life. They have lost, through lying, both moral conscience and the good of the intellect. In *Manalive* Sonnenschein's psychological jargon is honest poppycock, deducible, however feebly, from some kind of philosophical position. In *The Poet and the Lunatics*, the concepts behind psychology are completely fluid and its practitioners' venal. The lack of intellectual seriousness in the modern intellectual world, suggested in Saffron Park, has rotted the fibre of its inhabitants.

Compared with the doctors, the really mad in these later works are something of a relief. Consistent with his position in *Orthodoxy* and *The Man who was Thursday*, Chesterton still sees rationalism without common sense as one of the mainsprings of madness. It is not the eccentric poet Gale who is mad, but his 'agent' or rather patient Hurrel, the intensely practical man of affairs, full of financial schemes. Gale remarks that this is the most dangerous type of all:

Of all the maniacs I have tried to manage, the maddest of all was the man of business.[48]

Hurrel is bright, energetic, full of 'suggestions and proposals and possibilities' for the economic redevelopment of the derelict countryside around the Rising Sun inn. Moreover, his ideas sound plausible enough in themselves. This relentlessly optimistic and self-confident man 'making calculations on pieces of paper, and reeling off figures and answering objections and growing every moment more restless and radiant'[49] bemuses the squire. His effect on the depressive innkeeper is to make him try to hang himself. As Gale points out, the world of practicality and success has nothing to offer those whose personalities or joy in life has crumbled.

What can practical men do here? Waste their practical lives watching him day and night to see he doesn't get hold of a rope or a razor?[50]

He undertakes to cure the innkeeper's suicidal urge and in a twenty-minute interview is successful. Chesterton does not show this interview but conveys its content with an oblique subtlety in what follows. Gale, using a large piece of chalk, sketches on the inn-sign of the Rising Sun. Its optimistic emblem is altered to St Peter denying Christ, at the third cock-crow, with the sun rising in the background. As in Smith's dances and games in *Manalive*, Chesterton seems to be suggesting a language of gesture and representation, which, as Moon pointed out in the earlier book, is richer and fuller of nuance, than the conceptualising language of modern rationalism. The altered inn-sign implies, among much else, an escape from the success-failure polarity. Peter's failure was complete and humiliating and yet he was the chosen disciple. The innkeeper does not have to judge himself by a standard which is crude and impoverished as well as being impossible for him; a view of life, and glib emptiness of which Chesterton criticised elsewhere in such essays as 'The Fallacy of Success' in *All Things Considered* (1908) and 'On Making Good' in *All I survey* (1933). Having made this point, Gale can return to the care of Hurrel, the practical man, an incurable who needs constant care and attention.

The care of the individual lunatic by the individual keeper is another element in Chesterton's later view of mental illness. There is a suggestion here of the need for close observation of each case and the kind of attention to its needs and idiosyncrasies which can only be given in a one-to-one relationship. Gale watches Hurrel continually, to prevent his practicality and drive to succeed from becoming homicidal, as they threaten to do. In *Four Faultless Felons* the tutor John Hume watches his charge Tom Traill to guard against eccentric socially disruptive behaviour: Tom's tendency to come out with untimely truths. In neither of these two cases is the terminology of modern psychology of much help. Hurrel, far from being regarded as the maniac he is, conforms to the admired model of a successful man. Tom Traill, far from being really mad, is simply somewhat childlike and socially awkward:

He is only what they call a protected neurotic, which is their long-winded way of saying he has an extra skin that the Public School varnish won't stick on. . . . So much the better for him.[51]

Apart from the fluid and arbitrary nature of psychological terms and concepts which renders them open to exploitation by the unscrupulous, they produce that sense of fatalism which Chesterton had already noted as the disease of the time. Barbara Traill broods on a number of unrelated facts until she convinces herself that her whole family is tainted with insanity:

> Her mind was a hotch-potch of popular science about heredity and psychoanalysis, and the whole trend of her culture tended to make her pessimistic about everything.[52]

Enid Windrush in the second story in the collection, never yields the suggestion that her father is mad. She sees that Judson's pretentious jargon covers utter nonsense. Nevertheless she feels the case is hopeless. It is useless calling for help from either neighbours or the police 'against the machine of modern oppression':

> If two doctors chose to testify that Walter Windrush was mad they turned the whole modern world with them – police and all.[53]

The sense of an intellectual and moral chaos working through the machinery of the modern state has taken the place of the delusive conspiracy of *The Man who was Thursday*. The relatively straightforward effort against the refusal to joy in *The Man who was Thursday* or *Manalive* is replaced by particular action against particular problems, and by an attempt to relate insanity to contemporary social and philosophical needs.

Since Chesterton has been accused of an addiction to verbal cleverness and point, and by Bernard Bergonzi, of having a too rationalistic imagination,[54] it is interesting to note his continued concern with non-verbal and non-conceptual means of communication. This concern which figured in *Manalive* is retained in the paintings of Gabriel Gale and the 'riddles' of John Hume but without the earlier sense of joyful abandon. Gale is an outlaw and Hume is a tired man who cannot hate. One has the sense in the case-histories of *The Poet and the Lunatics* that it is still possible to reduce certain aspects of mental illness to philosophical errors. Underlying the particular manifestations, however, there is a more insidious enemy. Chesterton feels it is hardly possible to dignify this spirit, incoherent, vague and perverse, with the word error. Pessimism and materialism can be grasped and fought:

Materialists are all right; they are near enough to heaven to accept the earth and not imagine they made it. The dreadful doubts are not the doubts of the materialist.[55]

The process of intellectual dissolution has gone much further than this. The mere pessimists or rationalists in *The Poet and the Lunatics* such as Boyg in 'The Finger of Stone' or Noel in 'The House of the Peacock' are honourable, if limited men. There is, between them and Gale, a shared standard of respect for reason. The evil doctors represent something far worse.

Consequently the later writing of Chesterton on madness, in addition to community and mystery, has to concern itself with the foremost of first principles, such as the actual existence of the thing in itself or the admitted reality of the external world or the possibility of choice and action. His relatively late concern with the thought of Thomas Aquinas may be seen as part of a wish to elaborate a philosophical defence of the reality of phenomena[56] to counter the hazy subjectivism he felt had grown up in his lifetime. His most developed statement of his social and political theory, the significantly named *The Outline of Sanity*, (1926) concentrates, as a preliminary point on establishing that it is possible to act and choose at all.[57]

The much more difficult situation is, perhaps, symbolised by the change in one of Chesterton's favourite images, that of the tree. The giant beech of *The Flying Inn* in whose branches Pump, Dalroy and Dorian Wimpole sing their songs, surveying the whole country with its curving roads, suggests a central sanity and pleasure in life. The tall tree up which Innocent Smith shoots like a rocket at the beginning of *Manalive* has been neglected by the inhabitants of Beacon House for years, but it still recalls Yggdrasill or the Tree of Life. Long unnoticed, it can still unstop a spring of joy reminding Inglewood 'irrationally of something glowing in his infancy'. In *Four Faultless Felons* Walter Windrush's tree is 'forbidden', fenced off from the encroachments of the city growing up around his house, an attempt to preserve the mysterious and sacred in a now completely hostile environment. In *The Poet and the Lunatics*, however, the tree is given its most arresting meaning. Herbert Saunders in whom 'the inside has grown too big for the outside',[58] who is on the verge of seeing the world as a product of his own mind, is chased by Gale and pinioned by a pitchfork to a tree, representing the last reality, which cannot be ignored, pain.

Ultimately, in spite of the growing difficulties, Chesterton remains confident of the victory of reason. Madness is not natural to man and can at some point be checked by the will, if external factors break into the closing circle before it is too late.

> Remember that there is always something double about morbidity: the sound old popular phrase said the madman was 'beside himself'. There is a part of him encouraging itself to go mad; and a part that doesn't quite believe in the mania.[59]

An ultimate ground for hope is the greatest of all external factors, pain. The greatest danger of all is that of complete subjectivity, rejection of the existence of the material world, a kind of madness above all hostile to human nature and human happiness. The sense of things outside our own minds and of our own limits 'are the lines of the very plan of human pleasure.'[60] It is this delusion of omnipotence which for Chesterton is the form madness seems to be taking in his last years and 'there is no cure for that nightmare of omnipotence except pain; because that is the thing a man *knows* he would not tolerate if he could really control it.'[61] This somewhat austere, but unanswerable, doctrine of the necessary limit of human power is the final guarantee that the pursuit of sanity will, in spite of the lengthened odds, be successful.

XI

CONCLUSION: THE CASE OF ORAGE

Chesterton's analysis of the cultural division and cultural crisis of his time was, both intrinsically, and compared to the views of other commentators such as Masterman, original and penetrating. One is naturally inclined to ask how effective it was, ultimately. To such a question no completely satisfying answer can be given. How does one estimate the influence of a publicist who, for many years, held the attention of a large audience? It has been suggested that Chesterton's articles were one of the chief contributory factors in the rebuilding of the *Daily News*'s fortunes under Gardiner. There can be little doubt that his work then, as later, was read avidly. (Maycock remarks on the suggestive fact that twice as many readers took the paper on Saturday, when his column appeared, than on any other day).[1] This period was the foundation of a long and successful career as a merchant and critic of ideas. That the public had an appetite for reading Chesterton, however, may be readily granted without its becoming any clearer what in his writing amused and entertained them and what they took to heart. He chose the roles of a journalist and performer deliberately, because he felt ideas were more important than art, that communication was more vital and timely than the perfectionism of the isolated artist or cloistered academic. His arguments, to a fair-minded critic, have some show of reason, even if they run counter to still current prejudices. They would undoubtedly gain in force, however, if it could be conclusively proved that Chesterton's gamble, or his

235

deliberate choice, succeeded; that along with his freshness, flow of novel and entertaining notions, his brio and panache, the public accepted his analysis of and remedies for the cultural crisis of the time.

In spite of several outstandingly successful studies of particular aspects of his work, the question of Chesterton as a critic of culture has been, if not untouched, relatively neglected. When the reader considers the reams of often laboured exegesis that have stemmed from T.S. Eliot's phrase about the 'dissociation of sensibility', it is bewildering that Chesterton's really much more developed, humane and far less historically tendentious views of the contemporary cultural predicament should have remained in the shadow. Sometimes, perhaps rather than struggle for explanations, it is better to accept the place of the fortuitous in building and maintaining critical reputations.

This still leaves the problem of Chesterton's influence in the field of cultural ideas. On the analogy of his political influence, the answer would not, at first sight, seem too hopeful. A few years ago, the Distributist Movement must have looked like one of the, perhaps relatively few, ideas which die once and for all, without issue or effect. Maisie Ward's dismissal of the causes of popularism, small-ownership, the dispersal of property and population, to which Chesterton gave unstintingly of time, money and energy, as curiously dated,[2] seemed hardly open to dispute. The Distributist saga must have seemed a proof that it was perfectly possible to delight one's readers for years without affecting their actions in the slightest. But, as Margaret Canovan has pointed out,[3] the Oil Crisis, which has altered so much, has altered the view which may be taken of Chesterton's political and economic ideas. His suggestions may have been premature, like those of the Ecology Party now, but they can scarcely be dismissed as dead and buried. His work here may be less a matter of chasing shadows than of planting seeds in the public mind, which, after years of lying dormant, at last begin to stir. The whole affair illustrates the difficulty in assessing the significance of an intellectual influence.

Fortunately, in the cultural, as opposed to the political and economic field, we are, I would suggest, not quite so much at the mercy of surmise, however hopeful. It is possible, perhaps, to document a case of Chesterton's influence, a far from negligible one, and one which illustrates, from a single, clear example, his effect on the pattern of ideas of his time. In 1941, Chesterton's ally in the Distributist Movement, Maurice Reckitt, linked Orage and Chesterton as men who both avoided 'that sort of snobbery which disdains the transient,' and reflected that:

> it is a notable fact that two of the most profound and yet versatile men of their age... Chesterton and Orage should have given their chief energies not to any conscious cultivation of the permanent, but to the interpretation against the background of eternal values of the significance of every day.[4]

It affords a hint of a role for Chesterton not now fashionable in accounts of him, but which, as well as being undeniably significant, was close to his own design for living and writing. His own comments on Orage in a preface to Philip Mairet's *Memoir* of 1936 enlarges on the ground of their affinity. Orage's style was excellent because 'language was not being loved for its own sake, but used to an end.'[5] He wrote fine literature 'in the course of writing fighting journalism' yet in spite of the excellence of his literary style he 'managed somehow to avoid the awful fate of looking like a literary man', a fate which, it appears, Chesterton himself preferred to avoid. Orage's work was addressed to a public audience rather than a coterie like that of Sidney Colvin in former days or the Sitwells in the 1930s. Chesterton's opposition to literary cliques was repeatedly stated. But the chief ground of sympathy Chesterton discovered in Orage was his complete emancipation from 'a mass of middle-class prejudices preserved throughout Europe by the bourgeois freemasons, from which even Bolshevism was an escape into liberty.[6] This middle-class freemasonry (not, of course, Freemasonry) was a conventional adherence to certain ostensibly 'emancipated' ideas which had hardened into inhibitions on new thought. One *had* to believe in Free Trade or Secular Education just as one *had* to disbelieve in the possibility of the supernatural. Although Orage and he disagreed strongly on many subjects, Chesterton felt that none of Orage's thoughts were inevitable, part of a package. Orage really did think clearly, without prejudice, about whatever matter was in hand.

The importance of Orage's periodical, the *New Age*, as a clearing-house of ideas in the years just before 1914 is a truism. In the words of Wallace Martin's definitive study:

> The *New Age* provided a comprehensive record of the emergence of modern culture from its Victorian and Edwardian antecedents.[7]

It is worth emphasising that matter of substance did *emerge* from the debates which Orage organised in the *New Age*. He delighted in and utilised the repeated expression of strongly opposed opinions but this was not merely a matter of editorial technique. It was intended to, and no doubt did, boost sales, but it was intended also to discover truth. Orage, as his friend Mairet noted, was a man of strong religious impulse, with a deep desire for truth.[8] It is certainly possible to regret the form this religious impulse was to take after his resignation from the *New Age*, an acceptance of the teachings of Gurdjieff. But this, not, in fact, Orage's final position, does not, of itself vitiate and should not unduly colour what, as Martin's study makes clear, was the steady movement of the periodical, after the most exhaustive and intelligent debate, to definite positions on several subjects. To call these Chestertonian positions would certainly be a gross oversimplification and it would be quite wrong to state straightforwardly that Orage and the *New Age* moved simply because of Chesterton's arguments. Orage's changes of direction in politics and economics, in his view of the theatre and dramatic art, in his interpretations of the nature and possibilities of man, his ideas on culture, were the result of his own highly independent and intelligent mind operating on the body of evidence presented to it, evidence which principally took the form of strongly argued exchanges in his periodical.

Orage and Chesterton, then, both believed passionately in the widest public forum of debate and condemned coteries and the cultural fragmentation in which they resulted. Following from this, both Orage and Chesterton held very similar views on the dangers of specialisation and of the employment by cliques of code languages which excluded the majority of readers. They both held that ideas existed to be known as widely as possible so that they might be examined and judged and to that end felt that the employment of the clearest and most concise language was desirable. No argument or idea of substance would suffer by being expressed as simply as the case allowed. Both men believed passionately in the need for a coherent philosophy of man, embracing spiritual as well as social problems and that it should be based on common sense.

Apart from similarities between their views on the need for debate and discussion, Chesterton was drawn to contribute frequently to the *New Age* by its promise of intellectual freedom. Orage's only concern was with the quality of contributions and his editorial policy did not include the censorship and direction practised, however pleasantly, by Gardiner. (Belloc's dedication of his book, *The Free Press* (1918), a plea for small independent journals as a guarantee of freedom is, significantly, to Orage).

The first of the *New Age*'s debates and changes of position was political. Orage announced in 1907 the intention of the periodical to

> examine the philosophical basis of Socialism; by 1912 this examin-
> ation had been carried out, and the collectivist theory of the
> movement had been rejected.[9]

It is true that one of Orage's friends A.J. Penty had been advocating Guild Socialism, as opposed to State Socialism, for several years. It is true, also, that Hilaire Belloc used the *New Age* to broach those ideas on the economic and moral consequences of State Socialism, as currently advocated, which became, a few years later, in mature form, *The Servile State*. But while other influences than Chesterton's may well have affected Orage, it is hard to deny that much the most sparkling and vigorous phase of the *New Age* debate which pre-dated Belloc's attack, resulted from Chesterton's article 'Why I am not a Socialist' (4 January 1908), in the exchanges with Shaw and Wells which followed for several months, being 'carefully planned and sustained by Orage'.

Chesterton's contributions to the *New Age*'s debates on the theatre, the nature of art, the role of moral criteria in criticism, and the importance of tradition give stronger grounds for suggesting that he influenced Orage. In each case, Chesterton defended, in the periodical, views which he had already been advocating for years and in each case the *New Age* moved over to positions closely resembling, if not identical with those views. Between 1910 and 1914, for example, it turned gradually against the doctrines of Realism in both the theatre and the novel. Previously it had championed Realism but

> after 1910, this was no longer true. Orage began to attack [its] ideologies and basic assumptions about the function of art. He held that the proper subject of literature was not man's heredity and environment but his soul.[10]

Writing in the *New Age* on 25 January 1908, before Orage broke with Realism, Chesterton, taking up his comments in *Heretics* of three years before, criticised the documentary Realism of the slum novelists who studied the poor as if they were alligators, amassing facts and statistics about them yet missing their inner life.[11]

Orage's newly-announced view in his essay 'On Drama' (18 May 1911) is very close to views Chesterton had long held (expressed for example, in the *Daily News* article 'The Meaning of the Theatre', 1902). Chesterton's view, now held by Orage, was that the theatre cannot partake of rationalism and materialism, cannot in Chesterton's words document 'the dull and throbbing routine of our actual life', offer moral analysis or 'wield the scalpel'. It was a festival nourishing the soul by participation. It is interesting also to note that Chesterton anticipated both the ideas and phraseology of Ashley Duke's rejection of Shaw's drama in an article (23 March 1911) which, like Orage's piece a month later, marked a turning point in the *New Age*'s attitude. Ashley Dukes's essay, outdoing Chesterton in severity, portrays Shaw as a Puritan and Calvinist who 'sets ethics before taste, desiccates illusion, diverts all artistic emotion through the individual to a social end.'[12] The strong similarity between this view and Chesterton's discussion of 'Shaw the Puritan' in his book of a year before need hardly be elaborated.

The most striking instance of Orage's change of front, however, is his altered view, between 1908 and 1911, on the limits of human development. Orage has already been noted as one of the foremost English disciples of Nietzsche, the first to spread an accurate account

240

of the German philosopher's teaching in this country, in two pioneer books and the evangelist of the Superman cult of an unlimited transcendence of human limits, the significance of which Chesterton discerned and against which he struggled. These facts make Orage's reversal of view all the more striking. Two articles of 1911 repudiate his earlier ideas decisively. Man, he remarks in the first, (25 May 1911) is 'a fixed species'. In the second, (27 July 1911) he attributes much, if not most, of the modern crisis to the lack of acceptance of human definition. The notion that man is 'incapable of indefinite progress' is 'so contrary to the prevailing current of thought', the accepted notions of the time, that it is rejected as a mere perversity:

> The modern mind, being shameless, hates to think itself defined. For all that it is defined and very vigorously.[13]

Without a reliable starting point in the sense of what man is, needs and can do, nothing can be achieved:

> Starting from a false conception of the nature of man, the mind continually sees everything in a false light. Its whole object is to become something that it really is not, and can never be. . . . With human nature undefined nothing else is definable.[14]

These comments form a more striking instance than Orage's political doubts about State Socialism, to which other sources than Chesterton may admittedly have contributed. Remarks on human limits and the need for definition strengthen the case for suspecting that Chesterton's writings may have been, at least partly, instrumental in Orage's move away from Nietzscheanism. Orage's new views are remarkably close to those which Chesterton had been urging since the beginning of his career eleven years before. They. are, in fact, the very essence of Chesterton's constantly renewed attack on the myth of transcendence and the attendant refusal of the known human condition which, both men now agreed, was the 'prevailing current of thought of their time' and one of its chief dangers. Orage's new stress on the need for a definition of human nature and needs as an essential preliminary to useful action, too, echoes a point which Chesterton repeatedly made before.

The case of Chesterton's influence is further strengthened by

Orage's acceptance in this same piece of 27 July of the doctrines of
Original Sin and Redemption as the only 'theory which accounts for
all these cross purposes of the world' and his recognition that, as
Chesterton had pointed out, the myth of Evolution was, at root, a
superficially disguised version of Redemption, appealing to a real,
though distorted, religious emotion. As Martin points out, Chesterton had emphasised Original Sin as the only self-evident truth in
Christianity in two essays in the *New Age* in 1908 (22 February and
31 December) and pointed out its philosophical and psychological
significance. This, of course, predates Orage's change of view.

Very much attention has been given to the work of T.E. Hulme
and his influence in forming a certain astringent philosophical and
artistic position which, through T.S. Eliot, spread widely and
enjoyed great prestige. The Conservatism/Classicism synthesis has
been one of the leading English cultural elements throughout the
first half of the twentieth century. But 'Orage was ridiculing the
prevailing idea of progress and insisting on the importance of man's
limitation in relation to political theory as early as 1911, one year
before T.E. Hulme expressed similar views',[15] and, one might add,
Chesterton was doing this in 1908 and for years before.

If one accepts Martin's thesis, which there does indeed seem little
reason to reject, that Orage influenced Hulme, it is worth noting that
Orage held strong reservations about the turn Hulme gave the ideas
he transmitted to him.

> He urged several qualifications which reveal he was aware of their
> limitations. The world portrayed by Hulme... was indeed a
> gloomy one. The burden of original sin lay heavy on the worthless
> individual.... In disagreeing with this view, Orage utilized the
> doctrines of Christianity upon which it was supposedly based; an
> excessive concern with original sin led Hulme... to neglect its
> complement – the doctrine of redemption.[16]

Orage remained closer, if this suggestion is correct, to the original
positions of Chesterton which had influenced him. He retained
Chesterton's blend of cultural conservative with a radical, reformist
political philosophy. He retained, also, Chesterton's more cautious,
humane and balanced view of human limitation and Original Sin:

one unwilling to make a sharp polemical impression if the price was narrowing a view of life or over-emphasising particular aspects within it. Such a narrowing may obviously produce a more challenging and uncompromising ideological weapon, but it may, also, sacrifice too many qualifications and reservations necessary to truth. Chesterton and Orage were unwilling, for the sake of an immediate effect, to counter an obsession with endless evolutionary transcendence, by a correspondingly excessive stress on Original Sin and the resultant misery and bondage of man. Both men, although keen to establish the grounds of authority in morals, philosophy and politics, were cautious in adopting overtly authoritarian nostrums. Chesterton, although disappointed by parliamentary government, never rejected democracy or the liberal traditions of the years 1789 to 1871. Indeed a marked feature of his whole thought and of his opposition to the leading currents of his time, is that it retained an inherent moderation, a distrust of over-neat, schematised and too narrow statements even of its own positions. His attitude to the later High Anglican, 'Royalist' T.S. Eliot was characteristic. In his last radio talk in 1936, Chesterton gently suggested that the grim views of the younger man, though finer and subtler than the pessimism from which he had been converted, lacked 'repose', the simple happiness of being alive:

I will defend my own idea of the spice of life against even the spirituality that finds this ordinary life entirely without a spice.[17]

Eliot's own notorious comment that although Chesterton had plenty of ideas there was no proof he could think, helps to clarify the difference between them. By 'think' Eliot meant think ideologically, pulling no punches, accepting no qualifications, checks or balances and no humour, in the statement of an intellectual position.

It seems that this vital difference of temper between Chesterton and men like Hulme or Eliot explains that while his ideas fed the immediately pre-1914 reaction against the notion of the unlimited development and progress of a human nature capable of endless alteration, and prepared the way for a body of thought which stressed logic, limits, authority and tradition, he received little credit from the men who carved out kingdoms from fragments of his richer and more various world. If one accepts the theory that Orage *was* the mediator of many Chestertonian perceptions then clearly these were not without effect, but they did lose a warmth, a tolerance and geniality which their originator had not felt incompatible with serious thought.

Notes for pages 1–23

Introduction

1. Gilbert Keith Chesterton, *Autobiography* (1936; repr. London: Arrow Books, 1959) pp. 10–11. The 1959 edition is used throughout.
2. Maisie Ward, *Gilbert Keith Chesterton* (1944; repr. Harmondsworth: Penguin Books, 1958) p. 18. The 1958 edition is used throughout.
3. Chesterton, *Autobiography*, p. 14.
4. Ibid., p. 35.
5. Ibid., p. 30.
6. Ibid., p. 77.
7. Ward, *Gilbert Keith Chesterton*. p. 34.
8. Chesterton, *Autobiography*, p. 85.
9. Ibid., p. 84.
10. Ibid., p. 83.
11. Ibid., p. 85.
12. Ibid., p. 86.
13. Ward, *Gilbert Keith Chesterton*, p. 137.
14. Ibid., pp. 220–35.
15. Ibid., p. 186.
16. Leo A. Hetzler, 'Chesterton's Political Views 1892–1914', *Chesterton Review*, vol. VII, no. 2 (1981) p. 132.
17. Ibid., p. 133.
18. Lawrence J. Clipper, *G.K. Chesterton* (New York: Twayne Publishers, 1974) p. 181.
19. Ward, *Gilbert Keith Chesterton*, p. 381.
20. Ibid., p. 400.
21. Ibid., p. 401.

The Edwardian Cultural Crisis

1. G.K. Chesterton, *Simplicity and Tolstoy* (London: Arthur L. Humphrey, 1912).
2. G.K. Chesterton, *Tales from Tolstoi* (1903; repr. in *The Common Man*, London: Sheed and Ward, 1950) pp. 160–5.
3. G.K. Chesterton, G.H. Perris, et al., *Leo Tolstoy* (London: Hodder and Stoughton, 1903).
4. Ibid., *Leo Tolstoy*, p. 2.
5. Chesterton, *Simplicity and Tolstoy*, p. 3.
6. Ibid., *Simplicity and Tolstoy*, pp. 3–4.
7. Chesterton, *Leo Tolstoy*, p. 1.
8. Chesterton, *Simplicity and Tolstoy*, p. 18.
9. Chesterton, *Leo Tolstoy*, p. 1.
10. G.K. Chesterton, *Heretics* (1903; repr. London: John Lane, 1928) p. 11.
11. A.L. Maycock, *The Man who was Orthodox: a selection from the uncollected writings of G.K. Chesterton* (London: Dennis Robson, 1963) p. 135.

Notes

Notes for pages 23–34

12. G.K. Chesterton, *The Victorian Age in Literature* (1913; repr. London: Oxford University Press, 1966) p. 98.
13. Chesterton, *Heretics*, p. 15.
14. G.K. Chesterton, *What's Wrong with the World* (1910; repr. London: Cassell, 1913) p. 221.
15. Wallace Martin, *The New Age under Orage: chapters in English cultural history* (Manchester: The University Press, 1967) p. 136.
16. John Gross, *The Rise and Fall of the Man of Letters* (1969; repr. Harmondsworth: Penguin Books, 1973) pp. 250–1.
17. Chesterton, *Heretics*, p. 132.
18. Chesterton, *Simplicity and Tolstoy*, p. 15.
19. Ibid., p. 18.
20. Ibid., p. 23.
21. G.K. Chesterton, *Lunacy and Letters* (London: Sheed and Ward, 1958) p. 51.
22. Ibid., p. 53.
23. Chesterton, *The Victorian Age in Literature*, p. 69.
24. Ibid., pp. 70–1.
25. G.K. Chesterton, *The Common Man* (London: Sheed and Ward, 1950) p. 82.
26. Ibid., p. 83.
27. Ibid., p. 85.
28. Ibid., p. 86.
29. Maycock, *The Man who was Orthodox*, p. 94.
30. Ibid.
31. G.K. Chesterton, *All Things considered* (1908; repr. London: Methuen, 1928) pp. 7–8.
32. G.K. Chesterton, *George Bernard Shaw* (London: John Lane, 1910) p. 244.
33. Ibid., p. 247.
34. J.A. Hobson, *A Modern Outlook* (London: Herbert and Daniel, 1910) p. 282.
35. Ibid., p. 284.
36. Ibid., p. 318.
37. Ibid., pp. 82–3.
38. Ibid., p. 51.
39. Ibid., p. 241.
40. Ibid., p. 37.
41. Spencer's vast *System of Synthetic Philosophy*, one of the monuments of the Victorian era, published between 1862 and 1896, applied the principle of evolution to biology, sociology, politics and ethics, in a vast, ambitious attempt to unify our knowledge of the world and man.
42. Elie Halévy, *Imperialism and the Rise of Labour* (1926; trans. E.I. Watkin, repr. and rev. London: Ernest Benn, 1951) p. 21.
43. In *Socialism and Society* (1905), *Socialism and Government* (1909) and *The Socialist Movement* (1911). See David P. Marquand, *Ramsay MacDonald* (London: Jonathan Cape, 1977) p. 89.

Notes

Notes for pages 34–49

44. Michael D. Biddis, *The Age of the Masses* (Harmondsworth: Penguin Books, 1977) p. 52.
45. Hilaire Belloc, *Caliban's Guide to Letters* (1903; repr. London: Duckworth, 1920) p. 215.
46. John Passmore, *A Hundred Years of Philosphy* (1957; repr. Harmondsworth: Penguin Books, 1968) pp. 55–6.
47. Ibid.
48. Ibid., p. 56.
49. Ibid., p. 58.
50. Ibid., p. 59.
51. A.R. Orage, *Friedrich Nietzsche, the Dionysian Spirit of the Age* (London: T.N. Foulis, 1906) p. 75.
52. Passmore, *A Hundred Years of Philosophy*, p. 67.
53. Orage, *Friedrich Nietzsche, the Dionysian Spirit of the Age*, p. 76.
54. Chesterton, *George Bernard Shaw*, p. 43.
55. Ibid.
56. Maycock, *The Man who was Orthodox*, p. 108.
57. Ibid.
58. Chesterton, *Heretics*, p. 184.
59. Maycock, *The Man who was Orthodox*, p. 109.
60. Ibid.
61. Philip Mairet, *A.R. Orage* (London: J.M. Dent, 1936) p. 25.
62. G.K. Chesterton, *Alarms and Discursions* (1910; repr. London: Methuen, 1927) p. 133.
63. C.F.G. Masterman, *In Peril of Change: essays written in a time of tranquillity* (London: T. Fisher Unwin, 1905) p. 305.
64. Ibid.
65. Ibid., p. 323.
66. C.F.G. Masterman, *The Condition of England* (1909; repr. London: Methuen, 1911) p. 81.
67. Masterman, *In Peril of Change*, p. 174.
68. Ibid., p. 175.
69. Masterman, *The Condition of England*, p. 215.
70. Ibid.
71. Ibid., p. 84.
72. G.K. Chesterton, *Autobiography* (1936; repr. London: Arrow Books, 1959) p. 127.

The Journalistic Arena

1. George Sutherland Fraser, *The Modern Writer and His World* (1953; repr. Harmondsworth: Penguin Books, 1970) p. 81.
2. Margaret Canovan, *G.K. Chesterton: radical populist* (New York: Harcourt Brace Jovanovich, 1977) pp. 6–7.

Notes for pages 49–58

3. Ibid., p. 23.
4. Thomas Mann, *Doctor Faustus*, trans. H.T. Lowe-Parker (1949; repr. Harmondsworth: Penguin Books, 1968) p. 40.
5. Raymond Williams, *Culture and Society 1780–1950* (1958; repr. Harmondsworth: Penguin Books, 1971) p. 313.
6. G.K. Chesterton, *Lunacy and Letters* (London: Sheed and Ward, 1958) p. 134.
7. Ibid., p. 135.
8. Ibid., p. 136.
9. G.K. Chesterton, *Heretics* (1905; repr. London: John Lane, 1928) p. 94.
10. G.K. Chesterton, *All Things considered* (1908; repr. London: Methuen, 1928) p. 16.
11. Idem, *Lunacy and Letters*, pp. 115–16.
12. Ibid., pp. 182–7.
13. Ibid., p. 39.
14. G.K. Chesterton, *The Defendant* (1901; repr. London: J.M. Dent, 1922) pp. 158–60.
15. C.F.G. Masterman, *In Peril of Change* (London: T. Fisher Unwin, 1905) p. 160.
16. Ibid., p. 161.
17. G.K. Chesterton, *A Miscellany of Men* (1912; repr. London: Methuen, 1927) p. 87.
18. Idem, *What's Wrong with the World* (1910; repr. London: Cassell, 1913) pp. 247–9.
19. Idem, *The Glass Walking Stick* (London: Methuen, 1955) p. 3.
20. Idem, *Heretics*, pp. 110–16.
21. A.L. Maycock, *The Man who was Orthodox* (London: Denis Dobson, 1963) p. 137.
22. Ibid., p. 138.
23. G.K. Chesterton, *The Flying Inn* (1914; repr. Harmondsworth: Penguin Books, 1958) p. 86.
24. Ibid., p. 88.
25. Daniel J. Boorstin, *The Image: a guide to pseudo-events in America* (New York: Harper and Row, 1964).
26. Hilaire Belloc, *Caliban's Guide to Letters* and *Lambkin's Remains* (1903; repr. London: Duckworth, 1920) p. 15.
27. Ibid., *Caliban's Guide to Letters*, p. 19.
28. Ibid.
29. Ibid., p. 252.
30. Ibid., p. 215.
31. Ibid., p. 135.
32. Ibid., p. 85.
33. Ibid., pp. 15–16.
34. Ibid., pp. 233–5.

Notes

Notes for pages 60–72

35. Quoted in *Belloc: a biographical anthology* ed. H. Van Thal and J.S. Nickerson (London: George Allen and Unwin, 1970) p. 93.
36. Chesterton, *All Things considered*, p. 79.
37. Ibid., p. 78.
38. G.K. Chesterton, *Manalive* (1912; repr. London: Arrowsmith, 1926) p. 123.
39. Idem, *Lunacy and Letters*, p. 129.
40. George Sampson, *The Concise Cambridge History of English Literature* (1941; repr. Cambridge: University Press, 1945) p. 1036.
41. John Gross, *The Rise and Fall of the Man of Letters* (1969; repr. Harmondsworth: Penguin Books, 1973) p. 209.
42. Maisie Ward, *Gilbert Keith Chesterton* (1944; repr. Harmondsworth: Penguin Books, 1958) p. 114.
43. Quoted Ibid.
44. E.C. Bentley, *Those Days* (London: Constable and Co. Ltd, 1940) p. 221.
45. Ibid.
46. James Mark Purcell, 'The Edwardian Populism of Chesterton's Art', *Chesterton Review*, vol. VI, no. 2 (1980) p. 217.
47. Ibid.
48. G.K. Chesterton, *Autobiography* (1936; repr. London: Arrow Books, 1959) p. 169.
49. Stephen Koss, *Fleet Street Radical: A.G. Gardiner and The Daily News*, (London: Allen Lane, 1973) p. 66.
50. Canovan, *G.K. Chesterton: radical populist*, p. 14.
51. Ibid.
52. James Bryce, *The Hindrances to Good Citizenship* (Yale: University Press, 1909).
53. Wilfred Trotter, *Instincts of the Herd in Peace and War* (London: Allen and Unwin, 1916).
54. For example, Gerhard Masur, *Prophets of Yesterday: studies in European culture*, (1961; repr. New York: Harper and Row, 1966) pp. 89–105.
55. Alan O'Day (ed.), *The Edwardian Age: conflict and stability* (London: Macmillan, 1979) p. 2.
56. Ibid.
57. Ibid., p. 12.
58. Koss, *Fleet Street Radical*, p. 137.
59. Ibid.
60. Ibid.
61. Ibid.
62. Chesterton, *Autobiography*, p. 113.
63. Dudley Barker, *G.K. Chesterton* (London: Constable, 1973) p. 225.
64. Koss, *Fleet Street Radical*, p. 54.
65. Ibid., p. 31.
66. Ibid., p. 50.
67. Ibid., p. 54.
68. Ibid., p. 53.

249

Notes for pages 72–96

69. Ibid., p. 57.
70. Ibid., p. 24.
71. A.G. Gardiner, *Prophets, Priests and Kings* (London: Alston Rivers, 1908) p. 323.
72. Ibid., 330.
73. Koss, *Fleet Street Radical*, p. 115.
74. G.K. Chesterton, 'The Philosophy of Islands' in *The Spice of Life and Other Essays*, ed. Dorothy Collins (Beaconsfield: Darwen Finlayson, 1964) p. 120.

Symbol in *The Flying Inn*

1. Christopher Hollis, *The Mind of Chesterton* (London: Hollis and Carter, 1970) p. 141.
2. Ibid., p. 143.
3. G.K. Chesterton, *The Flying Inn* (1914; repr. Harmondsworth: Penguin Books, 1958) p. 8.
4. Ibid.
5. Ibid., p. 275.
6. Ibid., p. 274.
7. *Thus Spoke Zarathustra*, repr. in *The Portable Nietzsche*. trans. Walter Kaufman (1954; repr. New York: Viking Press, 1960) p. 251.
8. Chesterton, *The Flying Inn*, p. 274.
9. Ibid., p. 228.
10. *The Portable Nietzsche* op. cit., p. 233.
11. Chesterton, *The Flying Inn*, p. 14.
12. Ibid., pp. 186–7.
13. Ibid., p. 113.
14. Ibid., p. 127.
15. Ibid., p. 103.
16. Ibid., p. 280.
17. Ibid., p. 281.
18. Ibid., p. 86.
19. Ibid., p. 87.
20. Ibid., p. 94.
21. Ibid., pp. 20–1.
22. Ibid., p. 27.
23. Ibid.
24. A.L. Maycock, *The Man who was Orthodox* (London: Dennis Dobson, 1963) p. 64.
25. Chesterton, *The Flying Inn*, p. 56.
26. Ian Boyd, 'Philosophy in Fiction' in *G.K. Chesterton: a centenary appraisal*, ed. John Sullivan (London: Paul Elek, 1974) pp. 47–8.
27. Chesterton, *The Flying Inn*, p. 166.
28. Ibid., p. 58.
29. Ibid., p. 59.

Notes for pages 96–109

30. George Orwell, *Collected Essays: journalism and letters* vol. 4 (1968: repr. Harmondsworth: Penguin Books, 1970) p. 122.
31. Chesterton, *The Flying Inn*, p. 103.
32. Ibid., p. 102.
33. Ibid.
34. Ibid., p. 135.
35. Ibid., p. 83.

The Restoration of the Past

1. G.K. Chesterton, *A Handful of Authors: collected essays* ed. Dorothy Collins (London: Sheed and Ward, 1953) p. 25.
2. Ibid.
3. Salvador De Madariaga, *Don Quixote: an introductory essay in psychology* (1934; repr. and rev. London: Oxford University Press, 1961) pp. 173–85.
4. Chesterton, *A Handful of Authors*, p. 25.
5. Ibid., p. 27.
6. *G.K. Chesterton: a selection from his non-fictional prose* ed. W.H. Auden (London: Faber and Faber, 1970) p. 16.
7. Chesterton, *A Handful of Authors*, p. 111.
8. G.K. Chesterton, *Fancies versus Fads* (1923; repr. London: Methuen, 1925) p. 176.
9. G.K. Chesterton, *The Uses of Diversity* (1920; repr. London: Methuen, 1927) p. 110.
10. Chesterton, *Fancies versus Fads*, p. 177.
11. G.K. Chesterton, *The Everlasting Man* (1925; repr. NY: Image Books, 1955) p. 64.
12. A.L. Maycock, *The Man who was Orthodox: a selection from the uncollected writings of G.K. Chesterton* (London: Robson Books, 1963) p. 117.
13. De Madariaga, *Don Quixote*, pp. 137–57.
14. A dedication 'To Hilaire Belloc' in G.K. Chesterton, *The Napoleon of Notting Hill* (1904; repr. London: John Lane, 1928).
15. Chesterton, *The Everlasting Man*, p. 160.
16. Chesterton, *The Napoleon of Notting Hill*, p. 22.
17. W.H. Auden, *G.K. Chesterton: a selection*, pp. 17–18.
18. Chesterton, *The Napoleon of Notting Hill*, p. 289.
19. Maisie Ward, *Gilbert Keith Chesterton* (1944; repr. Harmondsworth: Penguin Books, 1958) p. 242.
20. Chesterton, *A Handful of Authors*, p. 23.
21. Ibid., p. 21.
22. G.K. Chesterton, *The Collected Poems of G.K. Chesterton* (London: Burns, Oates and Washbourne, 1927) p. 103.
23. Chesterton, *A Handful of Authors*, p. 21.

Notes for pages 109–127

24. *The Collected Poems of G.K. Chesterton*, p. 103.
25. Ibid., p. 104.
26. Chesterton., *A Handful of Authors*, pp. 21–2.
27. *The Collected Poems of G.K. Chesterton*, p. 102.
28. Chesterton, *A Handful of Authors*, p. 21.
29. *The Collected Poems of G.K. Chesterton*, p. 105.
30. Chesterton, *A Handful of Authors*, p. 23.
31. *The Collected Poems of G.K. Chesterton*, p. 105.
32. Christopher Hollis, *The Mind of Chesterton* (London: Hollis and Carter, 1970) p. 141.
33. John Coates, 'Symbol and Structure in *The Flying Inn*', *Chesterton Review* IV (1978) 246–60.
34. Chesterton, *The Flying Inn* (1914; repr. Harmondsworth: Penguin Books, 1958) p. 227.
35. Chesterton, *A Handful of Authors*, p. 21.
36. Chesterton, *The Flying Inn*, p. 56.
37. Ibid., p. 53.
38. Ibid., pp. 58–9.
39. G.K. Chesterton, *The Return of Don Quixote* (1927; repr. London: Darwen Finlayson, 1963) pp. 81–2.
40. Ibid., p. 39.
41. Ibid., p. 24.
42. Ibid.
43. Ibid., p. 26.
44. Ibid., p. 11.
45. Ibid., p. 139.
46. Ibid., p. 46.
47. Ian Boyd, *The Novels of G.K. Chesterton* (London: Paul Elek, 1975) pp. 112–39.
48. Chesterton, *The Return of Don Quixote*, p. 113.
49. Ibid., p. 33.
50. Ibid., p. 214.

Chesterton and Adventure

1. Francis Williams, *Dangerous Estate: the anatomy of newspapers* (1957; repr. London: Arrow Books, 1959) p. 126.
2. Evelyn Waugh, *The Life of Ronald Knox* (1959; repr. London: Fontana Books, 1961) pp. 178–9.
3. Raymond Williams, *Culture and Society, 1780–1950* (1958; repr. Harmondsworth: Penguin Books, 1971) p. 165.
4. Gilbert Keith Chesterton, *The Victorian Age in Literature* (1913; repr. London: Oxford University Press, 1966) p. 95.
5. C.S. Lewis, quoted in Ian Boyd, *The Novels of G.K. Chesterton* (London: Elek Books, 1975) p. 2.

Notes

Notes for pages 128–37

6. G.S. Fraser, *The Modern Writer and His World* (1953; repr. Harmondsworth: Penguin Books, 1970) p. 90.
7. It is interesting to note that in one of the few striking exceptions to the general critical neglect of such elements of fiction, Robert L. Caserio's *Plot, Story and the Novel from Dickens and Poe to the Modern Period* (Princeton, New Jersey: Princeton University Press, 1979), Chesterton is praised for his 'genuinely Dickensian sense of plot' [Caserio, p. 70] and for the soundness of his understanding of Dickens's art. Caserio relates the perceptiveness of Chesterton's Dickens criticism to his whole view of the nature of reality:

> His penetration to the archetype results from his conviction of the presence of the archetype as a fact of life. His archetypal criticism is simultaneously naturalistic criticism [ibid.].

8. G.K. Chesterton, *Autobiography* (1936; repr. London: Arrow Books 1959) p. 248.
9. G.K. Chesterton, *Orthodoxy* (1908; repr. London: Fontana Books, 1961) p. 140.
10. Ibid., p. 141.
11. Chesterton, *Autobiography*, p. 243.
12. John Gross, *The Rise and Fall of the Man of Letters* (1969; repr. Harmondsworth: Pelican Books, 1973) p. 174.
13. Ibid., p. 175.
14. Gilbert Keith Chesterton, *A Miscellany of Men* (1912; repr. London: Methuen, 1927) p. 203.
15. Ibid.
16. Ibid., p. 204.
17. Frank Swinnerton, 'Introduction' in Henry Seton Merriman, *Young Mistley* (1888; repr. London: Cassell, 1966) pp. xvi–xvii.
18. H. Rider Haggard, *King Solomon's Mines* (1885; repr. London: Thomas Nelson, 1956) pp. 170–1.
19. Morton Cohen, *Rider Haggard: his life and work* (1960; repr. London: Macmillan, 1968) p. 224.
20. Henry Seton Merriman, *Barlasch of the Guard* (1902; repr. London: Smith, Elder, 1903) p. 138.
21. Jocelyn Baines, *Joseph Conrad* (1960; repr. Harmondsworth: Pelican Books, 1971) p. 373.
22. Joseph Conrad, *Nostromo*, quoted Jocelyn Baines, *Joseph Conrad*, p. 374.
23. G.K. Chesterton, *The Napoleon of Notting Hill* (1904; repr. London: John Lane, 1968) p. 9.
24. Fyodor Dostoevsky, *Notes from the Underground*, trans. Constance Garnett (1862; repr. New York: Dell Publishing Co. Inc., 1960) p. 50.
25. G.K. Chesterton, *The Defendant* (London: R. Brimley Johnson, 1901) p. 20.
26. A.L. Maycock, *The Man who was Orthodox: a selection from the uncollected writings of G.K. Chesterton* (London: Dobson Books, 1963) p. 117.
27. Chesterton, *The Napoleon of Notting Hill*, p. 17.
28. Ibid., p. 16.

Notes

Notes for pages 138–47

29. Ibid., p. 17.
30. Chesterton, *Autobiography*, p. 44.
31. Ibid., p. 48.
32. Chesterton, *The Napoleon of Notting Hill*, p. 36.
33. G.K. Chesterton, *The Collected Poems of G.K. Chesterton* (London: Burns, Oates and Washbourne, 1927) pp. 70–1.
34. Maycock, *The Man who was Orthodox*, pp. 179–80.
35. Chesterton, *The Napoleon of Notting Hill*, p. 18.
36. Maycock, *The Man who was Orthodox*, p. 180.
37. G.K. Chesterton, *All is Grist* (1931; repr. London: Methuen, 1933) p. 92.
38. G.K. Chesterton, *Alarms and Discursions* (1910; repr. London: Methuen, 1927) p. 120.
39. Chesterton, *The Napoleon of Notting Hill*, p. 47.
40. Ibid., p. 79.
41. Chesterton, *The Defendant*, p. 25.
42. Chesterton, *The Napoleon of Notting Hill*, p. 90.
43. Ibid., p. 88.
44. Ibid., p. 193.
45. G.K. Chesterton, *Tales of the Long Bow* (1925; repr. London: Cassell, 1927) p. 217.
46. Chesterton, *The Collected Poems*, p. 232.
47. Wilfred Sheed, ed. *Essays and Poems: G.K. Chesterton* (Harmondsworth: Penguin Books, 1958) p. 204. [I am grateful to my colleague, Dr Bellamy, for the suggestion that Chesterton may have had in mind George Lindsay Johnson's *The Great Problem and the Evidence for its Solution* (Hutchinson, 1927 or 1928). The book was reprinted by Rider and Co. in 1935, the year of Chesterton's essay, which does seem to confirm the possibility. Johnson's work deals with spiritualist evidence for a future life. This instance suggests the detailed reference concealed behind Chesterton's often casual manner.]
48. Ibid.

A Right View of Myth

1. Ernst Cassirer, 'Language and Myth' in *Mythology: selected readings* ed. Pierre Maranda (Harmondsworth: Penguin Books, 1972) p. 24.
2. Isaiah Berlin, *Against the Current: essays in the history of ideas* (London: The Hogarth Press, 1979) pp. 8–9.
3. J.G. von Herder, *Treatise upon the Origin of Language*, trans. Anon. (London: Longman, Rees, Orme, Brown and Green, 1827).
4. F. Max Müller, *Comparative Mythology* (1856; repr. London: A. Smyth Palmer, 1909) p. v.
5. Idem., *Selected Essays on Language, Mythology and Religion*, vol. I. (London: Longmans, Green, 1881) pp. 308–9.

254

Notes for pages 148–59

6. Ibid.
7. Ibid., p. 311.
8. Ibid., p. 524.
9. Ibid., pp. 526–6.
10. F. Max Müller, *Thoughts on Life and Religion: an aftermath from the writing of Professor Max Müller by his wife* (London: Constable, 1905) pp. 67–8.
11. Nirad C. Chauduri, *Scholar Extraordinary: the life of Professor the Right Hon. Friedrich Max Müller, P.C.* (London: Chatto and Windus, 1974) pp. 5–7.
12. Müller, *Selected Essays*, vol. I, pp. 381–2.
13. Chaudhuri, *Scholar Extraordinary*, p. 7.
14. Sir J.G. Frazer, *The Golden Bough: a study in magic and religion* (1890–1915; repr. London: Macmillan, 1922) p. 55.
15. Ibid., p. 59.
16. Ibid., p. 55.
17. Ibid., pp. 55–6.
18. Gilbert Murray, *Five Stages of Greek Religion* (1912; repr. New York: Doubleday, 1955) p. 7.
19. J.E. Harrison, *Prolegomena to the Study of Greek Religion* (1903; repr. Cambridge: University Press, 1922) p. 6.
20. Murray, *Five Stages of Greek Religion*, p. 10.
21. Ibid., p. 11.
22. Ibid., p. 27.
23. Ibid., p. 60.
24. Edmund Leach, 'Frazer and Malinowski', *Encounter* (Nov. 1965) p. 29.
25. George Eliot, *Adam Bede* (1859; repr. New York: The New American Library, 1961) p. 176.
26. G.K. Chesterton, *The Victorian Age in Literature* (1913; repr. London: Oxford University Press, 1966) p. 46.
27. John Gross, *The Rise and Fall of the Man of Letters* (Harmondsworth: Pelican Books, 1973) pp. 149–54.
28. George Gissing, *Charles Dickens: a critical study* (1898; repr. London: Blackie and Son, 1926) pp. 10–11.
29. Ibid., p. 68.
30. Ibid., p. 39.
31. Ibid., p. 40.
32. Ibid., p. 82.
33. Ibid., p. 83.
34. Ibid., p. 85.
35. Ibid., p. 38.
36. Ibid., p. 81.
37. Ibid., p. 117.
38. Eric Stokes, 'Kipling and Imperialism' in *Rudyard Kipling: the man, his work and his world* ed. John Gross (London: George Weidenfeld and Nicolson, 1972) p. 94.

Notes for pages 159–73

39. Rudyard Kipling, 'My Great and Only', in *Uncollected Prose I*, Sussex Edition, vol. XXIX, 1937–9, pp. 265–6.
40. Gilbert Keith Chesterton, *The Defendant* (1901; repr. London: J.M. Dent, 1922) p. 20.
41. Ibid., p. 21.
42. Ibid.
43. Ibid.
44. G.K. Chesterton, *Charles Dickens* (1906; repr. London: Methuen, 1913) p. 67.
45. Ibid.
46. Ibid., p. 69.
47. Ibid., p. 68.
48. Ibid., p. 69.
49. Ibid., p. 71.
50. Ibid., p. 72.
51. Ibid.
52. Ibid., p. 14.
53. Ibid., p. 18.
54. Ibid., p. 24.
55. Ibid., p. 179.
56. G.K. Chesterton, *A Miscellany of Men* (1912; repr. London: Methuen, 1927) p. 90.
57. Idem, *Orthodoxy* (1908; repr. London: William Collins, 1961) p. 57.
58. Ibid., p. 53.
59. G.K. Chesterton, *The Everlasting Man* (1925; repr. New York: Doubleday, 1955) p. 112.

A True Sense of the Grotesque

1. Jorge Luis Borges, *Other Inquisitions 1937–1952*, trans. Ruth L.C. Simms (New York: Washington Square Press, 1966) p. 88.
2. G.K. Chesterton, *Robert Browning* (1903; repr. London: Macmillan, 1920) p. 149.
3. Idem, *The Defendant* (1901; repr. London: J.M. Dent., 1922) p. 114.
4. Ibid.
5. Ibid., p. 115.
6. Ibid.
7. Ibid., p. 118.
8. Arthur Clayborough, *The Grotesque in English Literature* (Oxford: University Press, 1965) p. 45.
9. Victor Hugo, *The Dramas of Victor Hugo*, trans. MM., Bido, Leloir, Pille, Maignan, Lalauze, Rochegrosse (London: H.S. Nichols, 1896) vol. VIII, p. 9.
10. Ibid.
11. Ibid., p. 10.

Notes for pages 173–85

12. Ibid., p. 12.
13. Ibid.
14. Ibid., p. 13.
15. Wolfgang Kayser, *Das Groteske; seine Gestaltung in Malerei und Dichtung*, cited Clayborough, op. cit., p. 61.
16. John Ruskin, *The Stones of Venice* (1851–3; repr. London: Routledge, 1907) vol. III, p. 141.
17. Ibid., p. 169.
18. Clayborough, op. cit., p. 49.
19. Walter Bagehot, *Literary Studies* (London: J.M. Dent, 1911) vol. I, p. 31.
20. Ibid., vol. II, pp. 342–4.
21. Thomas Wright, *A History of Caricature and the Grotesque in Literature and Art* (London: Virtue Brothers, 1865) pp. 8–9.
22. John Addington Symonds, *Essays Speculative and Suggestive* (London: Chapman and Hall, 1890) p. 245.
23. George Santayana, *The Sense of Beauty* (1896; repr. New York: Collier Books, 1961) p. 175.
24. T. Tyndall Wildridge, *The Grotesque in Church Art* (London: Andrews and Co., 1899), cited Clayborough, op. cit., p. 61.
25. Harold Bloom, *The Selected Writings of Walter Pater* (New York: New American Library, 1974) p. 220.
26. Ibid., p. 212.
27. Ibid.
28. Ibid.
29. Ibid.
30. Ibid., pp. 213–14.
31. G.K. Chesterton, *The Victorian Age in Literature* (1913; repr. London: Oxford University Press, 1966) pp. 19–20.
32. Idem, *A Handful of Authors* (London: Sheed and Ward, 1953) p. 36.
33. Idem, *The Victorian Age in Literature*, p. 96.
34. Idem, *A Handful of Authors*, p. 37.
35. Ibid., p. 40.
36. G.K. Chesterton, *Alarms and Discursions* (1910; repr. London: Methuen, 1927) p. 2.
37. Ibid.
38. Ibid., p. 4.
39. Ibid.
40. Ibid., p. 5.
41. Ibid., p. 6.
42. Chesterton, *A Handful of Authors*, p. 43.
43. Bloom, *Selected Writings of Walter Pater*, p. 216.
44. Chesterton, *Robert Browning*, p. 49.
45. Ibid., p. 48.

Notes for pages 185–99

46. Ibid., p. 49.
47. Chesterton, *The Defendant*, p. 49.
48. Idem, *Robert Browning*, p. 175.
49. Idem, *The Defendant*, p. 48.
50. W.H. Auden, *G.K. Chesterton: a selection from his non-fictional prose* (London: Faber and Faber, 1970) p. 154.
51. Ibid., p. 155.
52. Ibid., p. 154.
53. Chesterton, *The Defendant*, p. 118.
54. Auden, op. cit., p. 153.
55. G.K. Chesterton, *The Man who was Thursday* (1908; repr. Harmondsworth: Penguin Books, 1967) p. 160.

The Reaction against Impressionism

1. G.K. Chesterton, *Autobiography* (1936; repr. London: Arrow Books, 1959) p. 33.
2. Ibid., p. 36.
3. *G.K. Chesterton: a centenary appraisal*, ed. John Sullivan (London: Elek, 1974) p. 95.
4. Chesterton, *Autobiography*, pp. 36–7.
5. Ibid., p. 30.
6. Ibid.
7. Walter Pater, *Studies in the History of the Renaissance* (1873; repr. New York: Signet, 1959) p. 121.
8. *Selected Writings of Walter Pater*, ed. Harold Bloom (New York: Signet, 1974) p. 4.
9. Ibid., p. 3.
10. Walter Pater, *Marius the Epicurean* (1885; repr. Letchworth: Everyman, 1968) pp. 180–1.
11. G.K. Chesterton, *Selected Essays*, selected with an Introduction by John Guest (1936; repr. London and Glasgow: Collins, 1953) pp. 98–102.
12. George Moore, *Confessions of a Young Man* (1888; repr. London: William Heinemann, 1924) p. 118.
13. Ibid., pp. 173–4.
14. Ibid., pp. 118–19.
15. Joseph Hone, *The Life of George Moore* (London: Victor Gollancz, 1936) p. 184.
16. George Moore, *Conversations in Ebury Street* (London: William Heinemann, 1924) p. 118.
17. William Gaunt, *The Aesthetic Adventure* (1945; repr. Harmondsworth: Penguin Books, 1957) pp. 232–3.
18. Ibid., p. 231.
19. Chesterton, *Autobiography*, p. 83.
20. Ibid.

Notes for pages 199–214

21. G.K. Chesterton, *The Victorian Age in Literature* (1913; repr. London: Oxford University Press, 1966) p. 28.
22. Idem, *Heretics* (1905; repr. London: John Lane, 1928) p. 129.
23. Maisie Ward, *Return to Chesterton* (London: Sheed and Ward, 1952) pp. 203–4.
24. G.K. Chesterton, *William Blake* (1910; repr. London: Duckworth, 1920) p. 135.
25. George Santayana, *The Sense of Beauty* (1896; repr. New York: Collier Books, 1961) p. 100.
26. Anton Ehrenzweig, *The Hidden Order of Art* (1967; repr. London: Paladin, 1970) p. 26.
27. G.K. Chesterton, *G.F. Watts* (1904; repr. London: Duckworth, 1920) p. 97.
28. *G.K. Chesterton: a centenary appraisal*, p. 93.
29. Chesterton, *G.F. Watts*, p. 98.
30. Ibid., p. 104.
31. *G.K. Chesterton: a centenary appraisal*, p. 91.
32. G.K. Chesterton, *The Innocence of Father Brown* (1911; repr. Harmondsworth, Penguin Books, 1958; p. 131.
33. Ibid., p. 141.
34. Ibid., p. 150.
35. Ibid., p. 152.
36. Ibid., p. 154.
37. Ibid., p. 165.
38. Ibid., p. 172.
39. G.K. Chesterton, *The New Jerusalem* (1920; repr. London: Thomas Nelson, 1924) p. 146.
40. Ibid., p. 156.
41. Ibid., p. 146.
42. Ibid., p. 147.
43. Ibid., p. 160.

Ideology and the Individual Mind

1. G.K. Chesterton, *Four Faultless Felons* (1930; repr. Beaconsfield, Darwen Finlayson, 1964) p. 45.
2. Idem, *Orthodoxy* (1908; repr. London: Collins, 1961) p. 15.
3. Lawrence J. Clipper, *G.K. Chesterton* (New York: Twayne Publishers, 1974) p. 51.
4. G.K. Chesterton, *Autobiography* (1936; repr. London: Arrow Books, 1959) p. 91.
5. Samuel Johnson, *Prose and Poetry* (London, 1963) p. 282.
6. Jonathan Swift, *A Tale of a Tub and Other Satires* (London: Dent, 1955) p. 109.
7. Johnson, *Prose and Poetry*, p. 476.
8. Chesterton, *Orthodoxy*, p. 10.
9. Ibid., p. 27.

Notes for pages 214–28

10. G.K. Chesterton, 'On Certain Modern Writers and the Institution of the Family' in *Heretics* (London, 1905).
11. Chesterton, *Orthodoxy*, pp. 33–4.
12. Idem, *G.K.C. as M.C.* (London: Methuen, 1929) p. 205.
13. Idem, *The Man who was Thursday* (1908; repr. Harmondsworth; Penguin Books, 1967) p. 66.
14. Ibid.
15. Ibid., p. 67.
16. Chesterton, *Autobiography*, p. 160.
17. Idem, *The Man who was Thursday*, p. 10.
18. Ibid., p. 31.
19. Edmund Burke, *Reflections on the Revolution in France* (1790; repr. Dolphin Books, 1961) pp. 94–5.
20. Chesterton, *The Man who was Thursday*, p. 56.
21. Ibid., p. 18.
22. G.K. Chesterton, 'The Book of Job' (1929) in *G.K. Chesterton: a selection from his non-fictional prose*, selected by W.H. Auden (London: Faber and Faber, 1970) p. 151.
23. Chesterton, *The Man who was Thursday*, p. 96.
24. Ibid., p. 149.
25. Ibid., p. 129.
26. *G.K. Chesterton; a selection from his non-fictional prose*, p. 154.
27. Ibid.
28. Chesterton, *The Man who was Thursday*, p. 160.
29. Ibid., p. 180.
30. Ibid., p. 182.
31. G.K. Chesterton, *Manalive* (1912; repr. Beaconsfield: Darwen Finlayson, 1964) pp. 13–14.
32. Ibid., p. 14.
33. Ibid., p. 185.
34. Ibid., p. 29.
35. Ibid., p. 143.
36. Ibid., p. 184.
37. Ibid., p. 35.
38. Ibid., p. 36.
39. Ibid., p. 91.
40. Hilaire Belloc, 'On Translation' (1931) in *Belloc: a biographical anthology* ed. H. Van Thal (London: Allen and Unwin, 1970) p. 305.
41. Paul Hazard, *The European Mind 1680–1715* (1935; trans. J. Lewis May, 1953; repr. Harmondsworth: Penguin Books, 1964 and 1973).
42. Chesterton, *Manalive*, p. 109.
43. Ibid., p. 131.
44. Ibid., pp. 133–4.

Notes for pages 229–43

45. G.K. Chesterton, *The Poet and the Lunatics* (1929; repr. London: Darwen Finlayson, 1962) p. 176.
46. Ibid., p. 177.
47. Ibid., p. 178.
48. Ibid., p. 28.
49. Ibid., p. 15.
50. Ibid., p. 17.
51. Chesterton, *Four Faultless Felons*, p. 46.
52. Ibid., p. 45.
53. Ibid., p. 95.
54. Bernard Bergonzi, 'Chesterton and/or Belloc', *Critical Quarterly* (spring, 1959) pp. 64–71.
55. Chesterton, *The Poet and the Lunatics*, p. 90.
56. G.K. Chesterton, *St. Thomas Aquinas* (1933; New York: Image Books, 1956) p. 167.
57. Idem, *The Outline of Sanity* (London: Methuen, 1928) p. 46.
58. Chesterton, *The Poet and the Lunatics*, p. 85.
59. Ibid., pp. 87–8.
60. Ibid., p. 91.
61. Ibid.

Conclusion: The Case of Orage

1. A.L. Maycock, *The Man who was Orthodox* (London: Denis Dobson, 1963) p. 21.
2. Maisie Ward, *Gilbert Keith Chesterton* (1944; repr. Harmondsworth: Penguin Books, 1958) p. 336.
3. Margaret Canovan, *G.K. Chesterton: radical populist* (New York: Harcourt Brace Jovanovich, 1977) p. 148.
4. Quoted in Wallace Martin, *The New Age under Orage* (Manchester: The University Press, 1967) p. 293.
5. Philip Mairet, *A.R. Orage: a memoir* (London: J.M. Dent, 1936) p. vi.
6. Ibid.
7. Wallace Martin, *The New Age under Orage*, p. 3.
8. Mairet, *A.R. Orage: a memoir*, p. 13.
9. Martin, *The New Age under Orage*, p. 205.
10. Ibid., p. 108.
11. G.K. Chesterton, *Heretics* (1905, repr. London: John Lane, 1928) p. 279.
12. Quoted in Wallace Martin, *The New Age under Orage*, p. 78.
13. Ibid., p. 215.
14. Ibid.
15. Ibid., p. 219.
16. Ibid., p. 231.
17. G.K. Chesterton, *The Spice of Life* (Beaconsfield: Darwen Finlayson, 1964) p. 166.

INDEX

Index

Index

Johnson, Samuel, 212; *Adventurer*, No. 85, 213; *Rasselas*, 213
Joyce, James, 194, *The Portrait of the Artist as a Young Man*, 194

Kafka, Franz, 11, 220–1
Kant, Immanuel, 165; *Critique of Pure Reason*, 165
Kayser, Wolfgang, 174
Kenner, Hugh, 1, 63
Ker, William Paton, 212
Kipling, Joseph Rudyard, 10, 132, 134–5, 159–60; *Kim*, 134
Koran, the, 30
Koss, Stephen, 70

Laing, Ronald David, 214
Lang, Andrew, 155, 165
Leach, Edmund Ronald, 153–4
Le Sage, Alain-René, 227
Lévi-Strauss, Claude, 146
Life Force, 37
Lloyd George, David, 13
Lovejoy, Arthur Oncken, 36

MacDonald, James Ramsay, 34, 103
McLuhan, Herbert Marshall, 1, 63
Madariaga, Salvador De, (Madariaga y Rojo, Don Salvador), 99
Maeterlinck, Count Maurice, 52; *Pelléas and Mélisande*, 52
Mairet, Philip, 237
Marconi Case, 13–14, 87, 111
Martin, Wallace, 238, 242
Masterman, Charles Frederick Gurney, 41–5, 53, 235; *The Condition of England*, 41–3; *In Peril of Change*, 41
Mayock, A.L., 64, 94
Medcalf, Stephen, 193, 202
'Medievalism', 98, 100, 106, 113, 116, 119–20, 122–3
Merriman, Henry Seton, 127, 132; *Barlasch of the Guard*, 133–4
Mental illness, 210–14
Milner, Alfred, 1st Viscount, 35
Modern Art, 191
Moore, George, 196–9; *Confessions of a Young Man*, 196–7; *Conversations in Ebury Street*, 198; *Modern Painting*, 196–7

'Moral uplift', 29–30, 78–9
Morley of Blackburn, John Morley, 1st Viscount, 127
Morning Post, 59
Morris, William, 118, 177–8
Müller, Friedrich Max, 145–50; *Comparative Mythology*, 147
Murray, George Gilbert Aimé, 151–3
Music hall, 49
Myth, 144–68

Nation, 31
National Observer, 130
New Age, 238–41
'New journalism', 55–6
Newman, Francis, W., 179
'Newspaper Revolution', 54
New Testament, 148
Nietzcheanism, 15, 36–7, 40, 90–3, 111–12, 240–1
Noel, Roden, 27
Nonconformists, 66–8
Northcliffe, Lord: see Alfred Harmsworth

O'Connor, Rt. Hon. Thomas Power, 54
O'Day, Alan, 68–9
Orage, Alfred Richard, 25, 36–7, 40, 237–43; *Friedrich Nietzche: the Dionysian Spirit of the Age*, 25; 'On Drama', 240
Original Sin, 242–3
Orwell, George (pseud.): Eric Arthur Blair, 96

Paradox, 87
Pater, Walter Horatio, 28, 172, 178–80, 183–4, 189, 196–7, 198–9; *Marius the Epicurean*, 194–5; 'Postscript' to *Appreciations*, 178–80, 183–4; *Studies in the History of the Renaissance*, 178, 194–5; 'The Child in the House', 194
Pearson, Sir Arthur, 32
Pearson, Professor Karl, 17, 80
Phillimore, John Swinnerton, 58
Pilgrim's Progress, The, 11
Pinero, Sir Arthur Wing, 157
Polemicists in Edwardian Era, 65–6
Pope, Alexander, 212
Popular Culture, 43, 49–54
Popularist tradition, 48–9

265

Pound, Ezra Loomis, 50
'Psychological history', 102
Pugin, Augustus Welby Northmore, 177
Purcell, James, 65–6
Puritanism, 29, 38

Queux, William le, 12
'Quixote myth', 99–100, 106–7, 122

Racialism, 14, 28
Raleigh, Sir Walter Alexander, 130
Rand millionaires, 14
Realism, 21, 157, 183, 240
Reckitt, Maurice, 237
Redemption, 37
Relationship between adult and childish
    identity, 83–4, 95–6
Rhodes, Cecil John, 131
Rig Veda, 165
Robertson, Thomas William, 157
Roman Catholic Church, 17
Romanticism, 174, 181, 183
Ruskin, John, 28, 174–5; *The Stones of Venice*,
    174–5

Saintsbury, George Edward Bateman, 130
Sampson, George, 62; *Concise Cambridge
    History of English Literature*, 62
Santayana, George, 176–7; *The Sense of
    Beauty*, 200–1
Schopenhauer, Arthur, 61
Schumacher, Ernst, 16
Shakespeare, William, 52; *Hamlet*, 52
Shavianism, 11
Shaw, George Bernard, 11, 30–1, 37–8; *Arms
    and the Man*, 135; *Man and Superman*, 37–40;
    The Devil's Disciple, 37
Sickert, Walter Richard, 198
Simplification, 21
Slade School of Art, 5, 195–6, 199, 201
Sorel, Georges, 68
Speaker, 7, 10, 56, 58
Spencer, Herbert, 34
'Standard of excellence', 62
Star, 54
Steer, Philip Wilson, 197, 198
Stevenson, Robert Louis Balfour, 17–18
Swift, Jonathan, 62, 213
Swinnerton, Frank, 132

Symonds, John Addington, 176; 'Caricature,
    the Fantastic, the Grotesque', 176–7

Teetotalism, 87
Theatre, 52, 240
Tolstoy, Count Leo Nikolayevich, 20–2,
    25–6
Tolstoyanism, 22, 25
Tonks, Henry, 196–200
Tory tradition of the seventeenth and
    eighteenth centuries, 212
Toynbee, Arnold, 35
Trade Unions, 50, 115
Trotter, Dr Wilfred, 68
Turks, the, 77, 87, 90

'Ugliness' in aesthetics, 170–1

'Verax' (columnist in the *Daily News*),
    76–9, 82–3
Vere, Aubrey de, 27
Venture Annual, 83
'Victorian Compromise', 23

Wagner, (Wilhelm) Richard, 52
Ward, Maisie, 4, 6, 13, 107; *Gilbert Keith
    Chesterton*, 4; *Return to Chesterton*, 4
Watts, George Frederick, 201–3; 'Hope',
    202–3
Welfare State, 12, 16
Wells, Herbert George, 54, 65; *Anticipations*,
    103; *An Outline of History*, 17; *Tono-Bungay*,
    127
Weyman, Stanley John, 127
Whibley, Charles, 130
Whig view of history, 9, 15
Wilde, Oscar Fingal O'Flahertie Wills, 46,
    74, 180, 197
Wildridge, T. Tyndall, 177; *The Grotesque in
    Church Art*, 177
Williams, Raymond Henry, 50, 126
Wright, Thomas, 176; *History of Caricature and
    the Grotesque in Literature and Art*, 176
Wyndham, George, 129–30

Yeats, William Butler, 52
'Yellow Press', 55

Zarathustra, 90